LIVING EDUCATION

John Tomlinson

LIVING EDUCATION

ESSAYS IN HONOUR OF JOHN TOMLINSON

Edited by
Peter Mortimore and Viv Little

P·C·P
Paul Chapman
Publishing Ltd

Selection and Editorial material Copyright © 1997, Peter
Mortimore and Viv Little. All other material copyright as credited.

Paul Chapman Publishing Ltd
144 Liverpool Road
London
N1 1LA

British Library Cataloguing in Publication Data

Living education: essays in honour of John Tomlinson
1. Education 2. Educational change 3. Educational innovations
I. Mortimore, Peter II. Little, Viv
379.2

ISBN 1 85396 347 X

Typeset by Palimpsest Book Production Limited,
Polmont, Stirlingshire
Printed and bound in Great Britain

A B C D E F G H   9 8 7

CONTENTS

Part IV – Professional Concerns

FOREWORD

Writers of forewords to Festschriften are usually scholars of eminence in the same field as that of the person whose life's work is being celebrated by the contributors. Alas I do not fall into that category. On the contrary a journalist once accorded me the title, some would say justly, 'That illiterate Dainton', following my first public foray into educational policy matters nearly thirty years ago. The adjective must surely be a disqualification for writing about John Tomlinson whose mellifluous prose in speech and writing is the envy of many. But if his style is elegant he does not deserve Buffon's aphorism *Le style est l'homme même*; there is much more to John than that.

I first met John over a frugal lunch hosted by Edward Boyle who considered that we should meet. Whether Edward's motive was that he considered the encounter would civilise me, or whether his passionate interest in cricket drove him to devise a setting in which a Lancastrian and a Yorkist faced one another whilst he, Edward, umpired I have no means of knowing. But I do know that what John said on that occasion immediately commanded my respect for its clarity, wisdom and deep humanity. Since then our paths have often crossed and those encounters have deepened my regard for him and for his work.

The diversity of his contributions to education evokes amazement and admiration. He first taught and then spent twenty four years as an educational administrator, half of them as Director of Education for Cheshire, doing so with distinction whilst carrying out *en passant* with grace and efficiency many national tasks including those of chairman of The Schools Council and the National Schools Curriculum Award. In that period it seemed that no committee concerned with education or with the general good was adequately equipped to discharge its task without his constructive presence as a member. Then, in 1985, there was what seemed to many of us a surprising change of career from that of administrator to that of professor. In fact it was not so great a change as appeared for John was not to be just the *seeker for truth in the groves of Academe*; he was also Director of a large Institute of Education at Warwick and universities were changing rapidly. Nor was he one of Auden's professors who *talk in someone else's sleep*; for John's speech is never soporific but always a stimulus and energiser. It is little wonder that he was in such demand as a lecturer. With all his new preoccupations his stoic sense of civic duty did not desert him. His services to the Trust for Community Service Volunteers and the Council of the Royal Society of Arts as an energetic member and chairman were exemplary, as was his characteristic engaging diffidence with which he put forward his own ideas.

The roll of contributors to this book is eloquent testimony to the esteem in which John is held by the *cognoscenti* and to the range of his professional concerns. I suspect that for all of us, whether contributor or reader, who have known him it is true that we owe him a debt for the deeper understanding and friendship he has given us. We all hope and believe that retirement will in no way diminish his exuberant love of and participation in education and the formulation of policies for its enhancement and extension.

Dainton of Hallam Moors

A MESSAGE FROM: PROFESSOR THE RT HON BARONESS WILLIAMS OF CROSBY

I was tremendously impressed by John Tomlinson, whom I got to know through his work as Director of Education for Cheshire. His concern for all children, not least those with special needs, to achieve their potential, and his understanding of what makes schools succeed, were factors that influenced the decision to appoint him as Chairman of the Schools Council, a post he fitted with distinction and great sympathy for the hard and vital job of teaching.

John Tomlinson understood that education is a long term investment, and that standards only improve by steady and devoted attention to the morale as well as the skills of teachers. Never dogmatic, he measured those who worked with him by their commitment and their willingness to learn. Our educational system owes him a great deal.

Shirley Williams

ACKNOWLEDGEMENTS

We thank the seventeen authors who reacted so positively to our invitation to contribute to this Festschrift. By keeping to our tight deadlines they demonstrated the truth that if you want something done you ask a busy person. Our gratitude is also due to Lord Dainton and Baroness Williams of Crosby for providing the introductory notes for the Preface. Ranjna Patel managed the numerous scripts and diskettes with admirable patience. Finally we wish to record our appreciation of the enthusiastic way in which Paul Chapman, Marianne Lagrange and their colleagues at Paul Chapman Publishing responded to the idea of this book.

Peter Mortimore

Viv Little

LIVING EDUCATION: AN INTRODUCTION

Viv Little

Viv Little is a Lecturer in Education at the University of
Warwick. Previously she taught in secondary schools and
lectured in History at Coventry College of Education.

The proper study of a teacher is 'how to reach the mind of every boy' wrote
the distinguished Headmaster Edward Thring in 1883. Substitute 'person'
for the now unacceptable 'boy' and you have the reason why the title
Living Education was chosen for this collection of essays in honour of
John Tomlinson. Discernible throughout his extensive work in classrooms,
lecture theatres, offices, on platforms, heading committees and in professional
and even personal relationships is the concern to reach and to stir the deepest
aspirations of groups and individuals and to channel them in positive directions. John is a teacher from the core of his being because he is also a humble
and inveterate learner and because his goal is to offer insights and provide
techniques which actualise potential and equip groups and individuals to learn
and to act autonomously. John does not want disciples though he attracts the
hero-worshippers, groupies and indeed detractors that attend worldly success
in any field. He wants from those he seeks to influence commitment to the
causes of being human and becoming humane. He will define for you what
he means by these concepts and indeed his vision and his vigorous pursuit
of them are manifest in the pages which follow; but no-one is more aware
or excited than he that adoption of his stance can lead in directions he has
not envisaged and that changed circumstances will call forth interpretations
as yet unthought.

Nevertheless, despite the detachment of his inner attitude, won perhaps
from a subtle mind, a historian's training and the capacity to survive in local
and national corridors of power, John is undeniably a powerful exponent of

living education in that he has the gift of engaging with minds and hearts. Like many teachers, he might have been a compelling preacher or a moving actor and there are many testimonies to his inspirational powers: 'visionary'; 'idealistic'; 'overwhelming'; 'full of brilliant gems of observation and wit. It made one feel good to be in education'; 'one of the most wonderfully inspirational talks I've heard'; 'it was actually quite moving and I wish that the philosophy could be made clearer to a wide public'; 'what can I say, utterly marvellous!' These extracts are taken from feedback following HMI courses in the management of secondary schools, with which John has been associated since their inception in 1969, usually as opening or closing speaker. They can stand for responses from a wide range of audiences.

Such powers can, of course, delight and distract for an hour then yield before the mundane, but John's set pieces – openings, closings, keynote contributions at courses and conferences, project launches, commemorative lectures – resonate, reverberate and have consequences. People reach deeper, enlarge their vision, change their thinking and act after John has spoken to them. In this context 'living education' means achieving those moments Quakers call 'gathered' when the minds hearts and spirits of those present vibrate in understanding and accord; but it also means the translation of those moments into forms of action. The key reason for this is the effort that goes into the preparation of his lectures and addresses. John can be spontaneously eloquent and witty and, again like many teachers, he can think and speak well on his feet when necessary; but his talks and speeches are always the result of long study and careful thought. He will not waste the time of the professionals who come to listen. He will not tackle educational matters superficially. Moreover, because he is penetrating and trenchant in argument, his disquisitions always present an intellectual challenge. Further feedback illustrates this impact: 'one of the best speeches I have ever heard, concentrating on principle'; 'I have never heard an appreciation of an input anything like that which you received last Friday night. There were many very troubled people in that audience and you managed to offer them a realistic yet highly optimistic view of the future – and of their own personal futures. We are highly indebted to you'; 'It was tremendous to hear such a superb rationale for so many of the ideas we had been trying to discuss and implement'.

THE BEGINNING

Living education began early in John's life through the influence of his mother, a highly intelligent woman, who introduced him to books and to poetry and did all in her power later to foster and encourage his formal education. Its primary phase began later than most and was intermittently disrupted by the war. From these experiences, both positive and negative, stems John's deep awareness of the importance of the early years to intellectual as well as other aspects of development, a theme elaborated by Tricia David in her chapter. Stretford Grammar school provided secondary education and issued in a place at Manchester University. John's intention to become a historian had been expressed early, at age seven, if family folklore is to be believed. It was realised dramatically since he had the opportunity to study with one of the greatest – Sir Lewis Namier – who became a friend and remained an inspiration. John was drawn into the seminal work on the history of parliament and, as a post-graduate student at the Institute of Historical Research, produced an edition of the Grenville Papers, drawn from the period when George Grenville was First Lord of the Treasury between 1763 and 1765. This was published in 1962 and reveals the largeness of mind, insight and attention to detail so necessary to historical scholarship. Academe was certainly a possible theatre of operation, as John contemplated a career, but the National Service Act and family tradition led him into a commission in the RAF where, as a Flight Lieutenant, he demonstrated a flair for teaching, taking recruits through A level, Staff College entrance courses and a wide range of O levels in subjects as diverse as general science, mathematics, human biology and home economics! Service preferment beckoned, as had academe, but each seemed too enclosed for the ambition which by now (age 26) he admits had taken clearer shape. He wanted, needed (and with hindsight was clearly fitted) to make a difference to the world and to do so in a big arena, somewhere where he could both think and do in the hope of improving society and people's lives. The RAF had revealed a capacity for organisation and management, which, together with his love of teaching, seemed to point to educational administration as offering the best scope. After a further spell of teaching in state schools and in the WEA in the evenings, he applied for the post of Administrative Assistant in Shropshire, secured it and found his metier. Three years later he went as Assistant Education Officer to Lancashire. After five years he became Deputy Director for Cheshire and from 1971 to 1984 was Director of Education for Cheshire (in its reorganised form from 1974). Thus he served his apprenticeship and, in his prime, reached a position where *ipso facto* what he thought and what he did would make a difference.

DIRECTOR OF EDUCATION

John's period of service in Local Education Authorities (he is not embarrassed by the word service, nor does he see it as an anachronism) coincided with the reorganisation of secondary education in the direction of comprehension, the reorganisation of local government and latterly the beginnings of its erosion as Stuart Maclure shows in his chapter. It provided him with multifarious opportunities to display and hone his skills in organisation and negotiation and to draw on his intellectual resources to develop, modify and defend a philosophy and praxis of education in tough encounters with officials and elected representatives locally and nationally. He rose to the challenge admirably with energy, dedication and that blend of vision and realism so characteristic of his *modus operandi*. What is more he did it with a capacity to make friends both of colleagues and of those whose ideals and principles diverged from his own, which prompted the TES in a profile to describe him as the 'legendary former CEO of Cheshire'.

Most certainly during those years, John lived education. 'Fighting paper', as he puts it, chairing committees and meetings, setting up teachers' and outdoor centres, visiting schools by day and evening and arriving home late to work on routine administration into the small hours. Moreover, from the early seventies he was much in demand on the national scene for speaking engagements and to head national committees and projects such as the Schools Council.

Perhaps this is the moment to spare a thought for what all this meant for his wife and family. John was himself one of five siblings and he and Audrey have four children. In his Presidential Address to the Society of Education Officers in 1982, expounding the demands and lure of their calling, he acknowledged that it could be 'unless you are vigilant, destructive of home life!' In John's case it was not and that it was not must be due to that vigilance, but also in large measure to Audrey's generosity, understanding and personal strength, the resilience of his children and the forbearance of other close relatives. Public service of the kind John offers is not given without cost to the self, but above all to those closest and most dear. There must have been stresses and strains and heartache in sharing one's husband and father with such insistent and prominent public responsibilities, but Audrey provided the stability and continuity which enabled the family to distil from John's 'guest appearances', as I've heard her describe them, the high quality of love, care and stimulation which his experience and thoughtfulness (in all senses) could offer. With love, with patience, with humour and with, as the children grew, Audrey's dedication to the consuming career of social work, they developed a rich family life for which many in our troubled world can only yearn. They are the very model of a functional family and both account for and justify John's oft-stated conviction of the importance of small human groups – families, schools, local communities – to social development, moral growth and the health of democracy.

John's career in educational administration began under the leadership of Martin Wilson, whom he describes as an inspiration 'extremely lively, extremely intellectual, extremely demanding and very challenging to work for' (Bush *et al.*, 1989). In Shropshire John took responsibility mainly for Further and Adult education. He had considerable experience of the latter and has, rather neatly, returned to an aspect of the former with his Chairmanship of the Committee of the FEFC (Further Education Funding Council). This work in Shropshire fed one of his lifelong concerns, his sense of the unfulfilled potential in so many lives and his urge to help its flowering. In Lancashire his major responsibility was the reorganisation of secondary education into comprehensive schools – no mean task with 280 schools and a very strong Catholic-aided sector. All the 29 divisions of the county had to have two separate schemes, each of which had to be negotiated with the divisional executives, the teachers and the public and taken through the Education Committee and thence to the DES. It meant battering at building programmes and running the gauntlet of hostile public meetings as well as tackling the curricula and organisation of schools and the deployment of teachers. John approached the work with a will born of deep conviction of the rightness of the post Second World War project of building a welfare state on principles of justice and equality of opportunity and of education's role in this. (The conviction remains, though the arguments he now chooses reflect the shift towards instrumentalism of the past two or three decades). 'The economic need to raise the capabilities of our people, the perception that cohesive societies are more economically effective, the insight that an atomistic knowledge-based economy will be self-destructive unless each individual acts within a frame of social responsibility, will', he writes, 'all tend to drive policy makers towards . . . the comprehensive school' (Tomlinson, 1991). John pursued his Lancashire project so ably that the grand plan was completed in two and a half years. It would take many more to implement, but he could leave for a Deputyship in Cheshire in 1967 knowing that his successors had a strong base upon which to build.

As Deputy in Cheshire, John took on teacher staffing, teacher training, again the reorganisation of secondary education and a general deputising role. On the early retirement of his chief, owing to ill-health, the Committee decided (by acclamation, no advertisement!) to appoint John as Director for Cheshire in 1971; just as the Local Government Act was bringing about the creation of a new Cheshire, whose director he became in 1974. Thus, he found himself at the head of an organisation in a maelstrom of change. The decade or so which followed was to see not only the upheaval attendant upon reorganisation of systems, but a change in the ethos in which education lives. In the national press at least, consensus became confrontation and, on the ground, party political divisions were intensified and the clear understandings of the different but complementary roles of members and officers, characteristic of many local authorities, began to break up. By 1985, when John left Cheshire to become Professor of Education at the University of Warwick, the weakening of local government and the attenuation of LEAs were plain to see.

Forms of organisation change and decay but the legacy of patient, well-found work of teams such as those John headed continues to affect and enrich the lives of those who were their colleagues and employees. That scarcely a conference or public occasion passes without someone approaching John after a contribution or a speech, saying 'you won't remember me but I was such and such when you were Director in Cheshire' is testimony to this. Many also testify to his power to make people feel they were part of and partners in a great enterprise. And indeed they were, for John had a strong belief in 'the opportunities which a good county council had to bring health, social services, education and planning into a corporate view of the social and economic development of a whole community' (Bush *et al.*, 1989). Living education, as he did in this context, John achieved more, much more than can be told here, to ensure the health of that element of the organism and thereby to move in the direction of the ideals of social justice and active democracy he held so dear.

PROFESSOR OF EDUCATION

If, in his mid-fifties, reviving an earlier predilection for academic life and joining the University of Warwick, John cherished the prospect of more time to think and study at a depth impossible for those embroiled in the turmoil of day-to-day administration; he was not given long to dream. As Professor of Education and Director of the Institute, the Faculty of Education's place of interface with schools, LEAs and central government, he entered a decade of change unprecedented in Higher Education generally and scarcely familiar even in the less sheltered area of teacher education. It was characterised by growing government intervention, expanding student populations and diminishing resources, now old stories to him, but somewhat fresher to his new colleagues. Committed as he had ever been to teachers, to the nobility of their calling and to the seriousness of their responsibilities, he could not but be concerned to sustain the quality of their training and its location in Higher Education.

He brought to courses on policy matters for undergraduates and on management for post-graduates, a rare blend of learning and of knowledge of the world about which he theorised. He carried out research into effective schools, devising some conceptual frameworks not previously adopted in such work. He secured grants to further the research of colleagues. He did much, as John Eggleston shows, to further the link between teachers, teacher educators and industry, and he laboured through the Universities Council for the Education of Teachers to help keep colleagues at Warwick and elsewhere abreast of developments on the educational front. Moreover, he stumped the country in a determined endeavour to nourish teachers' self respect and dedication at a time when most of society's ills were being laid at their door. In 1991, he found himself, in addition to his role as Director, asked to undertake a level of detailed administration, as a chair of Department, which he thought he had long ago left behind for good. Subsequently in response to the creation of the Teacher Training Agency, financial retrenchment and contraction of student numbers and staffing and contemplating a year's study leave to add substantially to his already considerable written output – he was called upon, in 1994, to turn a University Faculty of five departments into one single department and Institute of Education in the Faculty of Social Studies, and to reposition it in the new world of teacher education governed by Circulars 9/92 and 14/93. It is well-known in the upper echelons at Warwick that the survival of teacher education there and its currently rosy prospects are largely due to his insight and leadership; the latter it must be said not always generally recognised or well-understood.

THE EXTRACURRICULAR ACTIVITIES

So John has lived education in two pre-eminent and exacting professional situations. The roles of Director of Education and Professor/ Director at an established University seldom, however, come alone, nor would John have wished it so. His life has long been divided like Gaul into three parts. The home base, a source of nourishment, welfare, concern and delight, but from which he is necessarily absent in body if not in spirit much of the time; the professional centre, the paid employment, whose concerns must take priority and be dealt with, if need be at the cost of sleep or pleasure, and the element to which he self-deprecatingly refers as the 'play-pen activities'. The latter, it should be understood, can range from giving talks at school speech days, to chairing important national committees on key educational issues and being Chairman (1989–91) of the Royal Society of Arts. Since the 1970s they have also encompassed chairing the Schools' Council (1978–81), spearheading the curriculum movement, which yielded HMIs *Curriculum Matters Series* and the white paper *Better Schools*, creating the Schools Curriculum award, supporting a number of projects concerned with the Arts in Education, steering the initiative for a General Teaching Council and producing the report *Inclusive Learning* for the FEFC. 'And this and so much more' (Eliot) – even the larger Who's Who entry is only a select list. Living education indeed. The host of activities undertaken illustrate the sincerity of his commitment, the breadth of his conception and the consistency of his principles.

They also show that he has lived education in the sense that he has given a very high proportion of his energy and time to its pursuit, ever widening the scope of his knowledge and experience and thus his ability to extend the benefits of education to others. It is evident that when John joins an organisation or a group, it is not long before he finds himself in a leadership role. Sometimes, to be sure, that is what he seeks in order to further some cause. More often, greatness is thrust upon him because of the sheer power of his mind. Recently a Chief Education Officer serving with him on the FEFC Committee conveyed to John her understanding of his manner of working with groups. She said that when, quite often, in meetings wrestling with complex concepts and problems, they ran into a morass, encountering conflicting arguments and seeing no way forward, John would allow the brainstorming to rage a while, a look of concentration on his face. Then he would say 'Well colleagues' and she would know that he had listened, ruminated and found a resolution. He would then explain, sometimes to their surprise, the essence and importance of the debate they had, its contradictions and the opportunities it afforded, and once again the work would take direction. This paraphrase echoes others and can stand for the experience over the years and across the country of many who have worked with him and indeed of the editors of this volume. John is remarkably good at working co-operatively and a horse designed by a committee he has chaired will belie the adage and become a trusty steed, bred of the best that all the members could offer and nurtured by an expert.

Many of the themes of John's thought and writings, stemming from his professional practice and manifold related activities, are considered in Chapter 4 of this volume and touched upon elsewhere in the collection. Two current projects upon which he is engaged are selected to illustrate further the quality and range of his thinking and doing. One relates to his interest in teacher professionalism, the other to his long-standing and central concern to understand how people learn and how they may best be helped to learn.

In 1990, John was invited to become the Chair of the GTC (England and Wales), a voluntary association, set up by teachers, employers and parents, seeking to have established a statutory General Teaching Council. Each of the constituencies had found that they had decided to propose the same person. Since these constituencies comprised all the teachers' associations including that of University teachers, and employers encompassing local government, the Churches and the Vice Chancellors, the invitation was in itself a measure of the generally high esteem in which John is held. The work he has done since then is also an index of his thoroughness, persistence and capacity to sustain goodwill and find safe routes through controversy and impediment.

A professional body for teachers in England and Wales has been long in the seeking, the first proposals appearing in the mid-nineteenth century. There was a number of abortive attempts during the subsequent hundred years but no GTC appeared in the 1944 Education Act. Again it almost came to be in the 1970s, but foundered on technicalities and faded before the economic crisis of that decade and 'New Right' distrust of 'combinations' in the next one. From 1983, however, the movement emerged again, its urgency exacerbated by teachers' loss of bargaining rights, increasing government intervention in teacher training and appraisal and in the school curriculum and its assessment. The GTC has accrued a strong body of support from both profession and public, from across the political spectrum and from a Select Committee of the House of Commons. The alliance involves some strange bedfellows and its object also has powerful enemies. That it has held through twists and turns of fortune during the past six years and now stands poised for a breakthrough owes much to John's leadership, his clear and consistent vision of the goal and its justification, his skill in debate and negotiation and his determination to fight on, whatever the odds and cost. Here more than anywhere, perhaps, his disposition to take the historian's long view has informed and sustained his mode of action.

John's most recent large-scale undertaking, is his Chairmanship of the Learning Difficulties and/or Disabilities Committee of the Further Education Funding Council. Again, a signal honour, it must have recalled for him his work in the mid-seventies on the Curriculum Development Council for F.E., his first national chairmanship. In September 1996 after three years' intensive work, the committee produced the report *Inclusive Learning* which, if its current reception is anything to go by, is likely to have an impact well beyond circumstances of its inception. The business of providing in classrooms for differences in learning style and orientation, stemming from individual psychology, class and racial background has moved through phases of assimilation and accommodation, via student centredness, entitlement, integration and differentiation to the wider notion of 'inclusiveness'.

Drawing upon the aspirations and experience of a host of individuals and organisations, John, with his knowledge of theories of learning and his intuitive grasp of the essence of good teaching was able to seize upon the somewhat fuzzy concept of inclusive learning, which was beginning to replace earlier more limited notions of match and integration, across the education scene, and help the Committee to clarify and expound it. He led them also to articulate its manifold and far reaching implications for practice, and to produce a set of cogent arguments for its furtherance in their sector. Inclusive learning is a concept which both admits the centrality and diversity of learners and insists upon the salience of teachers – discerning, sparking, framing, scaffolding, according to individual need and the nature of subjects. Elegant in conception, rich in analysis and example, the report carries many messages for other sectors and age-phases. Here was a further project in which John's intellectual prowess and capacity to make committee tasks a living education for all concerned were at a premium and the result was another major contribution to thought about learning and teaching:

> Ensuring that all pupils or students make progress demands that teachers do not treat them uniformly, but differentiate their approaches according to the previous experience and varied learning styles of those pupils or students. Providing audio-tapes for a blind learner, amplification or photographs for a deaf person or simplified text for a hesitant reader are matters of degree rather than kind.
>
> Moreover, teachers have to select materials and methods appropriate to the subjects being taught: artists must encourage visual awareness and skill with colour, shape and texture, scientists must foster observation and an experimental approach, historians must learn how to use evidence from the past. Each domain of knowledge has its different procedures for examining the world, different tests for truth. Each student must learn the ways needed to proceed in the chosen study and adjust their learning styles accordingly. The task of teachers is always to effect a marriage between the requirements of particular subject-matter and the predispositions, stage of development and capacities of those who would learn. The wider the spectrum the greater the insight and ingenuity called for.   (FEFC, 1996)

BY THEIR FRUITS YE SHALL KNOW THEM

How can one gauge the impact of such a person? The influence of most teachers reaches for good or ill, further and deeper than they ever know. John has operated in prominent positions and affected many lives from day to day. These, and his other activities have enabled him to create and develop a very wide network of contacts, friendships and shared values. His work and writings reveal a wide and subtle concept of what it is to educate, and commitment to a consistent set of values arising from respect for all persons and an open and imaginative conception of the potential of each for achievement. Much of his work has been set in circumstances where those values were hard to sustain and his leftward leanings politically have meant of late that his talents and efforts have not always been recognised or rewarded, as have those of people of lesser stature. Nevertheless, a true gardener in the field of human endeavour, he has sown seeds and given his all to their nurture. They will grow and bloom and propagate long after the gardener has put away his watering can. He has helped to improve society and improved people's lives.

This highly organised man, punctual, punctilious, disciplined, is yet profoundly intuitive and has something of the prophet about him. The mainspring of his mind and heart is spiritual and his compass needle is pointed at the greater good. His is the intelligence of feeling. He reads people and was helping them to seize control and solve their own problems long before the onset of counselling courses. He catches the direction in which things need to go and has been, via the All Souls Group, political lunches, the Boards of Charities and Trusts and other organisations, a mover and shaker behind many shifts and innovations during his career. Many of today's educational commonplaces: nursery education, environmental and residential education (a string of eight centres established in redundant schools) community education (with the community a resource for schools as well as vice versa) the training and induction of young teachers, devolved budgets, headship management training, school development planning were among the pioneering endeavours of Cheshire in his time. John Eggleston shows how John was prominent in the schools and industry movement, and his active interest in the curriculum of Cheshire's schools, uncharacteristic of LEAs at the time, gave him plenty of ideas to feed the HMI project of 1977–83 on *The Curriculum 11–16*, forerunner of the National Curriculum and, many argue, a bolder, fairer more radical and more manageable conception.

Moreover his thinking reached beyond education. Asked to be a member of the Child Health Services Committee under Donald Court, John drafted, with another member, the opening chapter of its report *Fit for the Future* in 1976. It is still regarded as a key statement of the purposes of health care for children and widely used in medical and social work training, ironically outside the UK in the main.

Long before the current panic about moral and citizenship education, John was pointing out the crucial importance of schools to moral growth in a turbulent and pluralist world. Indeed, since the late eighties he has been thinking and talking with teachers about values, education and values, and most recently, the values which underpin their own professionalism (Tomlinson, 1995, 1996).

WHO IS HE?

To say something about a person's work, however (though John is one of whom it can be said that the work is the life), is not yet to give you the man.

Dedicated to a high view of humanness and devotedly humane, John is also, in the popular usage of the word, a very human person. Notwithstanding his success, and the respect and affection he commands, he is truly modest; still capable of self-doubt, still surprised and gratified by small tributes or large honours. Despite his eminence and achievements, he is unassuming and approachable. As Director of Education he kept as far as possible an open door to colleagues in the authority and in schools and to parents, and at the University one rarely waited long for access to him. He is 'the old Prof.' to his pals at the pub, much in demand for quiz teams and not above treading the boards and floats in village frolics. He is a generous person, always first to buy a round, making the largest contribution to colleagues' leaving gifts and often paying himself for treats all assume to have come from the hospitality fund. A man's man, at home at formal dinners and in city clubs, a devotee of real ale; he is yet deeply understanding and appreciative of women and a champion of their rights at home and work. (With four sisters, a wife, two daughters, two daughters-in-law and six granddaughters, how could he be otherwise?) Nevertheless he has a paternal streak – 'a teddy-bear man' as a female colleague once described him. It is almost uncanny how, going about with him in course of business, he draws the fearful and the troubled. At some unconscious level perhaps they perceive the deep goodwill to all, which is the muscle of his heart and mind.

There are some, it must be said, who will not recognise this portrait, who see John as a remote figure preoccupied with memos and procedures; a bureaucrat, soulless, arrogant and tricky. They perceive his friendly approach as mere management-speak and the openness to argument as a pose, a cover for hidden and probably self-serving motives. Even his constructive approach to education, his enthusiasm and persistent optimism have been cynically dismissed as 'his hearts and flowers bit'. Much of this stems from the conspiracy theories and myth-making which perennially attend positions of authority and worldly success; but are there aspects of his behaviour or personality which provoke such responses? He is a formidable opponent in argument and well-versed in steering individuals and groups. To achieve good ends he believes that you have to be ahead of the game. Holy fools don't prosper. Some see only the game and the victory; not the commitment to principle or cause. He is extremely quick-thinking and it can be galling to discover he has leapt where you have limped. Frequently at the end of a discussion his ideas prevail, but only because he has mastered his brief and they have proved strongest.

He can be brusque in manner, especially under pressure, and asks much of those he works with, though never as much as he demands of himself. You have to be grown-up to work well with John. Paternal he may be in some situations, but paternalist he is not, though that term is also used of him with pejorative intent. He believes professionals should work collegially. He is truly a leader among equals. We are partners in a common enterprise which is greater than we are. 'If you see a job that needs doing', he is fond of saying, 'do it and do it as you wish; but keep me informed. If you can't do it alone, find someone to help or bring it to my attention'. Few are more sympathetic about illness or when personal concerns and responsibilities encroach on work, but, in the last analysis, when he delegates a job he expects it to be done. He has the perfectionist's concern for detail and will be blunt, critical, occasionally harsh in judgement if work for which he has ultimate responsibility is not well done. If you miss the mark, he will support you publicly, but in private, will let you know that you have fallen short. To him, in all such cases, and they are rare departures from a generally enabling stance, the attack is upon the deed, not the doer; but on the receiving end, it can seem otherwise. Following a brush with John in overbearing mode, only the well-acquainted, the brave, the bloody-minded or those who, perforce, must ask his help, discover the gentle man behind the fierce professional. As for his remoteness, if such there is, it is that of the supremely busy person, who controls the amount of trivia he will allow himself or others. Much of what he does is done unobtrusively, by necessity, because out of normal hours, or by design and there is something deeper. Like the 'superior man' of the Taoist oracle 'I Ching' he 'abides in dignity. He invites none, he flatters none. Those who come he accepts. Those who do not he allows to go their own way'.

While work and service are John's mainsprings, his interests range wide and deep. As with a good book, you don't discover all there is on first reading and you don't come to the end of him very quickly. Radical and progressive in his view of education and staunch in its defence through the period of reaction that has characterised the later part of his career, he has yet a deep feeling for continuities and for traditions. Contemptuous of currying favour at the expense of principle, he nevertheless relishes custom and ceremonial, delighted to have been offered the Freedom of the City of London and to have received it in the historic Guildhall, happy to be 'clothed in the livery' of the Goldsmith Company and proud to preside over the RSA and have his name added to the roll of honour stretching back over two hundred years. He feels related to human beings past and present, near and far and he can make that kinship palpable in a fireside tale for his grandchildren or in a deeply felt account of a visit to Egypt or to Africa. He savours things: here a piece of silver, a rare book or a fine glass for one of his collections, there the ravishing colours of his dahlias, or a new feature in a corner of his beloved garden. He enjoys music, painting, drama, literature, philosophy, science and wine and is no dilettante – what he knows he knows well. He contemplates experience, reaches for its essence and enhances the perceptions of those who share it with him. He is a good conversationalist, with a lively wit and sense of humour. He does not live entirely in his head, however. A rock climber and mountaineer in his younger days, he will now choose as relaxation a long walk, a few hours hard digging, or some D.I.Y.

It has been a privilege of which I am profoundly sensible and a living education to work closely with John Tomlinson for ten years. I am immeasurably enriched by his friendship and that of his family. All those who have contributed to this volume in his honour trust that he will accept it, as it is meant, as a token of their esteem and of their affection for him. It may also express the gratitude of many more, who count themselves the better for his touch upon their lives.

REFERENCES

Baynes, C F (1968) *The I Ching or Book of Changes – the Richard Wilhelm Translation*. Third edition. London: RKP.

Bush, T, Kogan, M & Lenney, T (1989) *Directors of Education – Facing Reform*, London: Jessica Kingsley.

Eliot, T S (1958) The Lovesong of J.Alfred Prufrock in *Collected Poems 1909–1935*, London: Faber & Faber.

FEFC (1996) *Inclusive Learning*. Report of the Learning Difficulties and/or Disabilities Committee, London: HMSO.

Thring, E (1883) *The Theory and Practice of Teaching*, Cambridge University Press.

Tomlinson, J R G (1962) *Additional Grenville Papers April 1765–July 1765* (ed), Manchester: Manchester University Press.

Tomlinson, J R G (1982) The Profession of Education Officer: Past Pluperfect, Present Tense, Future Conditional, *Sheffield Papers in Educational Management 25*.

Tomlinson, J R G (1991) Comprehensive Education in England and Wales, 1944–1991, *European Journal of Education*, 26, 2, 103–117.

Tomlinson, J R G (1994) Professional Development and control: a General Teaching Council. In H. Bines & M. Welton (eds) *Managing Partnership in Teacher Training and Development*, London: Routledge.

Tomlinson, J R G (1995) Teachers and Values, in *British Journal of Education Studies*, 23, 3, 315–318.

Tomlinson J R G (1996) A statement of Ethical Principles for the Teaching Profession. Unpublished draft GTC (England and Wales).

Tomlinson, J R G & Little, V M (1996) A Code of Ethical Principles for the Teaching Profession, unpublished paper, UCET Ethics Working Party.

PART I

Organisation of Education

1

THE TOMLINSON YEARS

Stuart Maclure

Stuart Maclure CBE was the editor of *Education* from
1954–1969 and of the *Times Educational Supplement*
from 1969–1989.

When Shirley Williams got her first big promotion from being Parliamentary
Under Secretary at the Department of Employment to Minister of State at the
Department of Education and Science, Sir Denis Barnes prepared her for a sea
change. 'You are going,' he said, 'from a department where the time-frame is
24 hours to one where it is eternity.'

If not eternity, then at least a generation. At any rate, that used to be
the assumption. More recently the quest has been for instant remedies and
paradigm shifts. But by definition it takes time to bring about long-term
change. Like the Chinese sage reflecting on the French Revolution, we
may be a bit close to the Thatcher educational revolution to distinguish
the lasting from the transient. Be that as it may, John Tomlinson's career
in educational administration (1960–1984) spanned a generation – the last
generation before the Deluge. It was the last before the Education Reform
Act; the last in which local education authorities had a leading role and young
men and women with ambitions in education could hope to realise them as
directors of education.

The period starts with some sort of political consensus – not conflict-free,
but for good practical reasons the political parties, nationally and locally, saw
eye to eye on many educational issues. It wasn't a consensus only between
the politicians; it also extended to the education professionals, who enjoyed
a wide measure of public trust. Centralising tendencies were already there to
see not very far below the surface, but the commitment to local education
authorities as the mainspring of educational provision and development was

genuine. Twenty-five years later it was not like that. The parties were at loggerheads, the local education authorities were about to be emasculated and the educational establishment sidelined.

In the early sixties the comprehensive issue was looming. It was one of the rocks on which the consensus would founder but some thought there was a sporting chance of shooting the rapids without holing the boat. Exit Edward Boyle, enter Margaret Thatcher and the Conservative hostility hardens. As for the curriculum, the period starts with the attempt to set up a Curriculum Study Group within the Ministry of Education and ends with Keith Joseph's last effort to achieve coordination without a legally imposed National Curriculum. All these dramas were played out against the back-drop of relentless social and economic change affecting the lives of children and their families, and therefore the schools.

I wish to discuss, then, these issues under four headings:

- politics and finance;
- organisation and structure;
- curriculum;
- social change: children and the family.

POLITICS AND FINANCE

In 1960 English education was still emerging from the immediate post-war phase. The main priorities were determined by a major Education Act passed only 14 years earlier. This was the nature and the explanation of the so-called consensus. The 1944 Act mapped out a programme for at least a generation. The only question was whether people could be patient enough to carry it out before embarking on the next generation's programme. There was an immense amount to do. It would be more than ten years before the school leaving age would be raised to 16. It would be thirty years before staying on beyond 16 ceased to be a minority activity.

A newly-appointed administrative assistant in Shropshire would have found the educational horizon dominated by the building of schools and the recruitment of teachers. Because it was a rural county there would also have been much talk of 'rural education' and further education would have a strong bias in the direction of agriculture and related crafts and trades. But the immediate aim was to complete 'reorganisation' which in the circumstances of the time meant the replacement of all-age schools with primary and secondary schools – the target set, note, a whole generation earlier by the Hadow Report of 1926.

But two years earlier there had been a change in the way education was financed which was to have far-reaching consequences. It marked the first stage in chipping away at education's privileged place in local government (Association of Education Committees, 1957). Under the old scheme, authorities received 'percentage grants'; for all approved expenditure on education they received a percentage grant from central government. There was a complicated rate equalisation scheme so the percentage each authority got back differed, but overall expenditure was split: about 60 per cent from central funds, 40 per cent from local.

The effect of this was to give the education committee of each county and county borough a special status. Education money was ring-fenced. The rate-payer only had to pay 40 per cent cost of any project. By the same token dropping an education project only saved 40 per cent of its costs for an authority bent on cuts. The Treasury had long disliked this formula and tried many times to get rid of it but it survived the financial storms of the inter-war years, backed by the Board of Education as the strongest and most effective instrument for defending educational standards and the one which most effectively matched the needs of 'a national system locally administered' (Cooke and Gosden, 1986).

The 1958, Local Government Act changed all this. For education, it meant that instead of a percentage grant, authorities were to receive the Treasury's contribution towards education spending in the form of a general grant-in-aid. The ring-fence was gone. The Ministry of Education dropped its opposition in return for guarantees about the future of the school building programme. The deal was brokered by the Ministry's Accountant General, David Nenk, widely regarded as the most gifted civil servant of his generation. (He developed cancer soon afterwards and died in 1960 at the age of 43.) (Cooke and Gosden, 1986, Maclure, 1984).

The education committees and their national association feared the worst which did not immediately materialise. They expected to see money for education cut and diverted to other local needs but there was no evidence of this. But the deal was sold to the counties and county boroughs as a means of relieving them of the central control the Ministry exercised through the Grant Regulations. In fact the local education authorities enjoyed no more real power because total funding was kept tight. What the change did do, however, was remove the power of Ministers to set financial priorities and add significantly to their sense of impotence.

Successive pieces of legislation on educational finance built on these changes, as did local government reorganisation in 1972 which undermined the education committees still more and fatally wounded their national organisation, the Association of Education Committees. The language of corporate management accorded with the modernising ambitions of the Heath Government, promising (but not achieving) stronger, more efficient local institutions. The same rhetoric weakened the hand of the Secretary of State, who was left only with the clumsy and legally uncertain powers in Sections 68 and 99 of the 1944 Act – powers only intended for use as a last resort.

The predictable consequence came in the 1970s when the sudden rise of youth unemployment focused attention on vocational education and the need for programmes to bridge the gap between school and work. The Department of Education was sidestepped; the money was channelled through the Department of Employment and its Manpower Services Agency. Britain's economic decline in the 1970s made matters worse. Successive chancellors sought to hold back local spending. Open confrontation between central and local government came in the first half of the 1980s with rate-capping which made a final nonsense of the Hailsham rhetoric a generation earlier about the gentleman in Wigan knowing better than the gentleman in Whitehall.

The changes in local government finance provide a running commentary on the changing political climate for education. The elimination of the education committee's privileged position also attacked the director of education's power base and, taken with managerial changes after 1972, encouraged local politicians to assert themselves in educational matters. The break-down of the system in the early 1980s with the ending of any pretence that local taxation might be allowed to fund serious local options, heralded the time for settling old scores with radical measures. For education this meant the end of the LEA as previously known; for local finance, it meant the debacle of the poll tax.

To sum up, the financial and political changes were interlinked. They undermined education's place in local government and denied the interdependence of local and central government on education. They undermined the relationship between politicians and professionals locally and between local education professionals and administrators in central government. And they weakened the Secretary of State's position in Cabinet. Beyond this they sharpened the political battle at all levels, polarised national and local politics on education and created the preconditions for a radical reaction.

ORGANISATION AND STRUCTURE

Few political slogans can have incorporated more ambiguities and confusions than Tawney's demand for 'Secondary Education for All'. It had all the hallmarks of a first-rate manifesto promise; a robust call for a universally recognised but conveniently undefined good. It is not clear that even Tawney knew what it meant. He like others was caught up in the toils of the psychology of individual differences when it came to translating slogan into policy (Simon, 1965). Did 'secondary education for all' mean a common school? Did it imply a common curriculum? Or could it mean a single educational phase, the needs of which might best be met in different kinds of secondary school?

The 1944 Act did not attempt to provide an answer. It simply promised everyone a secondary education in the post-Hadow sense that education was to be in two stages, primary and secondary, and all were to pass from the one to the other. For the public at large and MPs in the House of Commons, secondary education meant one thing – the grammar school, with fees to pay (or scholarships to win) and a curriculum geared to the School Certificate examinations. There was a widespread acknowledgement that such a curriculum would not be suitable for all pupils moving from the primary to the secondary stage.

The years since then have been spent in working out ways of meeting the spectrum of needs. In the immediate post-war period most authorities backed the prevailing view in the Ministry of Education which favoured separate types of secondary school, side by side, and a selection process at the end of the primary school to pick the ablest 20 per cent or so for the grammar schools (the exact percentage varied widely from authority to authority).

The attack on the selective system focused on the 11-plus procedures, the best researched tests in existence. The same research which backed the tests revealed their weaknesses and margins of error (Yates and Pidgeon, 1957). Labour, which from 1945 to 1951 had left the choice of secondary organisation to local education authorities, returned to office in 1964 with manifesto commitments to comprehensive education. The result was Circular 10/65 and All That – the beginning of another generation-long reorganisation programme.

The proponents of comprehensive education were not exclusively to be found in the Labour Party. Tory Leicestershire had been an early backer of the comprehensive idea with a two-tier system which avoided some of the snags thought to attach to the comprehensive model, like the need for big schools. Sir Edward Boyle, the departing Secretary of State, was leaning towards comprehensive solutions. For example, he had come round to the view that, planning from scratch in a new housing area, it would be a mistake to set up separate grammar and modern schools. But fairly soon it became clear that a change to comprehensive education could not be undertaken without a political row: the grammar school lobby was too strong and it had natural links with the Conservative Party. Edward Boyle was out on a limb and anyone who watched him battle against the tide in a Conservative Party Conference with rank and file whipped up by Angus Maude and a right-wing claque, can have had little doubt that the political divide would open up.

When Mrs Thatcher became Secretary of State in 1970, Conservative policy was held together by the principle that each local education authority should be allowed to choose its own system of secondary organisation. She saw no reason why grammar schools and comprehensives should not flourish side by side. To most people who spent five minutes thinking about it, 'co-existence' seemed to be based on a logical flaw. If one school was selective, a school alongside it could not, in logic, be comprehensive. But given the practicalities of the time, co-existence let Mrs Thatcher and her colleagues sidestep the main issue. They could continue to deal with the comprehensive schemes in the pipeline (and allow Mrs Thatcher famously to approve more comprehensive plans than any Secretary of State before or since) while offering their friends in local government support if they wished to hang on to their grammar schools.

Most Conservative-controlled authorities complied with Circular 10/65 and reorganisation went ahead in the patchy way you would expect given the decentralised nature of the system. But the ambiguities remained. What were the essential constituents of secondary education beside the age of the recipient? The grammar schools which remained, along with the independent schools (their number increased by the ending of Direct Grant), offered a yardstick of 'real secondary education'; the comprehensive schools were measured against it.

The only criterion for what constituted a comprehensive school was negative; no 11-plus selection. No fewer than six different models of comprehensive organisation were outlined in the Crosland Circular, ranging from the 'orthodox' all-through, 11–18 school through various forms of two- and three-tier systems. Resources specifically to smooth the way for comprehensive reform were extremely limited. Reorganisation schemes had to be carried through using the existing buildings – any new building had to be justified on other grounds such as additional population. Improvisation was the order of the day; split sites abounded. There was widespread disruption which took its toll on standards.

The character of the resulting comprehensive schools has been predictably diverse. Some are aspiring grammar schools; others are like striving secondary moderns; some start with every social advantage; others are severely deprived and face the accumulated consequences of poverty and delinquency. Academic results vary widely from the leafy residential areas to the urban and suburban slums. Clever parents, aware of this diversity, if they can afford to, choose to live in the right places. There is no way of avoiding the fact that some comprehensive schools are more (or less) comprehensive than others and to make them all 'fully comprehensive' would require an unacceptable degree of regulation.

There was no such thing as a comprehensive school curriculum in the minds of the reformers. Perhaps ideally Crosland should have first decided the curriculum and then devised a system to give expression to it. But such an idea was totally foreign to the world as it was in 1965; the curriculum was the responsibility of teachers and universities and examination boards. The comprehensive reformers simply had a gut feeling that the way to make education fairer and society more open was to organise secondary education so that children from all social classes and all ability groups went to the same school.

The one feature of the old regime which was abandoned without any regret was the 11-plus examination, and even now when politicians begin to talk openly of reintroducing selection in a variety of forms, nobody argues for the return of the 11-plus. The irony is, of course, that the 11-plus and its associated baggage, reflected the overriding aim of fairness – it was meant to attack privilege by making sure that everybody was considered. And in so far as psychometric tests were used, they were to discover ability which might otherwise be overlooked.

With all its shortcomings, the 11-plus was an attempt to counter the influence of class and family. That it failed should not obscure the fact that an attempt was made. Nor should it conceal the fact that selection by schools, responding to parental choice, is a tailor-made way of handing on educational advantages from one generation to another.

Comprehensive reorganisation – bringing it in and making it work – provided many of the ongoing preoccupations of the period under discussion. It remained incomplete when the Flood came – incomplete, literally, in the sense that there were still unreorganised local areas where grammar schools and secondary moderns survived; incomplete in the sense that the diversity within the system looks like increasing rather than decreasing and the quality gap between the best and the worst comprehensive schools is as wide as ever; and incomplete in the sense that the argument is still open about the character of secondary education and how best to meet the varying needs of the whole population.

CURRICULUM

Although there was no attempt to make comprehensive reorganisation conditional on choosing a suitable curriculum, curriculum reform became a priority in the early 1960s. In subjects like physics and chemistry there was an obvious need to review subject material and bring it up to date. One transatlantic response to the first Russian spaceship was an expensive reform programme for secondary school science. On this side of the Atlantic, the Nuffield Foundation earmarked funds for similar programmes.

For a decade after the end of the Second World War, Government policy had been to allow the secondary modern schools 'freedom' from the leading reins of external examinations. They were new institutions which had to work out their own curricular programmes without the outside pressures of examinations designed for academic-type secondary schools. In practice, however, the schools themselves wanted yardsticks to measure their progress and used what examinations they could lay their hands on – including technical examinations and those offered by such bodies as the College of Preceptors and the Royal Society of Arts, as well as the General Certificate of Education. It became obvious that the Ministry's policy of benign neglect could not be sustained and in due course a committee was set up by the Secondary Schools Examination Council under Robert Beloe, the Surrey chief education officer. What followed was a new examination, the Certificate of Secondary Education, tailored to the needs of the modern schools – this at the time when the drive to comprehensive schools was about to gather pace. (That, not untypically, it took another twenty years to bring GCE and CSE together speaks volumes about education's top management over the next two decades.)

If the secondary modern schools were going to have their own examinations, there were questions about what should be taught and how, which had to be considered before a new examination foreclosed them. Standing in the way of this were the inhibitions which conventionally excluded the Ministry from curricular decision-making. It took fully 25 years to mount a successful challenge to this exclusion, from the time in March, 1960 when David Eccles first mused to the House of Commons about a secret garden, to the replacement of Keith Joseph by the thrusting Kenneth Baker (Plaskow, 1985). The first moves inside the Ministry of Education were prompted by Ralph Fletcher, the civil servant in charge of Schools Branch, and led to the setting up in 1962 of a Curriculum Study Group to undertake the development work for the CSE. The interdisciplinary model was derived from the Ministry's Architects Development Group. Derek Morrell, a former head of the architects and buildings branch and another gifted administrator destined to die young, was given the task of bringing together a small team of administrators, HMIs and examination experts.

What followed was instructive and provides a key to the Tomlinson years. The Ministry had made its pitch. It set up a sensitive and intelligent mechanism for tackling the curriculum of the secondary modern schools and their new examination. It offered a way of bringing the curriculum back into the public domain. Other Ministers at other times would have brazened it out and pressed on. But in 1962–63 the Conservative Government's period of office was drawing to a close. In the face of concerted opposition from the teachers' unions and the education authorities, Edward Boyle allowed a working alliance between Ronald Gould, William Alexander and Derek Morrell to convert the embryo Curriculum Study Group into a very different animal – a Schools Council for Curriculum and Examinations, with a constitution devised by Morrell and Alexander which effectively preserved the teachers' curricular prerogatives.

Looked at thirty odd years later, the Schools Council appears as a twenty year parenthesis – a two-decade diversion on the path to a national curriculum. It demonstrated the power of what has come to be called the educational establishment in the context of the 1960s. Education was still a partnership. And as Alexander would argue, if any two partners – in this case the teachers and the local education authorities – combined they stood a good chance of holding back the third.

The Schools Council started with strong backing from the Ministry in the shape of Derek Morrell. He was a practical idealist with a passionate belief in public service. He was also clever and imaginative and highly regarded by his colleagues and by Ministers. But even if it took twenty years for its fate to be sealed, the Council's doom was guaranteed from the start. The Ministry had colluded in its creation but it represented a power base outside the control of what became the Department of Education and Science. Just as the Manpower Services Commission was bound in the course of time to be seen in the Department of Employment as an off-shoot which needed to be cut back, so too it was wholly predictable that in the course of time the DES would seek to take back what it had conceded to the Council.

In other respects, the life of the Schools Council follows the pattern of the period. It was ostentatiously unprescriptive. Its output carried no authority other than its own intrinsic merit. Projects went off in various directions without necessarily being consistent or sharing a single philosophy, though in tune with the times, liberal ideas predominated – discovery learning was in vogue; there was a bias towards individualised instruction. These liberal ideas were embedded in the Schools Council psyche and influenced the choice of projects and people.

But reaction was already afoot – it came at the end of the 1960s with public response to student unrest and the first Black Papers. Maurice Plaskow quotes

Mrs Thatcher's comment on Lawrence Stenhouse's Humanities project with its emphasis on the teacher as neutral arbiter of controversial discussion – 'when I was a girl we were taught to know the difference between right and wrong' (Plaskow, 1985). It was as if the Schools Council was also neutral: there was a reluctance to grapple with questions of balance within the curriculum as a whole because these were difficult and the Council was not constituted to tackle difficult questions. When the Council eventually got round to the curriculum as a whole it was at its least impressive.

It was a development body, a good organisation for getting ideas off the ground and then letting them fend for themselves. It was founded on the assumption that no executive decisions about the curriculum were needed. While the DES was in a non-executive mode, frustrated by its financial impotence and squeezed between the rival powers of the Department of Employment and the Department of the Environment, the Council had a limited lease of life. Come the Department's counter-attack in the 1980s and the Council's weakness and lack of friends in high places was revealed.

The final years of the Schools Council saw Tomlinson as the last chairman trying to keep the show on the road. The tale is one of duplicity and treachery as by devious means the Department set the Council up for the Secretary of State's *coup de grâce*. The Council and its staff were accused of not paying enough attention to the Secretary of State's agenda. To help them do better, DES representation was strengthened, but the senior DES officials whose job it was to give a steer, resolutely refused to do so, preferring to repeat accusations of the Council's unresponsiveness.

The life cycle of the Schools Council began in the optimism of the 1960s, a little mad and carried away by the excitement of a world turned upside down, but releasing a flood of ideas. The downturn came in the 1970s when the optimism evaporated and economic failure fed doubts about achievement and magnified concerns about the way schools prepared young people for working life. When critics rounded on the education system for its alleged failure to equip school-leavers for economic survival, they did not look to the Schools Council for answers: they pointed to central not local government for a response and to the Manpower Services Commission not the Department of Education and Science.

The rise in youth unemployment from the early 1970s was one important catalyst. Till then, youth employment had been more buoyant than adult. Fifteen-year-old school-leavers had no difficulty getting jobs in traditional industries without reference to their educational attainments. After the economic crises of the 1970s this ceased to be true. Youth employment became a buyers' market. Educational attainment (or lack of it) became a criterion for choosing who should and should not be employed. Unemployment was blamed on inadequately prepared young people – and the schools – not on the collapse of the smokestack industries and structural changes in the economy.

The Black Papers were the forerunners of much of the criticism – crude, poorly argued, blatantly populist in their appeal, they touched a nerve among the public at large. They focused attention on progressive teaching methods and, by implication, on many aspects of curriculum development. They helped to stimulate reaction – a nostalgic desire for the certainties of earlier times which, for all his denials, lurked in James Callaghan's Ruskin speech in 1976. From then on, the educational establishment was under notice, with the Schools Council conspicuously vulnerable. Government intervention was mooted and the next 10 years were spent exploring ways of bringing the curriculum under control, if possible by agreement.

Keith Joseph nearly pulled it off without nationalising the curriculum. Perhaps he might have done so with *Better Schools* had not the Conservative strategists decided to make radical reform of education a leading issue for the 1987 General Election. So the Tomlinson years ended with the nationalisation of the curriculum.

A basic premise of the radical reformers was that the schools had failed under the old dispensation and that the educational establishment had ignored the evidence of failure. There is some truth in this accusation. One reason for apparent complacency was that the evidence of success was so much more convincing – the steady rise in examination passes at 16 and 18, and the expansion of post-secondary education. Seven per cent of pupils got five or more GCE grades A–C in 1965; 38 per cent in 1990. The percentage attaining two A levels in 1960 was 6.5; in 1970, 13, and in 1990, 22 (Little and Tomlinson, 1993). The rapid expansion of higher education in the decade from 1986 to 1995 looked like a dividend on investment in education long before the radical reformers appeared on the scene. Even if some allowance is made for grade inflation this is hardly the record of three decades of failure.

Alongside the evidence of success, the evidence of 'school failure' – an emotive phrase which generates more blanket disapproval than acute analysis – is harder to assemble. But public anxiety, orchestrated by politicians and exploited by the media, is real enough. To reinforce this sense of anxiety there is now a powerful organ of the new educational establishment, the Office for Standards in Education, committed to the belief that the way to raise standards is to focus attention on signs of weakness wherever they can be found.

The evidence from international comparisons is not easy to interpret, but what there is, is not reassuring. It is at its strongest when direct comparison is made of particular levels and qualifications. When Professor Sig Prais and his colleagues looked at the evidence from the International Educational Achievement Study and backed it up with a detailed study of syllabuses and examinations in England and West Germany they concluded that pupils in the bottom half of the ability range in German schools did as well as the average for all children in English schools (Prais and Wagner, 1986, Green and Steedman, 1993).

Other studies have shown the superior mathematical attainment of German plumbers and electricians compared with English. It may be (as some say) that plumbers and electricians in Germany have more mathematics than they need; but what does it say about the schools which prepare them? There seems no reason to doubt that the standards in mathematics currently achieved by average students in Germany are higher than those expected of average students in England. This may well extend to other basic subjects. The evidence also reveals important things about industrial training. The standards achieved in school are likely to be related to those demanded by employers offering highly-valued training.

Of course, none of this casts any doubt on the proposition that the system as a whole has made great strides since the early 1960s – but so it should have, starting from a modest base; and schools in comparable countries have probably done at least as well. It has long been accepted that the gap between the best and the worst in English education is far too wide. Complaints about illiterate job applications are widespread but unquantifiable and like the poor, seem always to be with us. They refer to graduates no less than to applicants for apprenticeships and other jobs with training. If people have been through 11, 17, or 20-odd years of mainly literary education and emerge without the ability to write a few pages of connected prose without glaring mistakes, it seems obvious to those outside the education system that something is wrong. Few would deny that Keith Joseph's bottom 40 per cent get a poor deal in literacy and numeracy. Moreover, the system more or less guarantees that they will have their limited success shown up with painful clarity by a system of regular testing and the publication of results in competitive form.

At all events, it is probably a political fact of life that anxiety about educational standards and 'failing schools' is here to stay in England. It is not a temporary phenomenon, to be cured by radical treatment, but will have to be accepted as the political norm – a means of justifying the existence of secretaries of state for education. This inbuilt anxiety has certainly been the basic premise for educational debate in the United States for the past thirty years and more. The schools have become a necessary scapegoat for the ills of society, the multifarious effects of which make the job of the schools more difficult by the day.

SOCIAL CHANGE: CHILDREN AND THE FAMILY

It is impossible to consider any major aspect of education without also paying attention to social context. In the 1960s when sociology seemed to be queen of the sciences, social considerations dominated – some would say swamped – conversation about education. Reformers put forward the idea of compensatory education – education to compensate for social deprivation; the Plowden Report mooted the idea of educational priority areas where resources could be enlarged to meet the greater needs of poor children. Positive discrimination on a small scale became the orthodoxy of the day.

But if the 1960s were spent exploring the significance of social factors in education, the 1970s brought disillusion. It became clear on both sides of the Atlantic that nobody knew how much compensation was needed to be effective – except that it was more than could possibly be delivered by public systems of education. Moreover, education alone could not compensate; creating a level playing field for the schools (like guaranteeing 'real' comprehensive schools everywhere) depended on social reconstruction on a much wider scale – the kind of redistributive programme which no democratic political system could deliver. The message of the large-scale survey research in the United States was that, given the powerful influence of other factors in the social environment, schools made little difference.

This was a message which echoed the pessimism of the 1970s in Britain – a time when the decline of the British economy seemed to combine with the failure of British politics to hasten the drift into genteel decay. The broad-based search for a fairer society which had been one of the mainsprings of educational reform flickered, died down and flared again in sectarian terms of race, gender and sexual orientation.

As for the schools, they had to concentrate on the things which they could do something about – how to use the 15,000 hours of students' time they controlled, knowing that the art and craft of teaching was about refusing to let adverse social factors take over. The teachers who achieved most would be those who refused to believe their students were predestined to failure – who made students believe in themselves. As misplaced hopes for education as a self-generating well-spring of social renewal faded, there was a rediscovery of basic truths about the mechanics of teaching and learning and running well ordered schools.

Over the period the ethnic and linguistic composition of the school population changed out of recognition, bringing a slate of questions of a social, religious and educational character, some of them contentious, all of them demanding. Some of the least contentious but most demanding arose from the increase in the number of pupils whose home language is other than English. In Inner London the figure rose from 12–13 per cent to 25 per cent in the single decade of the 1980s. It takes time to adjust to changes on this scale, which are often localised in areas which are already severely deprived.

In a recent article in *Children and Society* Professor A. H. Halsey discussed the past thirty years of social change – years which have placed children at the centre of a revolution in manners and morals. Changes in women's roles have held a key to this social revolution, bringing smaller families, and changes in the workplace which have kept more women and notably more married women at work. With the collapse of many traditional forms of male employment there has been what Halsey calls a prolonged 'renegotiation of the division of labour'.

Changes in sexual mores associated with the contraceptive pill went along with the relaxation of other social conventions to usher in what was conveniently labelled the permissive society. As for marriage, between 1961 and 1989 the divorce rate rose from 2.1 to 12.7 per thousand married people. Marriage was deferred by many couples – three times as many women cohabited with their partners in 1987, as had done so in 1972. Births outside marriage rose from 5 per cent in 1960 to 28 per cent thirty years later.

The schools have seen the consequences in the form of a rapid rise in the number of children from one-parent families – 14 per cent of all families with dependent children by the beginning of the 1990s, more in many cities. In Inner London before its abolition in 1990, 30 per cent of the school population came from single-parent families. Children in such families are disproportionately likely to be poor and deprived. As Professor Halsey (1993) sums it up: 'such children tend to die earlier, to have more illness, to do less well at school, to exist at a lower level of nutrition, comfort and conviviality, to suffer more unemployment, be more prone to deviancy and crime, and finally to repeat the cycle of unstable parenting from which they themselves have suffered.' These are statements about averages not necessarily about individuals, though the average is made up from a totality of individuals. There is no simple way of measuring the effect of these changes on standards of achievement and the quality of school life, but few can doubt they have a bearing on the specific educational outcomes which now occupy the fevered attention of politicians.

If Professor Halsey's analysis is correct, what has been happening has to do with individualism – the 'superstition' that if 'ego maximises his or her choices we are all better off . . . the fallacy that individual freedom is collective good.' If the adult ego is self-sufficient, children thereby become 'commodities – quality objects to be sure – but nonetheless things like cars or videos or holidays which adults can choose to have in preference to other consumables.' For much of the period covered by the Tomlinson years the values of education have been at odds with the rise of these values. The Education Reform Act, which celebrates the victory of individual values over collective, has done nothing to resolve the conflict.

REFERENCES

Association of Education Committees: The Threat to Education 1957. Unsigned, but written by the present author.
Cooke, G & Gosden, P (1986) *Education Committees* AEC Trust, 75.
Green, A & Steedman, H (1993) *Educational Provision, Educational Attainment and the Needs of Industry, A Review of Research for Germany, France, Japan, the USA and Britain*, NIESR.
Halsey, A H (1993) *Children and Society*, Vol. 7, no. 2, p. 125.
Little, V & Tomlinson, J (1993) Education: Thirty years of Change – for Better or Worse? In *Children and Society*, 7, 2.
Maclure, S (1984) *Educational Development and School Building* 1945–73, London: Longmans.
Plaskow, M (1985) (Ed.) *Life and Death of the Schools Council, passim*, London: Falmer.
Prais, S & Wagner, K (1986) *Schooling Standards in Britain and Germany*, NIESR.
Simon, B (1965) *Education and the Labour Movement*, London: Lawrence Wishart.
Williams, S (1996) *Snakes and Ladders – A Political Diary*, Tape: BBC World-wide Ltd.
Yates, A & Pidgeon, D (1957) *Admission to Grammar Schools*, London: NFER.

2

CONSUMER RIGHTS AND COMMON PURPOSES

Tony Edwards

Professor Tony Edwards has been Professor of Education since 1979. He was Head of School of Education 1981 to 1989 and Dean of Faculty of Education at the University of Newcastle Upon Tyne from 1989 to 1996.

As a preface to his account of how a comprehensive, publicly-funded health service was constructed, Nicholas Timmins (1996, p. 101) quotes a comment by a future Labour minister that 'the gentlemen in Whitehall really do know better what is good for the people than the people know themselves'. In stark contrast, from the time when the first Thatcher Administration began to gather radical momentum in its efforts to dismantle the welfare leviathans, British government policy has been shaped by deep dislike of public services provided from above by those who 'know what is good for people'. The targets of that dislike have been both welfare professionals and the local and national public servants whose actions upheld their 'monopolistic' pretensions. Although a strong wish to curb the interventions of government became an international phenomenon, it was given distinctively confident expression by Margaret Thatcher. Asked by Parliamentary lobby correspondents after her second election victory how she would wish her government to be remembered, she chose as its most desirable epitaph that it had been the government which 'decisively broke with a debilitating consensus of a paternalistic government and a dependent people, which rejected the notion that the State is all-powerful and the citizens merely its beneficiaries . . .' (quoted in Kavanagh, 1987, pp. 251–2). Progress towards that objective might sometimes be slowed down or diverted by political expediency, but the objective itself was clear. It was to break the 'producer monopolies' in public services, and so compel the providers of those services to respond to consumer demand or suffer unprotected the consequences of losing custom.

This is familiar ideological ground, well trodden by believers and sceptics alike. Sceptics have much the harder time in argument. Convictions about the benefits of consumer sovereignty are easier to convey, having the clarity obtainable from an apparent absence of doubt, than are dilemmas about the balancing of individual rights and public interest. Consumer choice appears so obviously a good thing that those wishing to restrict it, for example to prevent what they regard as unacceptably unequal outcomes, may themselves be denounced as unacceptably paternalist. From a 'modified libertarian perspective', David Hargreaves (1996) defends the 'common-sense' view that choice should only be restricted or denied when there is strong evidence that the costs outweigh the benefits, and when there are also strong grounds for believing that those costs can be removed or reduced by limited government intervention. Real market enthusiasts however find it difficult to conceive of worthwhile objections to treating welfare services like any other form of consumption and leaving them, perhaps above some threshold of basic provision, to the interplay of demand and supply. They argue that to do so is more efficient because it subjects the providers of those services to the discipline of market forces, which inexorably reward success and penalise failure. It is also more democratic. 'Shopping is more effective than voting' as an expression of individual choice, because it is done much more often and the 'electorate' is much larger but also because it replaces incorrigible differences in cultural power which produce unequal access to welfare services with corrigible differences in spending power (Seldon, 1995).

From an unmodified libertarian position, John Tomlinson will appear as a many-dyed villain. As the last chairman of the Schools Council, he was a key figure in that interlocking educational establishment (dominated by teacher unions and LEAs) accused by its critics of resisting any real reform. As a former chief education officer, he has been an upholder of the LEA monopoly. As a professor of education, he will be presumed an uncritical advocate of 'progressive' teaching and other 'trendy' theories. As vice-chair of the Universities Council for the Education of Teachers through a period of radical change imposed from above, and especially as a prime mover in the campaign to establish a General Teaching Council, he will be heard as a voice of producer self-interest. Shorn of those pejorative expectations however, his is a career which has inclined him strongly to explore that difficult balance between private and public interests which recent government policies have tilted so sharply towards the rights of individual consumers (for example, in Ranson and Tomlinson, 1994). He and I were among the contributors to an 'alternative White Paper' the main theme of which was the inadequacy of unrestrained institutional self-interest as a basis for an effective, humane and equitable education system (Institute for Public Policy Research, 1993). It is within that frame of reference that this chapter has been written.

CONSUMERISM TO EXCESS?

Despite systematic ideological prompting of the government to be bold, the radical tide swept over education rather later than over health and housing. It then did so with extraordinary force. When my colleagues and I reported our evaluation of the Conservatives' first educational reform, we noted a continuing disappointment on the Right that nothing exciting had followed it and portrayed the Assisted Places Scheme as recreating a traditional scholarship ladder for the 'poor but able' rather than as a first step (as the 1992 White Paper was to claim retrospectively) towards restructuring the system (Fitz, Edwards and Whitty, 1986). Our analysis illustrates the risks of writing contemporary history, because its publication coincided with Kenneth Baker's announcement of a pilot programme of twenty city technology colleges – an initiative definitely intended to model both a new curriculum and a new kind of autonomous school free from Local Authority 'shackles'. Within months, a 'great' Reform Bill included an unprecedented increase in state control of the curriculum, an unprecedented delegating of financial powers to schools, an apparent opening of school enrolment, and a large escape hatch for parents wishing collectively to make their school self-governing. As the Economic and Social Research Council put it when inviting applications for a programme of research into 'innovations in teaching and learning', the exceptional scope and pace of educational change was creating a 'natural laboratory' within which to investigate issues of 'fundamental concern'.

How the prospects of upheaval were viewed at the time is vividly captured in Julian Haviland's (1988) compendium of responses to the government's consultation process. Apprehension was certainly high, proving to market enthusiasts how successfully vested interests were being threatened and the 'welfare mentality' was being challenged. A more sympathetic interpretation would identify deep anxiety that a public service was being rebuilt with too little thought about the shape and inadequacies of its replacement. There also seemed to be such a contradiction between the Act's centralising and deregulating tendencies that apparently incompatible components were attributed to quite different institutional and ideological workshops (Edwards, 1989) or explained as the government's reluctance to concede control over the curriculum until the consumers of education were fully empowered to exercise their 'common-sense' (Whitty, 1989). Certainly it was hard to reconcile the apparent enabling of consumers to choose the school they wanted with detailed prescription, throughout the entire public sector, of the only curriculum they could have. As John Tomlinson put it, 'a National Curriculum and a market in education cannot be compatible in any logic we understand' (in Haviland, 1988, p. 10).

Certainly the National Curriculum was often presented, sometimes by Ministers, as embodying a public interest in raising the level of common knowledge and understanding to which all children should have access, wherever they lived and went to school. As such, and especially for defining that level in such 'broad and balanced' form, it was attacked from the neo-liberal Right as a huge constraint on free trade and an ideologically objectionable departure from the government's general commitment to a free and competitive educational market (Sexton, 1988). Speaking to National Curriculum Council staff at an early staff development day, I argued that they had much less to fear from 'liberal educationists' whom Duncan Graham sometimes cast as irreconcilable opponents than from the ideologues of the Right for whom any national curriculum beyond a small core of basics stifled initiative and denied choice. Since consumer demand could not be regulated by price, any real competition required differentiated products and individual schools must therefore be 'free to become distinctive and to earn their custom on that basis' (Sexton, 1992, p. 2). The outcome would be a variety of forms of curriculum, but only those forms of curriculum for which there was sufficient consumer demand.

I have outlined a thoroughgoing libertarian position uncomplicated by concerns about any public interest other than the sum of individual choices freely exercised. One particular concern, however, prevented the conservative Right from going so far or at least presented a real dilemma. It might be necessary to constrain the choices available to teachers and parents in the interests of nation-building. The promotion of a stronger sense of national identity, most visibly through appropriately selected literature and history, was a main theme in Kenneth Baker's justification of a national curriculum. It is the theme repeated by the present head of the School Curriculum and Assessment Authority when he defended its proposals for 'British history, standard English and the English literary heritage' as being designed to 'reinforce a common culture . . . They help society to maintain its identity' (Tate, 1994). It is a purpose with obvious appeal to those whose anxieties about the effects of multiculturalism have produced some strikingly monolithic conceptions of British culture and ways of life (Madood, 1992). It prompted, for example, fierce criticism of those 'anti-racist' teachers to whom was attributed 'a desire to lock ethnic minorities in their own language and customs and to isolate them from the greater society of which they are a part'. Uninhibited support for 'new and autonomous schools of whatever kind parents desire' was therefore tempered by a belief that teachers' first duty is 'to impart our national culture' and that all children should be given 'the knowledge and understanding that are necessary for the full enjoyment and enhancement of British society' (Hillgate Group, 1987, p. 3). Such perception of a public interest obligation to impart or at least help to sustain a common culture fits uneasily with curricula determined by consumer demand.

Before returning to that dilemma in the second part of the chapter, I raise briefly a question confronted by several contributors to this book (in particular Stewart Ranson and A H Halsey) and by other recent analyses of the benefits and costs of an educational market (for example, Gewirtz, Ball and Bowe, 1995). In a system intended to be driven by competition between schools to attract custom and (in practice) by competition between customers for the school of their choice, where are collective expressions of public interest to find 'voice' and be contested? However imperfectly, Local Authorities have provided such a forum. Their deliberate weakening has created huge scope for state intervention, so that the priority given in the 1992 White Paper to diminishing them still further prompted a *Times* leader on the extraordinary sight of a Conservative government displaying 'such contempt for . . . the bonds that tie schools to their local communities through local democracy' but such faith in 'the rectitude of Whitehall planning' (29 July, 1992). Two years later, Newcastle's Education Committee was well aware of struggling against the tide when it affirmed its continuing commitment to 'a service which is distinctive of the City and reflects the Council's own priorities', and to maintaining 'a community of schools', despite successive initiatives intended to break that 'service' into competing fragments. The process of fragmentation is replacing political control by bodies elected with a responsibility for providing education for a whole population with quasi-autonomous schools which manage their budgets, shape their image, and (increasingly) select their intakes. This is claimed to depoliticise education. It does not. It embodies a different politics. Decisions not taken by central government are transferred from the public sphere and made into largely 'private' matters.

The extent to which school governors should think beyond the interests of 'their' school illustrates what is in contention (Thody, 1995). When a representative of the National Association of Governors and Managers argues that 'no governing body has the right to affect the fortunes of another school without a proper public process' (Walter Ulrich, reported in *The Times Educational Supplement*, 5 July, 1996), he is arguing against what market enthusiasts explicitly want them to do. Even the Secretary of State, who retains some regard for local government, foreshadowed the main theme in the 1996 White Paper when she asserted the right of grant-maintained schools to 'make their own decisions about how they operate and what sort of schools they want to be', and so to 'develop the character they judge will best suit the needs of their pupils and their communities without being told by anyone else what to do' (Gillian Shephard, 28 March, 1996). This is an exhortation to unrestrained institutional self-interest. In effect it says to schools – 'If you want to expand, or create a sixth form, or become selective, or specialise, then go for it. If doing so creates difficulties for other schools, then they either respond effectively or suffer the consequences. And those consequences are their problem and not yours.'

Despite the Secretary of State's passing reference to communities, local ties and loyalties are intended to be irrelevant in an open market in which consumers and producers seek to gain advantage. It seems to me, as to the Senior Chief Inspector for Schools when the 1988 Reform Act became law, that 'it is surely a triumph of hope over experience to expect that such self-interested, isolated, fragmented decisions, made in thousands of separate institutions, will add up to a sensible, effective and efficient national school system' (Bolton, 1993, p. 8). The alternative is not to return to a past confidence that those in authority 'know best', but to explore what limits might reasonably and fairly be placed on self-interest. Market enthusiasts tend to argue that while a market certainly produces unequal outcomes (or there would be no incentives for the enterprising), those outcomes are not 'unjust' because in their effects on individuals they are neither intended nor foreseen. But if it is foreseeable, for example, that already disadvantaged groups will be further disadvantaged by the emergence of a steepening hierarchy of schools created by various forms of selectiveness, then 'we can be held to bear collective responsibility for the outcomes . . . [especially] when the outcomes are capable of being altered' (Plant, 1990, pp. 17–19). Schools embody moral values in the ways in which they are organised and work, not only – indeed, not even mainly – through their teaching of 'right from wrong'. It seems somewhat perverse to urge schools to give more attention to developing their students' sense of social responsibility while ignoring the extent to which competition has been given such visible precedence over co-operation and the pursuit of self-interest made into a cardinal virtue.

IN DEFENCE OF COMMON PURPOSES

The more fervent libertarians seem to wish for a return to that nineteenth century model in which the state insisted that children should be educated, but neither provided nor prescribed their schooling beyond whatever minimum standards were deemed necessary for public safety and a sufficiently literate, numerate and biddable workforce. Attempts at more ambitiously inclusive schooling are then rejected as a certain path to mediocrity or worse. But much less dogmatic advocates of consumer choice have also claimed that schools directed from above by some form of public authority are both inescapably mediocre and incapable of significant improvement as long as education is still treated as welfare. First, the discipline imposed on schools by market forces is missing. Secondly, the supposedly democratic bodies which control them are themselves so subject to competing pressures that their directives either change as different interests prevail or are bound by uneasy compromises designed to avoid giving offence. Seeking to avoid offence to influential groups, they positively please none; seeking to serve too many purposes, they achieve none of them. Schools must therefore be free, it is argued, to be uncommon – that is, to respond to the preferences of particular parent groups and so display that clear sense of purpose which marks the effective school. Those preferences are seen as extending far beyond the content of the curriculum to pedagogy, ethos, and philosophy. In all those dimensions of schooling, real consumer choice requires real diversity of provision. From this perspective, traditional views of the socialising effects of common schooling are at best outdated.

Contributing powerfully to that stance is a view of modern society as too heterogeneous for supposedly common schooling to be anything more than a series of unstable, uneasy compromises. James Coleman (1990), for example, has concluded from a comparison of fee-paying, Catholic and neighbourhood high schools that the more effective are those based on 'communities of values'. His analysis seems to convey some regret for the passing of that tradition of public schooling which sought to avoid cultural enclaves by freeing children from 'the constraints imposed by accident of birth' and the often narrow cultural horizons of their home worlds. But he regards that tradition as fatally undermined by the multiple cultural identities of modern societies. Especially in cities, these make the intakes to supposedly 'common' schools too diverse to be manageable. He concludes that parents should choose schools and schools choose parents because of the particular values they share.

From this perspective, uncommon schooling appears as an appropriate response, part of a cross-national movement away from mass production and consumption of goods and services towards deregulation and diversity (Weiss, 1993; Whitty, Edwards and Gewirtz, 1993). In David Hargreaves' 'modified' version of that view, social cohesiveness in a pluralistic society is only possible through fostering and building upon 'more local and specific forms of social cohesion'. Whereas the neo-conservative Right maintain quite contradictory positions – that schools of faith and other special interest schools should be encouraged, but that a national culture should be imparted – Hargreaves (1994, 1996) wishes to complement ethically and culturally specialised forms of schooling with a common core of 'civic education' to counter what might otherwise be excessive fragmentation. Although its content is left vague, the proposal represents a considerable modification of a free market. It is because public education 'stands at the intersection' of competing and legitimate rights that the 'relationship of public and private benefits is endlessly complex' (Levin, 1989, p. 217). Market dogma removes the complexity by discounting any public benefits which might arise from interfering with the interplay of supply and demand. Less doctrinaire approaches are bound to be plagued by uncertainties about the 'right' balance between private rights to schooling of choice and public interest in a 'sufficiently' common educational experience. My own uncertainty was highlighted while preparing this chapter by visiting conspicuously multicultural Toronto. It is a city described approvingly as a mosaic rather than as a melting-pot, different ethnic groups maintaining distinct locations and so producing an invigorating cultural array. The image of a mosaic seems to fit David Hargreaves' view of British society as a federation of cultural communities, with its schools rightly encouraged to develop a corresponding diversity. The image also has less positive connotations, of pieces retaining their sharply marked edges so as to produce an overall effect only visible from a distance and preferably from above. But what if the overall effect is not intended to be a single picture? In the absence or decline of anything resembling cultural consensus, the democratic right of parents to have their children educated according to their own values and beliefs might seem to have the moral field to itself.

It is a right forcefully asserted by those who wish to see public funding made available for 'new faith' and other culturally (or pedagogically) specialised schools which are currently either stifled at birth by inability to meet the initial capital costs or are forced 'reluctantly' into the private sector (Carnie, Large and Tasker, 1995; Walford, 1995). The case is likely to be supported by referring to those statements in international covenants, often cited in defence of private education, which proclaim more generally the right of parents both to 'choose schools other than those provided by public authorities' and to ensure that their children's education is 'in conformity with their own religious and philosophical convictions'. Walford (1996) notes that the UK's acceptance of the latter obligation, contained in the European Convention on Human Rights, was made conditional on its compatibility with those clauses in the 1994 Education Act which seemed to subordinate parental wishes to 'the provision of efficient education and training' and 'the avoidance of unreasonable expenditure'.

I want finally to extend the definition of 'efficiency' to embody what has been a main theme in sociological analysis of schooling – its contribution to social cohesion. In my inaugural lecture at Newcastle University I commented that Durkheim's first lectures at the Sorbonne were about social solidarity and the 'conservation of societies' and noted the 'pleasing irony' that a discipline so often regarded as a breeding ground for troublemakers should have been the only one to have been compulsory at that University at that time. It is true that his influence on future lycée teachers was once denounced in the French Parliament as 'the gravest national peril our country has faced in recent times' but that was a Catholic reaction against the secular nature of the morality which Durkheim looked for in the schools. While his perception of a mounting intellectual and moral insecurity has some resemblance to recent accounts of multiplying cultural identities, the implication he drew out for schooling was very different. As I summarised them in that lecture, the critical questions of his time were these. As traditional ties and loyalties weakened and traditional communities broke up, how were new sources of social cohesion to be found? As individuals found more and more space to 'be themselves', how was some attachment to collective life to be maintained? Above all, how was sufficient common ground to be found for societies to hold together? Durkheim found the most hopeful answers to those questions in the schools (Edwards, 1988, p. 168). He therefore looked for something like Hargreaves' 'civic education' – for ways of making children sufficiently similar in behaviour and belief, and sufficiently aware of what linked 'citizens' across the otherwise widening social and cultural divisions, for society to hold together. In part he found it in teachers' obligation to transmit 'the great moral ideas' of their time, an obligation so central to their work that those not willing to do so should be denied the right to teach on the grounds that classrooms could not be allowed to add to the insecurity of the time by becoming a platform for contending private beliefs. Nearly a century later, it is unlikely that there would be agreement on what the necessary collective beliefs should be. Hargreaves' civic version of a core curriculum is also intended to support a common citizenship by connecting his 'local and specific forms of social cohesion' with a wider sense of belonging. But by not describing its possible contents and by arguing at the same time for schools to 'specialise along philosophical, ideological or religious lines' (and appoint teachers similarly committed) he makes that curriculum appear a rather meagre and contrived complement to what really matters. And unless its contents are almost entirely separated off into an entirely distinct sphere of civic virtues, there is likely to be some conflict with local parental values. In such situations, must the public defer to the private?

I noted earlier the dilemma which arises when belief in accepting whatever forms of schooling attract sufficient consumer demand comes into conflict with objections to letting teachers 'lock ethnic minorities in their own language and customs'. The objections should surely apply in principle to any attempt to contain children's education so narrowly within their teachers' or their parents' frame of reference. They arise most obviously in relation to religious education in a multifaith society. Thus Muslim parents have withdrawn their children from religious education in some Birmingham schools on the grounds that (in the words of one parent governor) – 'Multifaith education nurtures a spectator approach to all religions; it teaches you about religion, it doesn't teach you faith' (quoted in Narayan, 1996). From a very different perspective, that statement might be translated into an affirmation of schools' responsibility to 'teach you about the religion of others, not merely to lock you into your own'. I recognise the force of both objections to a curriculum so anxious not to offend that it seems to lack any convictions at all, and to a curriculum reflecting a homogeneous conception of British culture within which non-white, non-Christian groups may appear as intrusions (Madood, 1992). But I also believe that schooling in a multicultural society should be more than an extension of the parents' will and a reinforcing of local identities. Efforts to create publicly-funded Islamic schools illustrate the problem of balancing public and private interests, because such schools would reinforce a 'specific' identify at the risk of diminishing still further a 'collective consciousness' broader and more diverse than that of the local 'collectivity'. The market argument is that since all schooling involves some indoctrination, it is 'infinitely preferable' for that indoctrination to take a variety of forms than the state seek to impose common values through a monopoly of schooling (Flew, 1991, pp. 21–22). I do not believe that the complex balancing of public and private interests is open to so polarised a resolution – monopoly or an open-ended diversity. John Tomlinson believes that 'the kind of schooling we decide to offer our young is the clearest public statement we can make about the kind of society we want them to build' – that it is 'a form of control across generations' (Tomlinson, 1993, pp. 62–63). Conservatives wish to limit the freedom of the next generation to depart far from how things are. In that sense, Durkheim was conservative. But in conditions of much greater 'intellectual and moral' insecurity than those which so worried him, schools have still greater obligation to uphold the values of co-operation and tolerance and to explore with their students

– because there is no ready-made 'civic syllabus' – what common ground best deserves to underlie the diversity.

REFERENCES

Bolton, E (1993) Imaginary gardens with real toads. In C. Chitty & B. Simon (eds) *Education Answers Back: critical responses to government policy*, London: Lawrence and Wishart.

Carnie, F, Large, M & Tasker, M (1995) *Freeing Education: Steps towards real choice and diversity in schools*, Bath: Hawthorn Press.

Coleman, J (1990) Choice, community and future schools. In W. Clune & J. Witte (eds) *Choice and Control in American Education, 1*, Bristol, Pennsylvania and Basingstoke UK: Falmer Press.

Edwards, T (1988) Schooling, liberation and repression. In P. Gordon (ed), *The Study of Education: 3, The Changing Scene*, London: Woburn Press.

Edwards, T (1989) Benefits, costs and risks: some expectations of the National Curriculum, *Curriculum* 10, 2, 65–70.

Fitz, J, Edwards, T & Whitty, G (1986) Beneficiaries, benefits and costs: an investigation of the Assisted Places Scheme, *Research Papers in Education* 1, 3, 169–193.

Flew, A (1991) Educational services: independent competition or maintained monopoly? In D. Green (ed) *Empowering Parents: how to break the schools monopoly*, London: Institute of Economic Affairs Health and Welfare Unit.

Gewirtz, S, Ball, S & Bowe, R (1995) *Markets, Choice and Equity in Education*, Buckingham: Open University Press.

Hargreaves, D (1994) *The Mosaic of Learning: Schools and Teachers for the Next Century*, London: DEMOS.

Hargreaves, D (1996) Diversity and choice in school education: a modified libertarian approach, *Oxford Review of Education* 22, 2, 131–141 and 155–156.

Haviland, J (ed) (1988) *Take Care, Mr Baker: a selection from the advice on the Government's Education Reform Bill which the Secretary of State for Education invited but decided not to publish*, London: Fourth Estate.

Hillgate Group (1987) *The Reform of British Education*, London: Claridge Press.

Institute for Public Policy Research (1993) *Education: A Different Vision*, Institute for Public Policy Research, London: Oram Press.

Kavanagh, D (1987) *Thatcherism and British Politics: the end of consensus*, London: Oxford, University Press.

Levin, H (1989) Education as a public and private good. In N. Devins (ed) *Public Values, Private Schools*, Lewes & Philadelphia: Falmer Press.

Madood, T (1992) On not being white in Britain: discrimination, diversity and commonality. In M. Leicester & M. Taylor (eds) *Ethics, Ethnicity and Education*, London: Kogan Page.

Narayan, N (1996) Muslims set schools a spiritual test, *Observer*, 25 February.

Plant, R (1990) *Citizenship and Rights: Two Views*, London: Institute of Economic Affairs.

Ranson, S & Tomlinson, J (eds) (1994) *School Co-operation: new forms of local governance*, Harlow: Longman.

Seldon, A (1995) The economic fundamentals. In R. Murley (ed) *Patients or Customers?* London: Institute of Economic Affairs Health and Welfare Unit, London.

Sexton, S (1988) *A Guide to the Education Reform Bill*, Warlingham: Institute of Economic Affairs Education Unit.

Sexton, S (1992) *Our Schools – Future Policy*, Warlingham: Independent Primary and Secondary Education Trust.

Tate, N (1994) Off the fence on common culture, *Times Educational Supplement*, 29 July.

Thody, A (1995) The governor citizen; agent of the state, the community or the school? In A. Macbeth, D. McCreath & J. Aitcheson (eds) *Collaborate or Compete? Educational partnerships in a market economy*, London: Falmer Press.

Timmins, N (1996) *The Five Giants: a biography of the welfare state*, London: Fontana Press.

Tomlinson, J (1993) *The Control of Education*, London: Cassell.

Walford, G (1995) The Christian schools campaign – a successful educational pressure group? *British Educational Research Journal*, 21, 4, 451–464.

Walford, G (1996) Diversity and choice in school education: an alternative view, *Oxford Review of Education*, 22, 2, 143–154 and 159–160.

Weiss, M (1993) New guiding principles in educational policy: the case of Germany, *Journal of Education Policy*, 8, 4, 307–320.

Whitty, G (1989) The New Right and the National Curriculum; state control or market forces? *Journal of Education Policy*, 4, 4, 329–341.

Whitty, G, Edwards, T & Gewirtz, S (1993) *Specialisation and Choice in Urban Education*, London: Routledge.

3

THE CHANGING LOCAL DEMOCRACY OF EDUCATION

Stewart Ranson

Professor Stewart Ranson has been a Professor of
Education since 1989 at the University of Birmingham.
He was previously a Senior Lecturer in the Institute of
Local Government Studies at Birmingham.

The post-war world constituted a political order of social democracy based upon the principles of justice and equality of opportunity and designed to ameliorate class disadvantage and class division. Public goods were conceived as requiring collective choice and action. Thus the significance of systems of administrative planning (the LEA) and institutional organisation (the comprehensive school) grounded in professional judgement. John Tomlinson's educational leadership at local and national level epitomised this era with his commitment to and achievement in public service democracy. Public management and planning, shaped by his deep vision of education, was always made sensitive and responsive to the needs of the learner whether in classrooms, colleges or community centres.

During the 1980s these beliefs were called into question. A new political order of neo-liberal consumer democracy was proposed based upon different principles of rights and choice designed to enhance the agency of the individual, as consumer, empowered within a market at the expense of the (professional) provider. Public goods were now conceived as aggregated private choices. Individual (negative) freedom would, it was purported, better deliver the goals of opportunity and social change. The agenda of the Government has, therefore, been to reform the local governance of education by changing the relations of power, values and organisation between the individual and the system in the pursuit of a new social and political order.

© Copyright, 1997, Stewart Ranson.

This chapter draws upon research[1] into the emerging forms of governance and management of local education following the 1988 Education Reform Act. The study examined the patterns which formed in the process of implementation and the different kinds of local system of governance and management that emerged. The research proposed a longitudinal study to follow the stages of implementation of the new governance of education from 1988. At the outset the interaction of two dimensions of the local education system was chosen to provide a framework for studying development over time: a management dimension mapping the trend to deregulation, to delegating management of resources to schools (extent of PSB) indicating the orientation of the LEA to give up its traditional control of routine administration; and a governance dimension mapping the trend towards the self-governing school (extent of opting out) the degree of LEA ownership and control of the institutional system (diversification). Together the interaction of these dimensions capture not only the dominant characteristics of emergent education systems but, more particularly, by charting the growth of autonomy they describe the conditions for competition and market formation. Case studies were undertaken in different segments of the framework produced by the interaction of these two dimensions. If Government policy was committed to deconstructing the local system through market forces what impact did they have on different types of robust systems of 'new management', each resistant to the idea of gradual dissolution? Two LEAs were chosen in the high GMS/high PSB segment to allow more intensive explorations of the conditions of market formation.

| | | | **GMS** | |
		20+%	10+%	0%
	+85% PSB	Bromley Kent	Warwickshire	Manchester
LMS				
	−85% PSB		Brent	Enfield

Figure 3.1 The Framework

PHASES OF CHANGE IN THE NEW GOVERNMENT OF EDUCATION

Although there were, before 1988, considerable variations between LEAs in their organisation and practice there was nevertheless a common institutional framework and shared traditions which the Education Reform Act sought to reform radically. The traditional local education authority possessed the following characteristics. It was a unitary authority, with its schools and colleges forming one integrated system; controlling through routine administration of staffing and financial services delivered to institutions. Post-war LEAs had the formal powers to control their institutions and expressed values of professional expertise which placed their public in the subordinate role of client. Power lay with the LEA. It was a providing authority which produced all the educational services for its area, monitoring schools typically through advice to teachers in their subject departments rather than to heads and their management teams. Evaluation was typically informal and *ad hoc*. Who or what was achieving or failing would form private understandings amongst advisers (more than officers) and teachers, accountable for professional expertise and judgement through internal collegial discussion. The LEA was hierarchical in organisational arrangements and emphasised the virtues of 'segmented bureaucracy' with strong service departments (schools, further, special etc) located within an administrative hierarchy led by the chief education officer as head of profession. Education officers have been used to working within an office that centralised administrative decision-making while experiencing more discretion about professional developments within each particular service sector.

What was the impact of the 1988 ERA upon this institutional system of local education? Three phases of change in the local system of education can be identified following the Education Reform Act.

PHASE ONE (1988–1990): TOWARDS THE LOCAL MANAGEMENT OF SCHOOLS (LMS)

The Government regarded LMS as one of its most significant reforms, because it sought to secure maximum delegation of financial and managerial responsibilities to schools, while allocating these resources according to a public formula rather than political or professional judgement. The Government's strategy was to extend the scheme over time expecting LEAs to include in their LMS schemes, more schools, increased delegation of resources (85 per cent of PSB by April 1993; 90 per cent by 1995–96) and an increased proportion of resources to be distributed in relation to pupil numbers weighted by age (75 per cent initially; 80 per cent by April 1993). Statutory schemes came into force (in England, outside inner London) in 87 LEAs on 1 April 1990 and in another 10 on 1 April 1991. There were pockets of early resistance to LMS amongst a few LEAs who interpreted an opportunity for political opposition fuelled by a real anxiety about the implication of 'average (rather than actual) teacher costs' for school funding. The DES failed to agree Manchester's scheme for 18 months because it insisted on including actual teacher costs. This LEA, and a northern county, came in time, however, to radically revise their view of LMS believing it, essentially, to be an instrument of good management that encouraged flexibility and responsibility in the use of resources in schools.

	Bromley	Kent	Brent	Warwks	Manchester	Enfield
LMS 89	67	53	19	12	no scheme	
90	85	100(–'91)	70	20	100	54
93	100	100	100	100	100	100
PSB Del. –89	64	71.4	62	n/a	no scheme	61
89/90	76.1	80.4	78.7	n/a	no scheme	76.8
90/91	80.7	84.9	83.6	85.2	86.6	81.5
91/92	86.3	85.8	83.5	86.7	86.6	84.7
92/93	84.7	84.5	86.9	87.0	87.2	86.4
93/94	85.6	85.5	89.8	86.1	89.1	87.0

Figure 3.2 Local Management of Schools (%)

Most LEAs assented to LMS and were to be distinguished only by the relative scope and pace of implementation. The strategy in Enfield and Warwickshire favoured a gradual progression towards formula funding, beginning with small pilot schemes and choosing a gentle slope of delegation.

In many LEAs the initial scheme was planned by a Project Team led by a seconded head teacher and including advisers and officers with expertise on issues such as finance, law and information systems. In Warwickshire, for example, this team reported to a Steering Group which represented all parts of the service affected by LMS. A pilot project with schools provided invaluable experience about historic patterns of expenditure. Schools would be phased in to the LMS scheme: all secondaries by 1991 and all primaries (irrespective of size) by 1993. Warwickshire welcomed LMS believing that it would strengthen management within the system, targeting the use of resources in support of clearer policies based upon public evidence of needs. The processes of development planning would, it was believed, encourage cooperative working between schools so as to counter the pressures of market forces.

The formula was valued for the (painful) opportunity it provided to re-examine traditional patterns of resourcing amongst pupil age groups and types of school in order to arrive at a distribution that responded to their different educational needs. The formula had to be more sensitive, than hitherto, to the fundamental importance of the primary phase of education, while it was increasingly difficult to justify educationally small sixth forms when these students required a full range of learning opportunities. The formula linked to other LEA strategies would have to ensure that the needs of the 16 to 19 age group were addressed as a whole. More accurate and sensitive indicators of disadvantage would be required to inform the needs element of the formula.

Others LEAs, either early (Kent) or late (Brent), decided to introduce a much more accelerated programme of delegation. Kent's pre ERA pilot scheme reflected its enthusiasm for LMS: 'the Kent scheme . . . is more than a series of budget . . . procedures. It is part of a process to enable Heads and Governors to manage schools effectively and efficiently by providing the information and support they need . . . giving them the freedom to determine the use of resources to meet needs and identified priorities. LMS is a new form of partnership between the LEA and schools.' Kent originally planned a phased implementation of LMS, but in 1991 it was decided 'to go the whole hog': introducing 'all primary and secondary schools fully into LMS from April 1991 – certainly the largest LMS scheme in the country'. Kent chose to delegate more of its budget and to more schools than most other LEAs.

A number of LEAs, in time, began to follow this model, although the continuous progression towards delegation experienced a slight 'hiccough' in the 1990s. Some LEAs believed that the interaction of the Government's LMS policies on delegation taken together with the financial incentives built into GMS were onerous: causing an authority to pay GM schools twice for services: delegating funds and then paying over funds for maintenance.

Towards the New Local Management

Underlying the varying approaches LEAs adopted to implementing the ERA lay increasingly shared assumptions about the need to develop a new style of management (Ranson, 1992). The new management emphasised:

(i) *Strategy:* Many LEAs came to welcome the devolving of administrative responsibilities because it enabled them to focus upon strategic questions of policy and priorities for managing change for the service as a whole.

(ii) *Partnership:* LEAs' capacity to achieve any coherent sense of direction increasingly depended upon cooperative agreements with governors and heads, but also the wider public, about development priorities and plans. This has led some LEAs like Enfield to build their service around the values of partnership.

(iii) *Support:*   The emphasis in management shifts from producing services to providing advice and support to enable institutions to improve (e.g. governor information and training; management advice (legal, personnel, organisational); financial planning; information systems; marketing; training; quality assurance).

(iv) *Evaluation:*   The neglected role of quality assurance moves to the fore in the new perspective. Each of the case study authorities is developing mechanisms for a more comprehensive and continuous monitoring and evaluation of the performance of educational institutions (e.g. information systems; audits; performance indicators; value-added analyses).

(v) *Public Accountability:*   Quality is the purpose of accountability the mechanisms of which secure achievement and public confidence. LEAs were increasingly committed to a public system of reporting on a broad range of performance indicators that can lead to an understanding of what the service is achieving while revealing those points where action is required.

(vi) *Networking:*   New forms of organisational arrangement are being developed which seek to devolve but also coordinate administrative decision-making between schools and local areas.

This is Levacic's (1993, 1995) M-Form organisation, in which the old unitary LEA is replaced by a multidivisional structure strategically coordinated by a strong regulatory authority. 'In the M-Form firm, responsibility for operations is devolved to essentially self-contained operating divisions allowing the central (office/authority) to delegate administrative detail and focus upon strategic decisions of the organisation, involving planning, resource allocation among the divisions and by monitoring and evaluating the overall performance of the organisation. The shift to strategic and auditory functions can secure greater control for the central headquarters'. Just as this new paradigm of strategic, quality assuring, management began to gain acceptance within local government, the Government's legislative programme began to dismantle the powers and responsibilities of the LEA in favour of self-governing institutions.

PHASE TWO (1990–1992): GRANT MAINTAINED SCHOOLS: TO BE OR NOT TO BE?

While the 1988 Education Reform Act introduced the possibility of schools 'opting out' into grant maintained status it is a contested issue whether the originating conception of GM schools was as the future of all schools, or as a privileged sector like the old 'direct grant' schools, or as an exception (for schools seeking to escape purported 'undesirable LEAs'!) The Prime Minister and her Secretary of State for Education were apparently divided about the issue. The norm at the outset was, arguably, intended to be 'locally managed schools' within an LEA but accorded considerable discretion over the use of resources within local strategic policy planning. Yet since 1991 Ministers have been promoting a very different policy that 'GM status become a norm not an exception'. Institutional autonomy rather than discretion has now become the key value of Government.

GM initiatives were relatively slow to begin with but began to accelerate in a number of LEAs by 1990. By November 1991, 236 schools out of 26,000 (4,000 secondary) schools in England and Wales formally had voted to opt out, published proposals, or begun operating as grant maintained schools. One hundred and ninety were secondary schools; 71 per cent were in county, rather than metropolitan councils; and 66 per cent were in Conservative controlled councils. Progress of the GM movement has varied widely across the country. Figure 3.3 shows the trend in the case study LEAs.

	Bromley	Kent	Brent	Warcks	Manchester	Enfield
1990–91	5.0	2.7	5.5	0	0	0
1991–92	42.1	25.1	13.3	13.1	0	0
1992–93	63.6	43.5	43	22.2	0	19.9
1993–94	67.3	46.3	75	28.5	0	29.4

Figure 3.3   Trend of Grant Maintained Schools (%)

The case studies offered interesting differences in opting out. In two (metropolitan) LEAs no schools had begun proceedings to become grant maintained, while opting out had begun in the two county LEAs, one at an accelerating rate. Thirty schools have begun procedures to opt out of Kent LEA although a small number were not supported by parents and one has been rejected by the Secretary of State. Yet a trend was developing which, if it continued, accompanied by the financial regulations which, at that time, required an LEA to allocate 16 per cent of its central administration budget to GM schools, then the Authority believed it would, as one officer anticipated, 'go bankrupt'.

A number of dimensions need to be taken into account to develop an adequate explanation of opting out. Some of the proposals to opt out may have had their source in heads, governors and parents valuing the creation of a grant maintained sector with its rationale in strengthening institutional autonomy from local government as well as the purported growth of parental influence. It is clear however that none of the LEAs in the study has supported opting out although councillors in Bromley and Kent were constrained to adjust their initial hostility to a more neutral attitude of willingness to trade – without which their survival would be at risk. For a number of institutions opting out was clearly in their self-interest if they preferred survival either because they were threatened with closure or reorganisation or because a short term calculation of material advantage prevailed.

Evidence from a number of LEAs suggests that the contextual constraints tipped the balance of interest for a number of institutions towards opting out. While some, often urban, LEAs (for example, Enfield and Manchester) had reorganised their schools in the 1980s, thus approaching the ERA reforms both from a basis of stability and more significantly without the significant surplus capacity in schools which provide the conditions for competition, other LEAs were introducing schemes of institutional rationalisation late to respond to surplus capacity. A number of these reorganisation proposals threatened schools with closure and a number of these in turn responded with proposals to opt out which the government then acceded to.

While some of the initial applications to achieve GM status were caused by schemes of reorganisation evidence grows, others were clearly motivated by finance: by the growing financial constraints placed upon local authorities and the long period of under-funding education, reinforced, of course, by the considerable financial incentives (capital as well as revenue) central government has offered to schools.

The impact exerted by the constraints and the influence of the incentives depended however upon characteristics internal to the LEA system – in particular, the extent of integration and the value accorded to cohesion – as much as the constraints facing the LEA. While Enfield and Manchester had integrated institutional systems those in Warwickshire and Kent exhibited greater differentiation, especially in the latter, where selective schools created a hierarchical order of academic esteem. This LEA formed an interesting example of institutional systems which could contain within themselves the conditions for their own disintegration.

Whether differentiated institutional systems were vulnerable to fragmentation depended, however, upon characteristics of the management process within an LEA as well as cultural traditions. Warwickshire, for example, had a variety of institutions (some of which were selective) and a tradition of relative autonomy from County Hall, but the qualities of strategic leadership and the policy of partnership in the implementation of the Education Reform Act had, it appeared, been valued by schools and the collaborative response of all the education partners to charge capping indicated the development of a more cohesive service than the County has known hitherto. The lack of opting out in Manchester and Enfield (initially) could be attributed to a great extent to the culture of partnership between the Authority and its schools in the management of change. In Kent the Authority had tackled with consummate skill the challenge of establishing the conditions for managing a new and more effective customer oriented service, yet this required a time-span which was no longer available to it – the same objective had taken Enfield, for example, over a decade to accomplish with proficiency.

PHASE THREE (1993–95): BUSINESS PRESSURES AND THE EXTERNALISING OF SERVICES

Increasing Financial Disciplines

The introduction of LMS together with contracting local authority budgets has placed considerable pressure upon LEAs to radically enhance their capacity for efficient management of their activities. In one LEA increasingly tight financial constraints and the need for more efficient and effective monitoring and control of expenditure has led to the introduction of more rigorous financial disciplines, an influx of professionally (CIPFA) qualified staff within the Department as well as the introduction of sophisticated computerised systems (FMIS) to ensure accountability and control. Extensive budget management training has been provided for staff and cash limited budgets have been introduced. For some LEAs the pressure to improve efficiency has remained at this level of financial discipline. For many others, the response to the exigencies of financial efficiency has been to enter more completely into the disciplines of formal rationality, to generate a culture of contract management that replaces relationships based upon professional trust with those cast the mould of purchaser (client) and provider (contractor).

The Culture of Client and Contractor

One of the Government's key strategies for enhancing competition in local government has been to introduce into the public domain the contractual traditions of the private sector. Formal agreements or contracts make explicit what services and levels of service are to be delivered, and at what cost and quality. Relationships between client and contractor are formalised. The Audit Commission (1989) believed that LMS itself made LEAs clients of contracted out services: 'The division between LEAs and schools will, in some ways, parallel the client/contractor split needed in the case of local authority services subject to competitive tendering. The LEA will be responsible for setting objectives, the schools for delivering performance which makes those objectives a reality'.

Many authorities began their initiation into the contracting culture by introducing formal 'service level agreements' that specified what services would be delivered between departments. Now in many local authorities the culture of contracting has spread widely into the delivery of many educational services. While some LEAs have gone beyond particular contracts to redesignate the whole organisation in terms of formal client-contractor relationships: purchaser-provider relationships have been introduced with the departmental realignment in April 1993. The movement is towards specifying and purchasing services to be delivered by internal and arms-length providers, other corporate agencies or external providers where necessary. The formalising of contractual relationships together with the financial pressure to find new sources of income has led many LEAs to create self-financing business units or to plan for services to be 'externalised' or privatised.

Business Units and Self-Financing

Financial contraction has caused a number of LEAs to ensure that some of their services become income generating. This has occurred with a number of professional administrative services (such as finance and personnel services) but also with a number of educational services including advisers, professional development and training, careers, and adult education. Some LEAs have established formal business units for services.

In one LEA an Education Support Service has been established consisting of Finance, Personnel, Education Information Service and Curriculum Functions: ESS is an integrated service which is zero budgeted. Most income is from the Department (through serviced level agreements), from schools (for curriculum services) and some is generated from the GM sector and external customers. In the same authority a separate Curriculum Services Agency has been established as an accredited internal business unit which has to recoup all its costs including salaries and is thus wholly self-financing. Another LEA believed the response to financial pressure was to create more formal internal business relationship to ensure: 'services were rationalised and focused on customer demand; costs were defined and charging arrangements clarified; marketing of services was improved'. Some formal business units would be created with shadow trading accounts, but other services merely act in 'a business-like way, defining its range of customers, consulting and negotiating with them agreed levels of service to be incorporated in their development plans'. This authority contemplated but has, for the immediate future, decided against creating independent companies. European directives prevent an LEA negotiating a management buy out or trade sale and thus make it difficult for staff groups to raise the capital essential for independent operation. 'The only viable alternative was the creation of Local Authority controlled companies but there seemed no advantage in this because these would have not greater freedom than business units to trade with other LEAs or the private sector'. Other LEAs have taken the business, contracting, culture further and are proceeding to 'externalise' or privatise some of their services.

Externalising Services

The 1988 Local Government Act required local authorities to introduce compulsory competitive tendering for services provided by manual workers and the management of leisure facilities. The extent to which such contracts have been won by private sector tenders has varied. In Bromley and Kent there has been a steady progression to privatising cleaning (with Kent an exception), catering and grounds maintenance. In 1994 some LEAs are now planning to 'externalise' some of their educational services, perhaps in 1995/96, following a period of 'market testing' during which they have established the markets and the systems to survive independently in the private sector.

Emergent Patterns of Management

The contracting and restructuring of local education authorities has led many LEAs to review and clarify their fundamental role and function in management and local governance. The traditional authority owned institutions and produced services which it could control. When asked to describe what functions they would have prioritised in 1988 most authorities emphasised the significance of service provision, resource allocation and their strategic role of leading the LEA. The structural changes have precipitated very different choices about the function and organisation of education governance. By 1993 their chosen order of priority had often changed quite radically in response not only to the universal legislative restructuring but also their own shifting self-image. LEAs have created management systems which reflect their emergent choices about their primary role and function.

	Contractor	Enabler	Partner	Civic Provider
Values	Efficiency	Support	Leadership	Service producer, resource allocation
Configuration	Diversified	Loosely coupled	Association	Interdependent
Management *Structure*	Client-side, contractor-side	Support services, QA	Policy/planning, curriculum, community	Services, resources
Control	Deregulated	Devolution	Collaboration	Regulation
Rules	Contract	Contract	Service level agreement	Rule formalisation

Figure 3.4 Emergent patterns of management

The Contractor

Against a background of increasing competition from parents for school places and between institutions some LEAs, in this study exemplified by Brent, have clarified their management function for the authority as providing an efficient context for schools. The contract provides an appropriate form of rationality for effective management allowing specificity, regulation, evaluation and accountability.

The contracting LEA emphasises its function of defining and mediating contracts in support of services to schools. Administrative coordination may be provided where necessary. The authority will tend to act as provider of last resort, for example in special educational needs, but most of its traditional services will be contracted out to business units, while monitoring quality and taking remedial action. This is the Debenhams model of an LEA, a holding company, though establishing a local style of service while monitoring and evaluating standards of provision provided by the business units that hire space in its complex. It is Levacic's or Williamson's H Form of a divisionalised enterprise with the requisite internal control apparatus removed. In this model as Levacic argues 'great reliance is placed on the market as a regulating mechanism for ensuring that schools respond to customer preferences with inspection providing market information' (1993, p. 133).

The Enabler

In the new context of self-governing institutions, the LEA can no longer direct and must develop a very different conception of its role seeking not to impose its own view of policy upon its member organisation, but to provide advice and support to the multiplicity of autonomous and loosely coupled organisations. Its method changes from hierarchical control to the management of influence within a network of governance. For some, this role for an authority forms a significant, rather than an emasculated, role of influence within the new governance. Bromley is now emphasising this function of enabling support. It has reorganised from a traditional education phase structure (for example, 'schools', 'further education' etc) to an 'educational services structure' (pupil and student services; support services; training support services; planning; and the Inspectorate). Its preferred functions are consistent in their emphasis upon support to institutions and quality assurance while continuing to emphasise the roles of leadership and resource allocation.

The strategic role of the enabling LEA is to create the system of rules, the administrative infrastructure, which enables the local market to function without confusion and mutual frustration. The authority will seek to exercise a strong quality assurance role, evaluating the performance of its member institutions, to discuss its 'account' widely with the education partners and to take remedial action where necessary.

The Partner

A number of LEAs responded to the increasing legislative pressure to create autonomous schools and colleges by introducing during the 1980s arrangements that would support collaborative working between institutions, encouraging them to share resources, staff, equipment, and curriculum development. Partnership expressed the driving purpose of many LEAs during this period. These authorities believed strongly that despite the delegation of powers and responsibilities to schools their role remained to provide leadership on educational strategy and policy for the system as a whole. This approach strives to cling onto the new strategic management they believed the 1988 ERA inaugurated but subsequent changes have undermined.

The Civic Provider

Some LEAs have lost none of their institutions to grant maintained status and remain located within an Authority that continues to retain a strong corporate identity as an all purpose unitary local authority which seeks to meet all the educational needs of its area. The LEA has an enhanced commitment to provide the services and opportunities that will enhance the powers and capacities of all its young citizens. The LEA may have developed a sharper ethic of business efficiency but has not entered the culture of contracting and thus retains control of all its educational services.

The new corporatism is distinguished from the old by its readiness to willingly accommodate the 1988 reforms and to concentrate upon its strategic role, while delegating resources and routine administrative matters to its member institutions. It has sought to improve the support services it provides for its schools and colleges. The LEA has a strong conception of itself as an auditing and quality assuring authority in relation to its schools and educational services.

		high Diversification *low*			Institutional Control
	high	Market Formation (Privatisation) Contractor LEA (*Brent*)			Civic Provider (*Manchester*)
Deregulation			Enabler LEA (*Bromley/Kent*)	Partnership LEA (*Enfield/Warks*)	
Resource control	*low*				Unification

Figure 3.5   Patterns of Local Governance

The Extent and Limits of Market Forces

The Government's programme of legislative reform has sought, progressively during the 1990s, to transform the traditional system of local governance with its emphasis upon politico-professional planning into a self-regulating market of competing institutions and parental consumers. There is evidence from the studies that market formation has been responsive to the pressures exerted by 'contingencies' from the environment. Legislative change, for example the 1992 Education Act which privatised inspections and withdrew funds from public expenditure allocations, contracted resources available to LEAs and caused many to revise their conception of function. Financial contraction has further reinforced the need for LEAs to review the size and efficiency of their system.

The reforms have, however, been designed to incorporate an internal temporal trajectory with the components of the new system interlocking over time to reinforce the movement towards market formation. These organising principles assume that markets do generate internal forces, that there is a gravitational pull for institutions in market locations to continually adapt the system so that it is internally consistent and thus more likely to respond efficiently to the exigencies which it faces.

The research provides evidence to support the idea that there are pressures within systems to unfold toward their 'design type'. Self-governing autonomy, especially in conjunction with surplus capacity generates competition, which leads to diversification as institutions strive to create a niche in the market. The contraction of resources (both locally through GMS and nationally through public expenditure cuts) together with the deregulation of resources and services generates pressure upon the public authority (LEA) to 'externalise' or privatise services. This might be termed the 'parabola of privatisation': diversification together with deregulation creates a gravitational pull for LEAs to 'float off' or privatise some of their services.

Systems develop forward ratchets over time that structure the actions of their agents and prevent them 'turning back' to previous forms of action. LEAs which have been used to employing substantial advisory teams providing developmental support for schools, when confronted by major budgetary reductions are forced to shed staff and functions. There is no way back to the previous tradition of service provision. Actors become constrained by their spatial and temporal tracks.

In this case that there is pressure within market systems for the appropriate characteristics of the system to be created. An LEA experiencing the pressures of contraction, deregulation and diversification is constrained to restructure around a model of itself as a 'contracting' or 'enabling' authority. Because it now 'owns' few services or resources it can only constitute an indirect role in relation to the local system as an adviser, or a purchaser, or a facilitator rather than as a producer or strategic chooser for the system. Purchaser/contractor structures and processes, business units and externalisation become modes of formal instrumental rationality that appear given by the temporal trajectory that the institutional system is located in. The accelerating elaboration of the incipient trends in the market system, the Government hopes will become institutionalised over time: that control gives way to compliance and commitment. Markets rely less on regulation and more on culturally embodied *habitus* as prescription becomes sedimented in routine practice.

Agency, the 'Iron Cage' and Realms of Discretion

Weber's analysis proposed that modernity was in the grip of the forces of formal, calculative rationality which would not only sweep away entrenched traditions and values but become cemented in the structures of bureaucracy that would ensure their continuing reproduction. In this way contemporary rationality would become an 'iron cage' that trapped the creative agency of individuals and communities. The above account of market forces appears equally deterministic and pessimistic. Yet the research suggests that systems of formal rationality are never independent 'forces' but, in their accelerating development, are always chosen as much as given. Markets have to be 'willed' to become forces. Institutional systems are social constructions even if constrained constructions. The research suggests that a number of authorities even though subject to the ratchet effects of marketisation, nevertheless strive to set limits to its further development and to counter its momentum by articulating alternative frames of value rationality which express the educational or democratic values that provide legitimating meaning for them.

LEAs, though constrained, have choices: they have realms of discretion about the structures and processes they adopt. They are never merely determined. The pressures to adapt to the exigencies of efficiency never obliterate the opportunities for clarifying the values within their organising principles. The LEAs in the study have often exercised their discretion in how they have constituted their management systems and, more significantly, their conception of governance in the public domain. Bromley and Kent believed they faced the prospect of becoming, in the face of market forces, a mere local agency bereft of educational authority. Both have sought to construct a stronger role for themselves as an enabling authority. A contractor LEA could adopt a weak self-image as a facilitator of services for institutions, or a stronger self-conception as a purchaser of services on behalf of the public for whom it sought to act as advocate. The partner authorities have continued to assert a conception of their role as strategic leaders and coordinators of the local educational system despite encroaching market forces. The local systems, therefore, have expressed choices about public management. They have also continued to locate such ideas within frames of meaning about the public domain, about their role in a system of local democracy, for it is such principles of value rationality which, they believe, underlie and inform their legitimacy as local systems of public education.

Emergent Patterns of Governance and Democratic Choices

The traditional mode of governance constituted an all-purpose authority of the public's elected representatives who made decisions about provision of services and the distribution of resources based upon the advice of a substantial department of professional administrators. The reforms and the pressures for change may have eroded traditional forms of governance but not self-conceptions about the significance of their work for local governance. Different patterns of governance have begun to emerge over time.

	Neo-Liberal	Associative	Civic Representative	Participative
Institutional system	differentiated	differentiated	unitary	unitary
Concept of public	individual (active) consumer	individual/collective customer	individual (passive) client	individual/collective citizen
Public domain	public choice	public consultation	public action/service	public participation
Public management	contractor/ enabler	partner	civic provider	partner
Elected representation	weak	primus interpares	strong	duo-polity
Accountability	information	information/vote	the vote	discourse

Figure 3.6 Emergent Patterns of Local Democracy

Neo-Liberal (Consumer) Democracy

These local systems of governance form highly differentiated systems of schools and colleges. They constitute a market of institutions that are in competition for 'parental choices'. The public domain is conceived of as an aggregation of individual consumers who pursue their interests so as to maximise their private utility. Public management is modelled very much on the private sector striving to ensure efficiency in the local system through the regulatory mechanisms of the contract which embodies the culture of formal rationality. The contract allows the authority to specify and purchase goods and services which are designed to support and enable the purposes of individual institutions as they define them.

The public authority nevertheless is conceived in minimalist terms providing only a limited role for elected representatives in the local system. The democracy is expressed in the direct choices of individual consumers. The public role of the authority develops more as 'an agency' perceiving its role as offering an information service for its customers placing them in touch with the service providers they require. One LEA, contemplating the collapse of local government of education, began contingency planning to reform itself as a Trust, constituted as a charity, that could continue to offer the minimal support to local institutions believing they were essential to maintain the prerequisite foundation of administrative coordination.

The Associative Democracy

In the 1990s some authorities have taken the process a stage further and sought to broaden the defining of the education partners and to involve them directly in the deliberative process that would see their advice feed directly into the policy process. It develops a conception of an associative democracy whose characteristics are not dissimilar to the model of Hirst (1993). The developments have involved the creation of forums which involve the partners as associates within the traditional democratic process. The traditional decision-making process is extended formally to consult the partners. Two illustrations can be introduced from the study.

During 1993 Enfield planned to reconstitute its local polity and introduce a sophisticated model of associative democracy. 'The relationship between the Authority and the LEAs schools has been strengthened by the introduction of new democratic processes involving governors, parents, staff and employers, and by the development of joint planning and policy formulation with the head teachers'. A new vision for the LEA is articulated as 'an effective partnership of all those interested and involved in "x" so that people who live and work in the Borough will continue to learn and develop throughout their lives'.

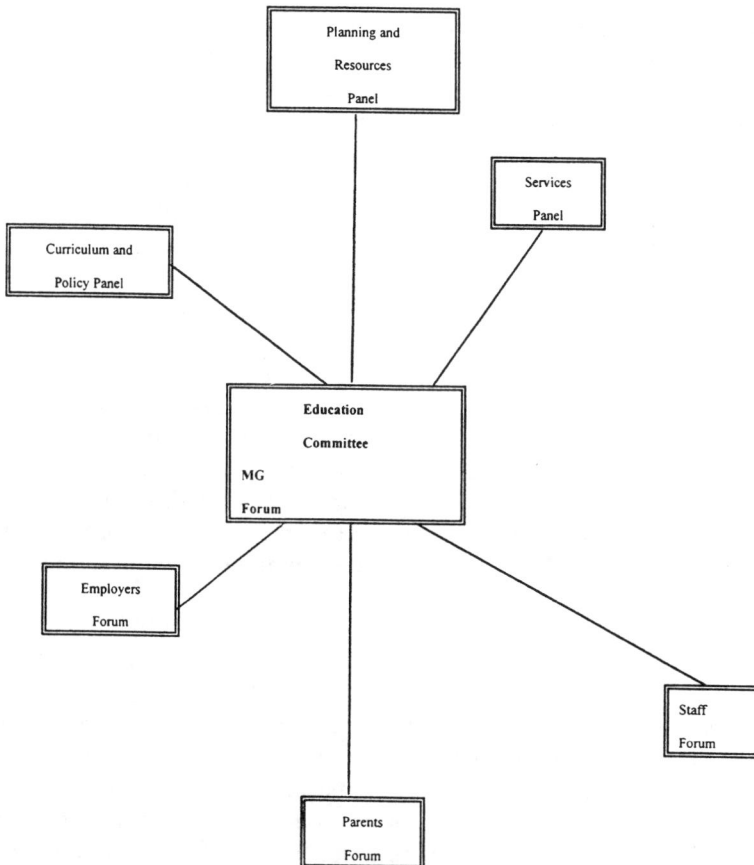

Figure 3.7　A model of associative democracy

A new forum comprising members of the Education Committee and representatives of governing bodies elected from local partnership groups is created to advise the Education Committee. This forum will, in turn be advised by three forums representing employers, parents and staff. The Employers forum will link the Council with the local Education Business Partnership, the Training and Enterprise Council, the Chamber of Commerce, and the Enterprise Agency. Representatives of the university, colleges and the careers service are also to be included. It is intended that the parents' forum will include two representatives from each local Partnership Group. Parents would serve on the forum for a two year term of office. The staff forum would include representatives of all the teachers' and headteacher unions and professional associations as well as non-teacher unions. It is planned that each forum should and would meet three or four times a year and present its views to the Member Governor Forum or the Education Committee as appropriate.

The Civic Democracy

This form of democracy elaborates upon a tradition of corporate leadership of the local authority. A unified institutional system underpins a firm conception of the public domain as forming an integrated whole. The new civic authority is recognised as a plural polity made up of diverse communities and ethnic minorities. The interpretation of the political processes of local governance, however, remain rooted in the tradition which believes it is the role of the elected representatives in political caucus to interpret, judge and decide the policies and plans which are best for the commonwealth of civil society. It is the conception rooted in the Hegelian tradition of the role of the state to synthesise and integrate the diverse interests that are expressed in civil society.

The role of the local state is to produce the services which provide for the needs of its diverse local communities. The public is still conceived passively although because the legislative reforms have necessarily created a devolved institutional system the public authority has learned to listen and become more responsive to the articulation of needs and become more public service oriented. But the central thrust of this civic democracy is to create the framework of values and rules that constitute the conditions for realising the common good on behalf of the public. Accountability is expressed in the test of the local ballot box.

The Participative Democracy

The response of one LEA to the need to clarify and develop its fundamental function has been to strengthen its commitment to the democratic processes of local government believing them to be integral to the quality of local education. The role of elected representatives remains central, though their role clarified and enhanced – 'it is in the sorting out of values and the willing of ends that a locally elected and accountable body is most needed'. Yet this authority, drawing upon the ideas of Putnam (1993) believes that if the democratic process is to work as a whole with the contribution of representatives enhanced then a participative dimension is needed to reflect the growing differences of interest and voice across increasingly diverse communities. The response of this authority was to create a series of Area Community Education Councils. These councils would be located within a Charter of Community Education the vision of which encourages 'opportunities for personal and community development and the participation of all members of the community in a process of life-long education'.

Membership would include representatives of elected members of the County, District and Parish Councils together with representation of community groups and education users. The councils would meet four times a year. A minimalist position for the councils, merely acting as a conduit for County pump-priming activities was rejected in favour of a positive approach which accorded the councils a developmental role in representing local communities, identifying needs, acquiring resources and planning their use. They would prepare and implement an integrated area development plan and advise on agreements with providers so as to identify and fill gaps, and ensure proper monitoring and evaluation of the plans. The community councils development role was to enable new projects to get started and become free standing rather than become part of another nascent bureaucracy, albeit at community level.

	Marketisation		
Active Public (individual)	Neo-Liberal Consumer Democracy	Associative Democracy	Active Public (collective)
	Civic Democracy	Participative Democracy	
	Unification		

Figure 3.8 Patterns of governance and democratic choices

CONCLUDING ANALYSIS

The pressure of legislative and local change has led LEAs to review and clarify their fundamental role and function in managing the system. Patterns of local management of education have developed over time shaped by contextual pressures but also choices about function. The systems are expressed in the dominant management role of the public authority:

• Contractor: a market system regulated by the principles of efficiency and contract.

- Enabler: a market system loosely coupled by networks of influence and support.
- Partner: cooperative associations led by a strategic planning authority.
- Civic Provider: a controlling authority producing services for civic need.

These patterns have been influenced by market forces which interact over time to reinforce the internal development. An LEA experiencing the pressures of contraction, deregulation and diversification generates a further gravitational pull along a 'parabola of privatisation'. The authority is constrained to restructure around a model of itself as a 'contracting' or 'enabling' authority. Because it now 'owns' few services or resources it can only constitute an indirect role in relation to the local system as an adviser, or a purchaser, or a facilitator rather than as a producer or strategic chooser for the system. Purchaser/contractor structures and processes, business units and externalisation become modes of formal instrumental rationality that appear given by the temporal trajectory that the institutional system is located in. The creators of markets hope that in time they need to rely less on regulatory controls as practices become taken-for-granted cultural routines.

Systems thus develop temporal 'tracks'. Their form unfolds over time according to the dominant organising principles as they become embodied in the structures and decision procedures. Market systems in particular appear to constitute internal self-regulating mechanisms. Yet the research suggests that markets have to be 'willed' to become forces. Institutional systems are social constructions even if constrained constructions. The LEAs though constrained had choices and they exercised their realms of discretion about the structures of management and more significantly the system of governance. They were never merely determined. The emergent patterns of local governance of education became:

- Neo-liberal democracy: values an active public of individual consumers of public (market) services.
- Associative democracy: involves public groups in a consultative process of partnership.
- Civic representative democracy: the local state synthesising the diverse interests in civil society.
- Participative democracy: the diverse interests must be given their voice in a multilayered polity.

The local systems, therefore, have embodied choices about public management. They have also continued to locate such ideas within frames of meaning about the public domain, about their role in a system of local democracy for it is such principles of value rationality which underlie and inform their legitimacy as local systems of public education. John Tomlinson's work illuminated this understanding. His vision of a civic representative democracy recognised the inescapable social and political conditions for learning, that there is no solitary learning: we can only create our worlds together. The unfolding agency of the self always grows out of the interaction with others. The possibility of shared understanding requires individuals not only to value others but to create the communities in which mutuality and thus the conditions for learning can flourish. The *telos* of learning is to learn to make the communities without which individuals and others cannot grow and develop. John Tomlinson understood and helped to illustrate for us the way that a strong LEA within a flourishing local democracy is the condition for this vision to grow.

REFERENCES

Audit Commission (1989) Losing an Empire, Finding a Role: the LEA of the future. Occasional Paper no. 10, London: HMSO.

Hirst, P (1993) *Associative Democracy*, Oxford: Polity.

Levacic, R (1993) Local Management of Schools as an organisational form: Theory and Application. *Journal of Education Policy* 8, 2, 123–141.

Levacic, R (1995) *Local Management of Schools: Analysis & Practice*, Milton Keynes: Open University.

Putnam, R (1993) *Making Democracy Work*, Princeton University Press.

Ranson, S (1992) *The Role of Local Government in Education*, Harlow: Longman.

Ranson, S (1995) From Reform to Restructuring of Education. In J. Stewart & G. Stoker (eds) *Local Government in the 1990s*, London: Macmillan.

NOTE

1. ESRC Sponsored Research (Grant RWO 231879) – Report (1994) The New System of Government for Education, Swindon: ESRC.

4

FOX OR HEDGEHOG?

John Mann

John Mann was Secretary of the Schools' Council from
1978–1983. He was also Director of Education for the
London Borough of Harrow from 1983–1988.

'The fox knows many things', John Tomlinson would say, quoting a much
loved Russian proverb, 'the hedgehog knows one big thing.' He liked to
see himself as something of a fox, and even more a hedgehog. Speaking
to the Royal Society of Arts he described his work 'as a chief education
officer, whose job is always to reconcile the ideal and the pragmatic; the
political and the professional – even when they are irreconcilable.' As an
education officer he needed the fox's supposed ability to handle a dozen
problems simultaneously. But he had too the 'vision thing', so notoriously
lacking in President George Bush. John's mission was perhaps to reconcile
the pragmatic and the ideal. Of a philosophic turn of mind, and as he would
say 'a man of the eighteenth century', like the hedgehog he constantly sought
an overarching, integrating principle.

Hill walkers know how often they can be misled by bog grass and false
summits. With hindsight, the teams John Tomlinson led in the late 70's and
early 80's when he was Director of Education in Cheshire, and successively
Chair of the Further Education Curriculum Development Unit, Chair of the
Schools Council, President of the Society of Education Officers, and Chair
of the Royal Society of Arts, can see that he was leading them across a
treacherous and marshy watershed. The Yellow Paper, Callaghan's Ruskin
Speech, and the 1979 election were the first mileposts on a tortuous trek
through difficult terrain. In his Charles Gittens Memorial Lecture John
Tomlinson himself said 'We all have a sense of being at a watershed on
the question of who makes and controls the school curriculum'. Late in 1979

the government had published their report on the LEA responses to Circular 14/77 which had asked LEAs about their attitude to their responsibilities for the curriculum. As John Tomlinson observed, 'Para 14 of the preamble contains the remarkable statement: "The Education Department will draw up and circulate a draft policy document suggesting the form a framework for the curriculum might take and the ground it should cover"'.

It was once commonly assumed that if a visitor from Mars were to ask anyone in the British education service to 'take me to your leader', the only reply would be a stunned silence. That is perhaps a fair reflection of the system of dispersed powers which was said to typify the government of English education for forty years or so from the 1940s to the 1980s. The assumptions underpinning this edifice were challenged by Para 14. The structure proved more pregnable than anyone had thought. The foundations crumbled, and in ten or fifteen years the edifice came tumbling down. In a system of dispersed powers there was, unsurprisingly, no Moses to lead the people out of darkness, no Mao to hold them together during their Long March, no Mandela to epitomise an alternative kind of society. If there was a single voice articulating an alternative it was perhaps that of John Tomlinson. By virtue of his inspiring search for unifying principles, and the offices he held, John Tomlinson had many public opportunities to develop his vision of childhood, family, society, curriculum, schools, teaching, professionalism, and government. He did this in a series of speeches and papers between 1978 and 1981.

In, for example, the final section of his Lockyer Lecture at the Royal College of Physicians, he sketched his 'vision of a conceptual framework embracing views of childhood, the family, theories of learning and good practice for co-operation between our two professions.' 'The danger of "scientific reductionism" has been the besetting sin of both our professions,' he told his audience of doctors. 'Since the Renaissance, knowledge has indeed grown, but it has become more splintered in the process' and both professions had tended to lose sight of what he called 'the total human individual and his social connections'. The essential components of a unifying philosophy were:

- a view of the nature of childhood
- a view of the family
- a view of parenthood
- a view of when and how best to convey both knowledge and attitudes to children and adults
- a view of a good relationship between the individual or family and the statutory or voluntary services who impinge upon them.

CHILDHOOD

For our contemporary view of the essential nature and needs of childhood, I cannot do better than quote the opening chapter of the Court Report:

It is the hall mark of the human species that our young are born incomparably more 'immature' than the young of other species. Man is the only species which has gone all-out for general immaturity and open mindedness: they are his particular strategies for development. The human baby and child faces a long period of development and dependence during which he develops the fundamental human attributes of speech, thought, self consciousness and reflection. During these stages the child is a biological organism with biological propensities which needs constant inter-action with his environment, especially the adults around him, so that he can learn in innumerable ways and emerge a social as well as an individual being. As the human child grows he is in many important ways being created by the slowly forming imprint of experience, the essential tension between the biological and the social, hereditary and environmental influences. That is why the rearing of the young is the fundamental issue in a human society – and why the quality and philosophy of health, education and other care available to the child and his family are so important.

Tomlinson developed his thinking about child development and teaching in greater detail in a paper for the International Journal of Health Education:

Much remains to be learned about the way children think and its implications for schooling. But it seems clear that for a long time children develop ideas and skills by action rather than abstraction and can solve advanced problems in this way provided the substance is within their grasp. The power of abstraction and formalization then grows; but on entering new fields children (and, I would suggest, adults too) often find concrete problem-solving approaches the best starting point. We have undoubtedly underestimated the importance of the arts, the imagination and the real world's problems in our western education systems so far. Finally (in this preliminary sketch of how teachers try to work in these days), I must emphasize that there is strong evidence that the best regimes involve setting realistic expectations, with their outcomes being confirmed by approval (rather than the harsh punishments of yesteryear, still advocated in some quarters), so that children gain a satisfactory picture of themselves and confidence in their own competence.

CURRICULUM

John Tomlinson developed his views on the curriculum more fully in his Gittens Lecture. His starting point then was the framework papers recently published by HMI and DES in 1979. Both were, he thought, defective, because, perhaps, of an understandable wish to keep the subject manageable.

For example: [a] The HMI paper says 'the curriculum in its full sense comprises all the opportunities for learning provided by a school.' But it then says that it will discuss only the formal school programme and ignore the extra-school activities and the hidden curriculum (ie the incidental transmission of attitudes and values). It further asserts that teaching methods and the way schools organise and manage their time are specifically excluded from consideration. I find that quite astonishing and clearly HMI found it impossible, because their paper in fact, and admirably, pays much attention to the importance of teaching methods.

[b] The DES Consultative document, by contrast, admits the importance of assessment but also pays no attention to teaching methods or school processes generally.

LEARNING

The unresolved conundrum at the centre of our secondary schools is how to redeem, in practical terms, the political promise of Secondary Education for All. That promise was made in 1944 and the framework for it provided by raising the minimum leaving age to 16 in 1973–74 – only six years ago. Until our generation, secondary education was given solely for the brainy by the brainy. It stood faithfully and securely in a tradition of 2,000 years. Its practitioners felt that significance of their task which is essential for motivation and personal satisfaction. The abstract and intellectual, pursued honestly and for its own sake, awakens the mind to the principles of beauty and truth which have sustained the human spirit. It is a tolerant, life-enhancing stream of thought and action sweeping those who can ride it through the minds and spirits of men past so that we may grow through them. The Republic, The Divine Comedy, The Discourse on Method, The Magic Flute and the Interpretation of Dreams constellate the mind.

But even intellectually able people do not learn solely through the brain. In an audience such as this we have probably all been educated, so far as our formal education is concerned, in the way I have just described. Look into your inner self and ask whether the deepest knowledge that has stood you in good stead through the greatest crises of your life has not come largely otherwise – through the experience of life, through the act of loving and being loved, of giving and receiving sacrifice? And is it not observable that some of the cleverest among us seem most helpless before the permanencies of the human condition – fear, cruelty, rejection, jealousy, pusillanimity, the need to care for others at the expense of ourselves?

For the truth is that, whatever its glories, the intellect has always been the avenue to knowledge – of self and the world – for a minority. Most of us learn through the heart not the brain. 'What gives me hope', said Andre Gide, 'is that by his very nature, man is compelled to feel ten times more than he thinks.' And Archbishop Temple once said, 'Teach people to feel together and to think for themselves, instead of thinking together and feeling alone'. The dismissal of the emotions is, I would say, the greatest incubus conferred by the scholastic tradition. For most of the history of mankind the skills and understanding needed to live life have come through the culture in which one grew up – home and village or town; pastoral or nomadic, or urban society. Family and friendship, relationships at work, the texture of society at large, have contributed more to the raising of a new generation than have the conscious acts of a professional minority; the teachers.

If now society in late twentieth century Britain says to its education service 'educate all our young, full-time, up to the age of 16', one thing only is certain – that the model used in the academic tradition will not be sufficient.

It was, he said, argued that 'inappropriate pedagogy has not only failed to educate many youngsters adequately but has also given the formal and theoretical a precedence and prestige compared with the practical and the applied which has been socially and economically harmful.'

The second strand of criticism of the traditional secondary school curriculum links with and reinforces the first in an interesting way. It comes from work in psychology. Its best exponent, in my experience, is Margaret Donaldson. It says simply that the kind of human intelligence which is generated by practical, problem-solving approaches to learning is not a second rate kind of intelligence. It is the *same* as is generated, in those who can learn that way, by the abstract and formal approaches. Children learn by making use of the information and concepts already learned. That is, they try to make 'human sense' of every new situation. Formal approaches to education are, by definition, deprived of all human sense aspects. They therefore fail to connect with many children who could easily understand the issue if it were represented in concrete form.

Two things seem to follow for the secondary education curriculum:

1. Even the cleverest children, who can learn easily through the formal system, would be the better for learning in practical ways also;
2. The notion (hallowed, for example, in the Hadow Report of 1926 and still believed in many quarters) that there are two kinds of knowledge or ability, one of which is greatly inferior to the other, ought to be abandoned once and for all.

This, it seems to me, clinches the case for having a common secondary school curriculum (in terms of the areas of experience to be approached) and for paying attention to methodology of teaching as well as content.

THE HIDDEN CURRICULUM

'The third part of the secondary curriculum must be concerned with the personal and social development of the youngsters. Unless they are helped to become self-confident and caring they will not be able to develop fully or make their best contribution to society.' As John Tomlinson wrote (*International Journal of Health Education*), of *Curriculum 11-16: Health Education in the Secondary School Curriculum*, 'The striking thing about this paper, compared with previous "official" statements, is the emphasis it gives to the "hidden curriculum", that is, the attitudes and values which a school conveys to its pupils (and to its teachers, the parents and the community) by the way it actually treats people – whatever its advertised intentions.'

TEACHING

John Tomlinson's concern for the 'hidden curriculum' is matched by a fitting scepticism about the effectiveness of didactic teaching.

I still recall my sense of shock, early in the life of the Court Committee (1973, that is) when it became apparent that some health service experts in high places firmly believed that the 'health aspects' of human behaviour could be changed, on a large scale, by direct, didactic, teaching. The formula was simple: information causes change. Moreover, they were looking to the schools to undertake a good deal of the teaching and hoped that the Court Report would legitimize this approach. As a teacher, I felt much more modest about what can be achieved and stressed the need for greater subtlety in the teaching and learning process. No doubt those of the other conviction considered me pusillanimous and typical of the weakness in this respect in the educational world.

As I got deeper into the literature, however, I came to realize that I had many allies inside the health profession. I particularly enjoyed reading the paper of 1975 by Guy Stewart, Professor at North Carolina University: 'There is one major obstacle I shall deal with immediately: the deeply entrenched and simplistic notion that health-related behaviour is susceptible to change primarily via health information accompanied by exhortations to change. The solution, in short, is seen to lie in the education of the public, in the rather traditional sense of cognitive change, as a *sine qua non* of subsequent attitudinal and behavioural change – precisely in that order.

The literature of health education is replete with surveys of the knowledge and attitudes of target populations about specific health problems, designed to serve as foundations for action. However, the inevitability of this duck-like sequence of change in knowledge, attitude, and then behaviour has been seriously contradicted by research and experience. Frequently it could be argued with equal force that change in behaviour will precede exchange in attitude and knowledge.'

BETTER SCHOOLS

Realistic yes, and cautious too, but, as he showed in addressing the College of Preceptors, firmly confident in the capacity of teachers and schools to influence outcomes.

I believe that we have most of the knowledge and techniques required to provide an excellent public education system for all children – provided we can spread that knowledge to where it is needed and make those who must support the schools understand their real needs.

The survey of Primary Schools by HMI in 1978 showed how well the basic subjects were attended to and how well children were helped to grow up, individually and socially. Yet it also showed several things which we must now take account of:

1. It was the 20 per cent of teachers who used a mixture of didactic and exploratory methods who achieved the best results. That means, simply, that 80 per cent of our teachers need to expand their professional armoury;
2. It was the schools with the broad curriculum who achieved most, including the best results in the basic subjects. This is a finding of the highest importance and justifies totally the view that narrowness is never good for children. But it means that the majority of our schools need to be helped to widen their curricula.
3. Teaching in humanities and science was inadequate, all too often.

The survey of secondary education 14–16 by HMI also showed things which help to form our agenda for the 80s:

1. The system of subject options has in many schools become over ramified. In the attempt to provide choice ('You may take any combination of subjects you wish' said the school brochure), schools have lost the necessary balance and coherence;
2. Indeed, only 11 per cent of our secondary schools have conscious and deliberate ways of ensuring that they consider the coherence, balance and progression of the total curriculum, as experienced by the individual pupil;
3. Add the findings of Michael Rutter in '1500 Hours', that many of the most valued school outcomes were achieved by the ethos of the school, and it becomes clear that secondary schools need to counterbalance the effects of excessive reliance upon subject teaching and departmental autonomy.

PARTNERSHIP

John Tomlinson went on in this address to applaud the fact that the College of Preceptors and the Schools Council were proposing joint action in two areas, school management and industrial studies. The potential benefit of partnership, between bodies like the Preceptors and the Schools Council, between health and education professionals, between both of these and parents, was one of his recurrent themes.

John Tomlinson refers to the enthusiasm and commitment of the Court Report

> which showed the practical ways in which a child health service might be more effectively developed as a working partnership between parents, children, doctors, nurses (including the all-important health visitor) and teachers – and what this implies for organisation, training, relationships and the availability of information. And, if it might work for children then, *mutatis mutandis*, why not for adults also? ... Without good health, children cannot benefit fully from their education; and their education must make a contribution to keeping them healthy. The link between education and health is, therefore, strong and reciprocal. The child health and education services ought to see themselves as largely engaged upon a common task and co-operate closely.

In his opening address to the School Council John Tomlinson explored this theme in greater detail:

> For England and Wales, the Court Report has demonstrated how uneven are the life chances of children, depending on where they are born by class and geographical area. A child born into the family of a semi-skilled or unskilled worker is twice as likely to die in the first year of life (when environmental factors count for so much) as one born to parents in social classes I and II. Moreover, this gap has been widening steadily for 25 years, despite improvements, or so-called improvements, in services. Two and a half times more children die in our lowest two social classes than in the top two, of certain infectious diseases. And children born in inner cities are likely to be physically and emotionally less healthy. Yet services in the urban areas get proportionately fewer resources – what I discovered the cognoscenti of the health service had grimly coined as 'the law of inverse care.'

> The last theme I want to explore, regrettably briefly. How far, and when in their life's experience, can we help people to be better parents? As a teacher, may I end by stressing that I am more and more convinced that all health is ultimately mental health. That is why I place such emphasis on the self-image which society helps a growing youngster to create of himself. But let no one doubt the difficulty because in so many societies

the inner, spiritual life is in a process of transition which for many gives the appearance of a void.

He was to develop this theme in his Lockyer Lecture.

> All we have learned about children suggests that we ought to concentrate in the first place on their personal and social development. A sense of identity, security and purpose is an essential prerequisite of self confidence and success in learning the intellectual and vocational skills which are the traditional pabulum of schooling. This has always been true and was understood by good schoolmasters even in the days when schooling was only available to an intellectual minority. Once society says to its teachers 'Educate all our children full-time, at least until they are 16', an understanding of the psychological, physical, emotional and social development of the child and teenager becomes essential for the teacher. Seen in this light, how lamentable has been the false dichotomy, created by Black Papers and popular press, between 'traditional' and 'progressive' education.

This was particularly so for those with disabilities, as the Court Report had explained:

> As congenital and hereditary conditions become more significant in the totality of illness and as more children survive with handicapping conditions, new demands are made on services. Families with a chronically ill or handicapped child need to be in a continuing relationship with health workers and this relationship demands new sensitivities.

The report contrasts short term acute illness, and what it calls the treat-and-cure model, with the care of the handicapped, which

> demands on-going support and specialized knowledge at a level immediately, easily and continually available to parents; the support and knowledge will not be purely medical – nurses, teachers, therapists, social workers all have a part to play. Most important of all, services for the handicapped child must include the parent as part of the assessment, decision-making and management team.

He combined this belief in partnership with a facility for identifying the ground people had in common. His Lockley Lecture illustrates this talent. In it he sketched parallels between doctors (a title derived from the Latin doceo, I teach) and teachers, and between health and education in contemporary society. 'The establishment of the national health service and of a national requirement that children should be educated, have brought both professions into the political arena. The funding and government of both services' he said presciently, 'is continually on the political agenda and remains problematic ... Both our services live in a flux of movement between the poles of allowing the profession to run the service and insisting on lay involvement in the names of democracy, accountability or retrenchment.'

THE SCHOOLS COUNCIL

The remodelled Schools Council whose Chairman John Tomlinson became in 1978, was perhaps Britain's most imaginative attempt to create a national forum for education. In his Opening Address to Convocation, the Council's consultative assembly, he said,

> I think we are all conscious today that we are at a turning point. Perhaps, like me, you feel gratified but also overawed and not a little nervous. I wonder if historians will say of our efforts that they justified the intention and the hope of enabling constructive public debate of big educational issues, after the sharp, but possibly superficial, disagreement of recent times? Shall we be seen as this generation's educational monument – alongside 1902, 1918, and 1944?
>
> The Convocation of the Schools Council has been created so that there can be a national meeting place between those whose job is to 'do' education and those who want it done. Our discussions ought always to bear in mind that it is the relationship between these two sectors which either enhances or impairs the health of the education service – and therefore of a good part of the way we are raising the next generation.
>
> In this note, for the first meeting of Convocation, I have tried to set forth some of the issues which, in my estimation, are and will continue to be crucial in that relationship. Issues upon which neither 'society' should (or can) 'dictate' to its teachers, nor teachers claim (or expect) the right to act autonomously. Issues which go to the heart of how we in this country regard ourselves and one another and upon which, therefore, the teacher can only act with approbation if there is an explicit or, at least, implicit consensus. I believe that it is the task of Convocation to face such issues and, by discussing them without the posturing and vested interest which attaches to so much public debate of education, set a scene in which the decision makers may be able to act to better effect.
>
> Some appear to believe that our view of human nature, as it has developed by the late 20th century, and the fractured nature of our society, make the idea of a consensus not only impossible but absurd. For such people social institutions can only exist to contain conflict, not to create good. I reject such a pessimistic view. I grew up and started work as a teacher and administrator in a society which believed that hope lay in the child and held in common many simple but fundamental beliefs about what human beings need for spiritual and mental health. Those beliefs or their contemporary analogues need rediscovering in the

context of our fluid and anxious world. To believe that these have been suddenly cut off from the historical sources of humane wisdom is more arrogant than to set out on the argosy now required of us.

MANAGING THE EDUCATION SERVICE

In his Gittens Memorial Lecture John Tomlinson referred to the government report on LEA replies to Circular 14/77 about local authority arrangements for the curriculum. This had said the Education Department would draw up a 'draft policy document suggesting the form a framework for the curriculum might take and the ground it should cover.'

> The reasons for doing this are quite clear. 'Not all authorities have a clear view of the desirable structure of the school curriculum, especially its core elements'. Government should give a lead and 'an agreed framework could offer a significant step forward in the quest for improvement in the consistency and quality of school education across the country.'
>
> At Convocation in December 1979 occurred what may prove to be the last discussion in which 'teacher-control' and 'national control' are polarised and presented as incompatible. The spokesman for the NUT declared that teachers have always seen their job as serving the interests of the child and his parents and not the national interest. To this the DES spokesman retorted that there was a temptation for the NUT 'to believe that they are representing a long-established orthodoxy of educational principle and practice. I believe that what they are propagating is a heresy which has not been accepted by the people of this country.' He went on to argue that Central Government has always taken an interest in curriculum and that the historical list of DES/Ministry of Education pamphlets proved it. Moreover, all three levels of government – Central, LEA and School ought to be involved in different and appropriate ways.
>
> It was left to a Chief Education Officer (perhaps because CEOs stand at the pivot in such matters) to say that the truth is that central government interest in the curriculum has ebbed and flowed during the 100 years of compulsory education, that the reality is that it is flowing at the moment, and that the job in hand should be to ensure that some good comes of it.
>
> I happen to believe that about sums it up . . . A national framework for the curriculum is an idea whose time has come. The constituent members of the Schools Council – central and local government, teachers associations, CBI, TUC, parents and co-opted lay members from many walks of life had already decided that, as long ago as May 1979.

He explained the case for a national framework to the Professional Association of Teachers in these terms:

We no longer have a consensus about what schools should be trying to achieve and it is dysfunctional to leave 30,000 individual schools to make their own lonely decisions and then defend them against a hostile and largely uncomprehending local environment. But that is not to say that the framework should be conceived and imposed by a single element in the power structure of the educational system. Indeed, that would be to attack both the principles of pluralism and professionalism, on which I have said a democratic education system should be based.

A body constituted as the Schools Council was could meet these needs. The Schools Council, he told PAT,

> has existed for 15 years, been reformed at least once and is sometimes the subject of speculation about further reform or even abolition. From that I take comfort, since it must mean that it has become one of the unassailable parts of the British establishment – like the Monarchy, the House of Lords, and British Lions.
>
> I shall try to explain why I think the Schools Council ought to have an unassailable place in the educational establishment and then say something about its current work and especially its methods of working – which, again, connect directly with the individual teacher.
>
> I take it as agreed, in an audience such as this, that the schooling of the young is a most responsible activity. Teachers are given the privilege of intervening in the personal development of the new generation. That has significance for the individuals and for society. Of course, this forceful intervention is intended for beneficent ends. But it is, potentially, an instrument of tyranny. It is therefore essential that two conditions should prevail, if we are to remain a democratic and compassionate society: the power which activates the educational system should be dispersed rather than concentrated, and the teachers should be highly professional. By professional I mean simply trained well enough and given sufficient independence to be able to make sound judgements in the interests of their clients.
>
> But the Schools Council also has a wider role than being an instrument for reaching agreement about a framework for the curriculum – though it should certainly be that instrument. It should also, as a minimum:
>
> 1. work on the issues which are worrying society and the profession at any time;
> 2. work in ways which connect it naturally to the educational system and especially the schools. Thus the problem of dissemination of curriculum development, encountered and largely unresolved in all western countries, may be approached;
> 3. provide a network of information about good practice for the profession;
> 4. maintain the educational verities against the tides of fashion.
>
> Thus conceived, a central body such as the Schools Council is essential

for the health of a decentralised system. It is a safeguard for, not a threat to, pluralism and professionalism. That is an ironic but profound truth.

We have analysed the work of the system into:

1. Schools as whole institutions, and how they achieve their effects;
2. The teacher as an individual practitioner, and how he can be helped to be more effective;
3. The curriculum, conceived as subject content and educational experience;
4. Individual pupils, especially those with special needs;
5. The methods by which we monitor, evaluate and record our work. That includes knowing more about evaluation of schools', teachers', and the pupils' progress. Currently it also means reforming our examinations.

That analysis has, I believe, several strengths. By definition, it is inclusive. Therefore any future activity which may be desired can find a logical home which immediately relates it to the system as a whole. It will force the Council, in reviewing the content of programmes from time to time, to consider the totality of the educational experience and not just the fashionable parts. It also provides a dynamic way of organising work so that momentum and learning are less easily lost when a particular project finishes.

John Tomlinson urged

the use of existing institutions to regenerate public confidence in the education system . . . and create a healthy and mature relationship between the public and the profession. By that I mean a system with three characteristics:

1. Objectives are debated and settled by both public and profession;
2. These objectives are pursued by a profession adequately trained and untrammelled by external interference;
3. The results are measured according to agreed criteria and examined honestly by both public and profession, and in a constructive rather than rancorous spirit – for the future improvement of the service.

Historical awareness and optimism combined a few months later in his speech to the College of Preceptors on behalf of the new Charter Fellows. The 1980s was to be a period of contraction in the education service. The number of primary school children would continue to fall, by a total of 1.5 million. The fall in secondary school numbers had hardly started, and that would be 1.25 million.

Over and above the shrinkage caused by demographic change Government is determined to cut back public expenditure. We therefore face not only relative, but also absolute decline in size and resources per pupil. That would be bad enough in itself. But it comes, historically, after a period of public heart-searching about the purposes and practices of education. The Events of May in 1968 in Europe and America signalled the start, I suppose – in this country the Prime Minister's Speech at Ruskin in 1976 opened our (so-called) Great Debate, and questions about objectives, methods and accountability have filled the air since then.

Faced with such a period it would be easy for a profession to turn inward, become excessively defensive, and eschew the very innovations required for survival. I take it to be the job of educational leaders to try to prevent that from happening – in the interests of the rising generation.

In an article in *Education in Cheshire* he wrote 'we need the best possible partnership between elected members and professionals so that these important decisions can be taken against a background of real knowledge and professional experience.' He regretted the need for cuts to be made quickly in the summer of 1979–80, because they had to be made where money was still unspent, and were based on expediency not principle. The decision to give no more discretionary awards had removed a once for all opportunity for some youngsters, and gave further grounds for anxiety, because a local decision not to use a discretionary power conferred by parliament raised in question the whole system of local government. Cuts in education were difficult because

> We cannot choose which pupils we will take (as independent schools can), we cannot put it off till next year (as road mending can be put off), teachers cannot decide how big their classes will be (as doctors can close their lists), and parents and public expect that the Authority (and not only the school) will monitor the quality of the education and hold itself accountable . . . If the curriculum in secondary schools is to be reduced in range, are the Cheshire schools to make their own 80 different decisions (and, by implication, 5,000 in England and Wales) or must we agree on some common approach? Perhaps the diversity between schools did not matter so much when resources were sufficient to ensure at least an acceptable minimum of similarity.

THE EDUCATION OFFICER IN A DEVOLVED SYSTEM

The symbiotic relationship between local authorities and their officers seemed, as John Tomlinson explained in his Presidential Address to the Society of Education Officers, to lie at the heart of responsible local government:

> The essential features of the education officer's work and attitudes are still rooted in the traditions of the service, refined in the crucible I have just described. The education officer takes public responsibility for the advice he gives his authority.

This is enshrined in and required by the duty and the right of the CEO to report to his Education Committee at their public meeting. The importance of this constitutional position cannot be too much stressed. From it flows the personal responsibility of each officer in the department and the characteristic visibility of the education officer in public meetings and policy discussions. It is different from the Civil Service tradition in which advice given to ministers is not only confidential from the public but not revealed to ministers of the next administration. By contrast we are servants of the Authority, not of any individual party or other grouping within it. And the Authority is deemed to have a continuous existence regardless of changes in control. It puts us into the public debate more than civil servants and it forges in us special skills and sensitivities. For, like the civil servant, we must survive to fight another day, and the only sure armour is integrity and intelligence – backed up by a good digestion.

CONCLUSION

Much of what John Tomlinson said in the 70s and early 80s seems in the mid 90s as redolent of Olde England as village cricket and warm beer. But when the pendulum swings, as it seems to do every fifteen or twenty years, his holistic hedgehog vision of the relations between growing children, the adults responsible for them, and the communities which provide their schools, could form the platform on which to build a professional service in an open society.

REFERENCES

Tomlinson J R G (1979) Address to Convocation on 14 November 1978 as Director of Education, Cheshire. Cheshire Education Committee.

Tomlinson J R G (1979) An educationalist looks at health education, *International Journal of Health Education*, 22, 3.

Tomlinson J R G (1980) Reflections on Curriculum Development (The Charles Gittens Memorial Lecture), 19 February.

Tomlinson J R G (1980) The Schools Council: address to the Professional Association of Teachers, 29 July.

Tomlinson J R G (1980) Charter Fellows, Presentation Ceremony (College of Preceptors), 15 October.

Tomlinson J R G (1980) Reflections on Education and Medicine (The Lockyer Lecture to the Royal College of Physicians), 16 October.

Tomlinson J R G (1980) The Director's Bin (Article from Education in Cheshire).

Tomlinson J R G (1981) Present State of the Curriculum Debate in England (Address to American Association of School Administrators), 16 December.

Tomlinson J R G (1981) Ideas into Action, or The Empire Strikes Back (Address to Secondary Heads Association), 31 March.

Tomlinson J R G (1981) Education in the 80s (Address to Royal Society of Arts), 3 June.

Tomlinson J R G (1981) The Schools Council : A Chairman's Salute and Envoi (Schools Council Lecture to British Association), 1 September.

Tomlinson J R G (1982) The Profession of Education Officer: Past Pluperfect, Present Tense, Future Conditional published *Sheffield City Polytechnic Papers in Education Management*.

ENDPIECE 1

Justice Shallow

Justice Shallow was a regular contributor to *Education*
until its demise in 1996.

My dear Silence

Passing through Hatfield on the train the other day, I caught a glimpse of Hatfield House, and, at the main gate, of the statue of Robert Cecil, third Marquess of Salisbury, who, like Melbourne and Disraeli, had those most desirable of qualifications for the office of Prime Minister, being highly intelligent, sardonic, and with no illusions about the ability of politicians to change anything at all for the better. It was during his administration, in 1888, that the County Councils Act reached the statute book – not, I think, that he cared tuppence one way or the other, since he was as bored by local government as F.E. Smith would have been at a temperance meeting. Were he to return, over one hundred years on, he would, no doubt, still be yawning and amused to find that another Conservative government had as little faith in that form of local democracy, believing it to be, in his words, 'lax and costly'. The long years in between seem to count for nothing, and their achievements as sand.

Whatever vast responsibilities County Councils and Borough Councils carried, none was greater than education, and its importance grew until unkind souls became jealous of its status, covetous of its funds, and suspicious of its influence. Many elected members were ambivalent about it, unsure as to whether education was the jewel in their crown, or the cuckoo in the nest, or just a mixed metaphor which stimulated emotion but not thought. Certainly, in the 1970s, the haughty satraps of the ACC and the boyars of the AMA determined to cut the upstart down to size, and so, in a move of competent brutality worthy of Bismarck, they put to the sword the Association of Education Committees, replacing it with their own marionette, CLEA, which sensibly and from time to time, danced merrily to its own tune.

The dark clouds continued to mass. Sometimes, the concerned observer thought that the system would self-destruct. Education budgets appeared to spin out of control, until even the most accommodating Treasurer became as irritable as a dyspeptic rattlesnake. Teachers went on strike, some with a blood-curdling enthusiasm which made Arthur Scargill look like Lord North. Crackpot governors began to cull school library shelves of politically incorrect books, as though Noddy were a plague bacillus which would strike dead any mixed infant who came within five paces. Parents gathered at school gates, muttering darkly about the philosophical and practical inadequacies of Piaget's theories, and demanding of the Head that he give more weight to the writings of Czerniewska in his schemes of work.

Like the miasma from a primaeval swamp, all these odours swirled up to the nostrils of the shining ones at the DES, who decided to abandon their traditional policies of sublime inactivity and transform themselves into activists. It was all of a piece with a Conservative government ditching conservative principles and, instead of leaving things alone – 'How small, of all that human hearts endure, that part which laws or kings can cause or cure' – set about reorganizing them, or reducing them to rubble. Onto the midden heaps of history went trade unions and nationalized industries. Saved, but sent to rehabilitation, like some drunk still loved by his family yet whose beery eccentricities could no longer be tolerated, was the education system.

The first task was to sap the powers and confidence of the local education authorities, and this was achieved by subjecting them to petty interferences, and instructions of the 'nanny-knows-best' type sent out in their thousands by demented officials. Chief Education Officers were no longer consulted. The various education associations were left to moulder impotently, and secretaries of state appeared at their conferences only to reprimand them in the shrill tones of a headmistress from an Ealing comedy film. The second tactic was to leave the word to take away the substance of 'authority' from the local authority. Some schools were removed altogether from the LEA sphere of influence, and given grant-maintained status – a thing which appeared seductively chic to a number, but as applicants rapidly dried up and government targets shown to be as unrealistic as Stalinist figures for tractor production, so ministers took to subtler methods – hectoring, bullying, offering selection, and promising to stuff with gold the mouths of opt-outs. When all that fails, as it surely will, then the government will simply tell all schools that they are now grant-maintained, a stroke of splendid bureaucratic simplicity, speedy, thrifty and undemocratic. One other interesting variation of institutional independence came with the building of City Technology Colleges, to be funded solely by business and industry, and with a curriculum centred on electronics, balance sheets and computer-assisted lathes. In practice, the bill has been presented to the tax-payer as industry moved on to other interests or into recession; some colleges had no connection whatever with a city, and others none with technology pursuing instead idiosyncratic roles devoted exclusively to the arts, with students who delight in words not word-processors.

Colleges of Further Education and Polytechnics, raised from infancy to sturdy maturity by town and county halls, were declared free of their suffo-cating parents. Some, like the prodigal son, soon wasted their inheritance with riotous living – and, without the LEA, there was no-one to pay the creditors or mediate with the bailiffs – whilst most, like his elder brother, led sober and righteous lives, their tranquil days troubled only when the apparatchiks of the Funding Councils came to scrutinize their accounts or judge the efficacy of their teaching methods. Government policies have thus done little more for these institutions than move them from the rule of Tsar Nicholas II to that of the Politburo.

But of all the changes, none was more damaging to local authorities than the granting of financial independence to schools, who, as the argument ran, were groaning under the lash of local tyrants, men and women so lacking in financial acumen that millions or rate-payer pounds were being squandered through restrictive contracts, bungling administration and political obduracy. Then, at one bound, Jack was free. Schools took control of their own budgets, and could decide to buy a teacher or a trampoline without having to send in a requisition in quadruplicate only to have it turned down by a spotty youth in the finance department. To help them use their discovered freedoms prudently, new-style governing bodies sprang into existence. In place of the Alderman Hardcastles and Lady Arabella ffytches from the party lists came elected parents, managers, company directors, city agents, churchwardens and rotarians all of whom, to their great surprise, have had to slave like coolies on the sub-committees, working parties and *ad hoc* groups without which no progress can be made in any British venture. And, lest these bodies acquire delusions of grandeur, they were made accountable to parents, to whom each year they had to send an account of their stewardship, some at length and in prose so leaden that you could roof churches with it, and others with a brevity which would make Calvin Coolidge sound prolix. Additionally, the full governing body had to present itself to an annual meeting of parents, there to be subject to interrogation, and, when appropriate, abuse. As might have been expected, however, parents stayed away, much preferring the comforting fictions of Coronation Street to the cold realities of hearing about budget shortfalls and the oracular pronouncements of the Chief Inspector of Schools.

As if all that were not enough, local authorities were then compelled to cooperate with bodies called Funding Agencies which have powers over money and school places, and which are packed with government nominees to an extent which might have made nervous even that unrivalled master of unscrupulous patronage, the 18th century Duke of Newcastle.

So, as the millennium approaches, the organization of education has become what the French call *mouvemente*. There are simply too many groups struggling to be in charge, and, as in the Balkans before the Kaiser's War, border conflicts crackle and burn, and may eventually lead to a more furious and widespread conflagration. Up to 1988, local authorities had managed to keep some cohesion and absorb whatever shocks and discontents emerged, but, and serve them right, central government is now the whipping boy when matters go wrong, with no one between itself and parent rage. The old shire and borough councils, bereft of real education responsibilities, appear, like Tolstoy in his last days, to be stumbling around looking for somewhere to die, but – who knows? – reincarnation is not impossible, and the old skills, which the best had, of peace-keeping innovation, encouragement and responsiveness may be sought once more.

PART II

Curriculum Development and Practice

5

OECD CURRICULUM LESSONS

Margaret Maden

Professor Margaret Maden is Professor of Education
and Director of the Centre for Successful Schools at the
University of Keele. She was Director of Education for
Warwickshire 1989–1995 and Head Teacher of Islington
Green Comprehensive School from 1975–1982.

Educational tourism has its exhilarations as well as its dangers. Thrilling to
the deferential charm of Taiwanese or Russian school children is one thing,
trying to replicate such behaviour and practice elsewhere is an altogether
different matter, as well as impossible. However, the analytic distillations
of a mediating international agency such as the Organisation for Economic
Co-operation and Development (OECD) begin to make sense of the exotic
and the apparently irrelevant.

The need for the OECD emerged from the Marshall Plan and the reconstruction of post-war Europe. It was finally set up in 1960, with its headquarters in Paris. Its original purpose was mainly to promote economic
growth in member states, initially Western Europe and the USA, through
research and development activities. Soon, however, the OECD spawned
the Centre for Educational Research and Innovation (CERI) which is now
the world's leading source of information about education and training
systems globally, as well as being a major *animateur* in supporting and
evaluating innovation within and between member states. Japan, Australia,
New Zealand, Mexico and soon, the emerging democracies of the former
Soviet Union and Warsaw Pact countries, are now part of the OECD's remit.
Membership depends on a country's commitment to both a free market
economy and to a government system based on free elections.

In 1994, OECD-CERI published *The Curriculum Redefined: Schooling for the 21st Century* (TCR). This is the culmination of a decade's work across more than 25 countries, led and synthesised by expert researchers and evaluators in CERI, many of whom are on 2 or 3 year secondments from government ministries, universities and research and development (R&D) institutes in member states. International conferences and seminars, involving politicians, practitioners and researchers periodically checked and steered this major project. Incidentally, it is odd that in 1993, the final conference had 8 delegates from the United Kingdom and all were from either the Department for Education and Science and Scottish Office or from the Office for Standards in Education (OFSTED). No one from either the Schools Curriculum and Assessment Authority or from any University or Research Institute, except for one from the University of Ulster. Interestingly, however, 5 of the 15 independent experts invited by CERI were from the UK and included the former chief of Her Majesty's Inspectorate, Eric Bolton, and the originator of the early pupil assessment methodology when the National Curriculum was first established in England, Professor Paul Black.

For OECD purposes, the school curriculum is taken to include everything that 'happens in school as a result of intention' (TCR, p.51). Thus, both the what and how of pupils' learning are considered and the skills and status of teachers are important parts of the investigations and deliberations. So, too, are the skills and role of parents when these are the subject of school developmental studies and school–community innovatory practices.

Perhaps the most illuminating and clarifying component of the document is its context statement. This provides a robust underpinning to more mutable curricular structures and forms. It also demonstrates most vividly the benefits which accrue from an independent international body which now has an unparalleled database and is also able to utilise and refine high level evaluative and research techniques. The organisation's arms-length relationship with its main funding source, the governments of member states, is also a strength just so long as the two are loosely coupled.

For those of us who have experienced radical and fairly tumultuous educational reform in recent years (mainly in the UK and New Zealand) having access to such a thoroughly considered and rooted context statement is both reassuring and elevating. The statement includes references to dramatic developments in the globalisation of the economy and, in relation to these, the emergence of more co-operative alliances such as the European Community, the Asia-Pacific Economic Co-operation grouping and the North American Free Trade Association.

'On the other hand' we are reminded, 'societies formed by tightly-bound disparate elements are breaking up into smaller, more coherent, more homogeneous groupings, sometimes bringing about inter-group strife in that process' (TCR, p.29). We can all recognise such a paradox; global economic forces and integration in sharp contrast to more narrowly defined and exclusive ethnic, religious and cultural groups. No curriculum artefact can ignore such issues. Also ubiquitous appear to be the emergence of more varied family patterns, an increasing gap between rich and poor, insecure and unpredictable career profiles, as well as societal changes which, we are told, include:

- negotiation of rules, e.g. between parents and children, is more significant, but schools are not well placed to do this,
- social control has diminished, leaving schools to formulate continuity and to forge collaboration,
- new forms of social and economic exclusion mean that the full benefits of education are denied to some groups of children,
- society is more dynamic with situations more loosely structured so that people have to define and solve their problems themselves,
- there is an increasing need for more reflective and critical approach to knowledge.   (OECD-CERI, 1995, p.8, Para 15)

This leads to a helpful account of more specifically educational context elements and these reveal as much commonality as diversity between countries, which each, no doubt, believes itself to be unique. Thus we are told that the

> implications of the change from education of an elite to mass education are still being worked out, and as schools grapple with dealing with the whole range of society's needs, more seems to be expected of them as other institutions lose their influence. The lives of the young people in schools are also changing rapidly, at a pace and in ways which neither the school nor politicians are able to control. Thus the expectations, the social and family pressures, and the means of support, which mould the lives of pupils are all very different from those on which present school programmes were based.   (OECD-CERI, 1995, p.8, Para 14)

Other trends that are evident in all of the participating countries include greater school autonomy, linked to more explicit forms of public accountability, with greater emphasis on outcome standards being the means by which governments, national or regional, express their relationship with schools. The delegation of resources and managerial discretion to schools is certainly not unique to our own country although the extent of such delegation and the variety of practices described yield some fascinating insights into political value systems and the histories of different countries. We are advised that:

> it was possible in the past to speak broadly of systems being centralised or decentralised with respect to the control of issues such as curriculum, staffing and finance. Thus, countries such as USA and Britain were decentralised while others such as Japan and Sweden were centralised. Changes over recent years have blurred these distinctions, with initiatives to centralise and decentralise both occurring, often in the same countries.   (TCR, p.31)

Rising rates of student participation following statutory schooling and in higher education represent another common experience. A special study of Dynamic Asian Economies (DAEs), provides a dramatic example of the powerful pace and impact of this latter phenomenon. In South Korea, the relevant age group in universities rose from 3 percent in 1953 to 35 percent in 1985. We are told that, 'much of this growth was fuelled by the very high rate of economic growth and the consequent heavy demand for graduates' (TCR, p.33). Can this explanation be applied with equal certainty to a very similar UK trend? In South Korea, the school system responded in such a way as to create their own form of hyperinflation. The number of qualified but unsuccessful candidates for university education grew from 70,000 in 1970 to 700,000 in 1985. Disillusionment and anger resulted amongst both the rejected and the increasingly overcrowded and mass-instructed successful candidates. Such pressures are observable in most advanced industrial and post-industrial societies as the transition from an elite to a mass higher education system unfolds. The implications for the school curriculum are unavoidable, if not always obvious. These include issues of curriculum content and standards, as well as modes of delivery.

Indeed, it is interesting that OECD surveys and analyses indicate that between 16 and 20 percent of school children have special educational needs and that 30 percent are defined as being 'students at risk', due to social disadvantage or ethnic minority status. Whilst there is considerable overlap between these groups, the curriculum statement makes it clear that for reasons of equity and justice as well as for economic and broader social reasons, these students need to be included in the drive towards a mass further and higher education system. 'No society can afford 20–30 percent of its working age citizens to be unproductive' (TCR, p.157). We are also urged to understand the curricular implications of our contemporary understanding that we cannot take the distribution of intelligence on the Gaussian curve as 'normal' and regard IQ as fixed. It is not entirely certain that most schools or, indeed, the public in general in the UK accept this truth.

The more active influence of the business community – and an increasingly wide range of special interest groups – is another widespread phenomenon, included in the consideration of context. We are reminded that 'Educators have frequently proclaimed the importance of schooling to society in general and must now expect to be taken at their word' (TCR, p.34).

In the UK we may be surprised that in so many OECD countries, business and industrial interests include trade unions, as well as employers, and that both are vociferous in their claims to be full participants in a continuing dialogue. However, it is not only in the UK that educationalists have a sense of unease about an undue emphasis on vocationalism which might be expected to emanate from such sources. Conceptually, at least, the OECD curriculum analysis is helpful in reviewing and resolving such concerns. We are told that:

In many countries, vocational education has been the Cinderella of the education sector, dismissed as being involved merely with training and not with education. In the vocational world of today and tomorrow, that distinction becomes increasingly irrelevant. Vocational education cannot be limited to a set of skills imparted before commencing work and used thereafter in a career. The pace of technology change means that vocations require new sets of skills continually and the capacity to learn and to keep on learning is more crucial than particular competencies.   (TCR, p.34)

The importance of a systemic dialogue between the business–industry sector and education clearly needs to be understood in this context and a reconstructed vision of what is meant by 'general education' also follows. Such a dialogue is also stressed as crucial from another, more pedagogic, viewpoint:

Increasingly, much vocational education occurs on working-sites, contextual learning as many business leaders call it. With the expansion of education for those for whom school environments are not conducive to learning this is important. It is important, too, to make available to schools a wider range of situation and of technology than they will be able to provide . . . there is a lack of research and analysis on important ideas such as contextual learning or situational learning. Both these deserve more attention.   (TCR, p.34)

Other stakeholders and pressure points are also cited by OECD as being more evident and insistent than previously. In OECD member states, generally, there are often strident demands being made of schools by evangelical and fundamentalist religious groups, by lobbying interest groups with particular moral viewpoints on health education, ethnic and race relations, 'green' issues and so on. 'Now, and in the future, major social issues will make their claims for attention because of the perception that education is an effective agent of change, in concert with other processes such as legislation. How schools and curriculum agencies work creatively and responsibly with such an array of interests is a contentious and unresolved matter. 'Partnership' has to have more meaning than as a fine-sounding slogan and an important warning-note is issued when it is suggested that currently, 'the place of such issues owes more to the power of advocacy than to any comprehensive consideration either of the claims for a place or of the capacity of education to provide effective responses' (TCR, p.34).

In both the larger matters of curriculum reform and in the particularities of process, lessons have been learnt and a full account is given of these. When major curriculum development is embarked upon, the key factors which have been identified as requiring equal attention and articulation are initial teacher education, curriculum framework and resources, professional development and assessment.

In addition, we are advised that these principles are important in any such development or reform if it is to work:

- statements of purpose, such as goals, aims and objectives need to be clearly stated and understood,
- such statements need to relate to widely held values and widely agreed needs,
- the active interest, engagement and support of major stakeholders, including teachers particularly, are necessary for success,
- national level, government-led reform measures need to address a major, widely perceived need and to offer benefits to large numbers or to specific groups experiencing great hardships. (TCR, p.27)

These precepts and principles have emerged from a welter of case studies and innovation exchange across more than 20 countries. The OECD has commissioned three 'country clusters', each comprising 10–12 different member states, to investigate further the processes of curriculum reform as they differentially interpret and apply these basic principles. One of the clusters has been examining the role of teachers and their professional development in facilitating or impeding curriculum reform. The Japanese speak of the teacher as *sensei*, a figure of respect. Others describe the multiplying tasks wished on, or assumed by teachers. The need to be clearer about the teacher as teacher, rather than as social worker, counsellor, facilitator or curriculum designer appears to be widely supported.

It appears, then, that these variants of the teacher's role do not simply represent another example of 'a very peculiar practice', limited to the English. Nonetheless, the greater concentration on the teacher as teacher does not mean that teachers can be left unmolested by the urgent drive towards curriculum and pedagogic reform. International evidence indicates that ambitious top-down reforms place enormous burdens on teachers, because their working practices and their relationships with pupils – as well as with parents and outside agencies – have to change.

These matters are fully explored and are being investigated through ongoing research in the CERI/OECD programme of work in 1995–96, reported in *Teachers and Curriculum Reform in Basic Schooling*. In this report we are told that if pupils are to become more active learners, taking on enhanced responsibility and initiative, the nature of the teacher–pupil relationship has to change. We are also advised that the capacity of more autonomous schools to manage curriculum reform, when this has been formulated elsewhere (at national or regional level), requires extensive and particular forms of support for teachers. The idea of teachers being programmed automatons, merely 'delivering' new curricula, is dismissed with the back-up of plenteous empirical evidence. Teachers have to be key agents of change and 'continuous professional development, encouragement and protection' are needed for this to become a reality. Widespread case studies show that 'no reform policy can proceed faster than teachers are able to cope with its practical realisation'.

An interesting and relevant postscript to this report relates to emerging problems of teacher supply. As economies recover and where there is already a new baby boom, it is seen to be important that the status and attractiveness of teaching as a career are ensured. It is suggested that 'over-hasty reforms, top-down prescriptions which are not based on consensus, a narrow emphasis on accountability and on blaming teachers for shortcomings, can all threaten the future'.

Bringing together, in these ways, the collective evidence of curricular change and educational reform more generally, is enormously illuminating. Whilst a conclusion is drawn that 'the dynamics of change are not well understood', enough appears to have been observed and evaluated, to lead to the observation that 'school systems cannot respond to rapid and radical change'. The 'social culture' of the teaching profession is advanced as a major reason for this, but such a critical issue surely warrants a fuller account of available research evidence, not simply of and about schools, but of how change occurs in other organisations as well.

A familiar conundrum is attached to this universal problem of effecting change; that whilst 'political leaders need to recognise the necessary complexity of the curriculum process and the long time-scale of educational change', schools and teachers, on the other hand, 'must recognise the contending force of political life and the need to define and achieve short-term goals, as inherent parts of our democratic pattern'. (TCR, p.212). A refreshing rider to this series of reflections and studies of educational and curricular change is the requirement that the resources needed to effect change should be quantified and best practice identified in terms of value for money. It is encouraging that the leading edge in such an approach is acknowledged to be our own Audit Commission.

Our own National Curriculum is strongly aligned to traditional subjects and recent pressures at key stage 2 (8–11 year olds) are extending and emphasising this further down the age range. The OECD approach runs counter to this and in the presentation of 4 main models of curricular structure, this subject-based model is criticised. Whilst it possesses certain pragmatic advantages, a particular disadvantage is seen to be its inherent difficulty in addressing 'new aims needed by society and the need to reformulate subjects to strengthen links between the academic and the practical and vocational aspects'.

Such a generalised critique is spelt out in a more vivid and illuminating way in an account presented of the CERI/OECD Project on Innovations in Science, Maths and Technology Education. From this major project have arisen a wide range of responses to social concerns about environmental quality. In 19 countries, a linked CERI/OECD programme, Environment and School Initiatives (ENSI) demonstrates how connections between scientific and technical fields, on the one hand, and political, social and economic considerations, on the other, can be treated. In a few countries, a new subject, environmental studies, has been created. In many places, the better established subjects have been modified to incorporate environmental issues. However, the impact on teachers' professional development and on initial teacher education of such initiatives is complex and demanding. The four main targets of the ENSI programme confirm this to be the case:

• to envisage the environment as a sphere of personal experience,
• to examine the environment as a subject of interdisciplinary learning and research,
• to shape the environment as a sphere of socially important action,
• to accept the environment as a challenge to initiative, independence and responsible action.   (TCR, p.153)

In assessing pupils' more dynamic qualities; responsibility, initiative, co-operativeness, creativity, our more traditional examination subject syllabi and assessment instruments are stretched to breaking point.

However, it is inspiring to learn of such developmental projects and the case studies which underpin them, with these glimpses of work in progress:

• at Evo, in Finland, the vocational school has planned and set up a nature park, following negotiations with the local council and industry board;
• at Serre, in Italy, a primary school investigated pollution in a local wetland and pursued their findings with local industry. Improved industrial practices subsequently continue to be discussed and monitored;
• at Bredstedt, northern Germany, a study group of teachers and secondary pupils converted a disused school into a nature information centre and continue to provide many of its publications, including research studies, and handle its public relations.

These accounts need to be considered in relation to the high priority the OECD attaches to the 'many students who are progressively detached from their school learning, seeing it as unrelated to their interests or as beyond their capacities' (TCR, p.155). The potential power of imaginative curriculum reform to reach pupils who are not motivated by more traditional subject and book-centred approaches should not be forgotten. Improving performance and jacking-up standards do not result simply from published league tables of exam results or from a tightly prescribed national curriculum. The seriousness attached to these questions of motivation and pupils as active, rather than passive, participants in the learning process permeates all of the curricular innovations sponsored by CERI/OECD.

In the ENSI project, the case studies reveal a diverse range of learning contexts, from a 'bolt-on' strategy, using science or geography lessons as a subject base for more active experiential learning, through to quite separate modular courses. The usual problems associated with each are well documented; the former is unable to bring forward sufficient time or multidisciplinary expertise, the latter is marginalised in terms of traditional, higher status, single subjects. In both, however, there is concern about interdisciplinary boundaries in problem-solving and research. Interestingly, much of the most exciting, leading-edge work in universities is now interdisciplinary (geophysics, biochemistry, criminology, for instance), but in schools there are problems of a practical, operational, kind and evidence suggests there is a need to avoid a *mélange* which lacks cohesion or rigorous thought. Similar problems arise in health education or in moral and civic education.

The increasing marginalisation of such approaches in English and Welsh schools, especially in secondary but also evident in primary, is a worry to many teachers. They feel unable to engage the commitment and interest of a significant minority of young people whose sense of belonging to a 'learning society' is non-existent. Thankfully, there are several curricular projects which CERI/OECD is co-ordinating and evaluating which aim to combat unequal access and low achievement in basic schooling and which try to prepare students for later, lifelong learning.

New delivery systems, either based in school or loosely coupled with school are also being studied. Case studies which address the issue of self-directed learning, assisted by new interactive technologies, represent a particular priority. The cost-effectiveness of such less conventional forms of learning are being evaluated and the important socialisation role of schools is being considered in terms of alternatives to the conventional '9am–4pm' school.

An important part of such enquiries is the need to identify learning strategies which serve the needs of an increasingly differentiated client-base. It is not only white, male members of the proletariat who are, on occasions, disaffected and for many students, some of the time, in some parts of their study programme, there will be benefits in accessing I.T. and other self-directed learning strategies. Accelerated learning methods, not necessarily dependent on what a whole class is concerned with, need to be more commonly available. Likewise, these case studies are examining learning technologies and opportunities provided outside school hours and terms. Much of this appears to fly in the face of some recent advocacy, in England, of a more standardised 'whole class' approach, apparently based on the precept 'keep it simple stupid!'.

The development and exploitation of a wider range of teaching and learning strategies, does not, however, deny the efficacy of classroom practice being clearer and more focused. But the beleaguered teacher who yearns for a simpler golden age will not be helped by solutions which appear to deny the existence of a huge range of individual motivation, readiness and need. In England and Wales, a sharper focus on what the teacher intends and expects to achieve with pupils is one of the better practices more recently revealed through careful classroom observation by inspectors, evaluators and others. Nonetheless, the place of such good practice, lesson by lesson, needs to be seen as a small gleaming chip in a larger, well structured and eventually, coherent mosaic. The best teachers have always kept an eye on this larger pattern, to which they are contributing. They know that an exclusive concentration on one term's results, or a school's GCSE performance for 16 year olds, can be harmful and is certainly insufficient.

CERI/OECD seeks to hold such elements in balance and constantly stresses that in all its case studies, the concept of lifelong learning places compulsory education in a new setting. Rather than being a unique period of schooling leading on to vocations or further education, it is a phase in a lifelong process.

That phase, however, has two key requirements: one is to provide a basis for further learning; the other is to ensure a continuing motivation for it. This may imply a greater organisational variety and more flexibility in approach than is the case with current schooling. It certainly implies the need for greater and more constructive student involvement in the planning and conduct of their education.   (TCR, p.159)

It is sad that this kind of thinking is currently unfashionable in England and Wales and is often associated with the 'trendy seventies' and other ideological demons. The fact is that CERI/OECD is chronicling practical innovations, in over 20 countries, which seek to engage the interest of pupils in their own continuous learning and raise their achievement levels. This is what all countries associated with the OECD recognise as an urgent and supremely important task.

Innovations are needed, of organisational structures, of pedagogies, of curricular and disciplinary configurations and of how teachers, pupils and significant adults other than teachers, relate to each other. In the conclusion to the CERI/OECD study we are reminded that:

Our reason for working together is not because of an existing consensus, but because of controversy and conflict. Our work is a continuing search for a consensus as an unfolding task, the unfinished and unfinishable task of building a curriculum for the future . . . We should not underestimate the magnitude of the task of curriculum reform. The school's part of the social contract is to create high quality education and training for all. We should neither minimise or shirk the task, but recognise that the alternative, a bitterly divided and unjust society, is not acceptable.   (TCR, p.213)

It is the combination of these larger insights and the breadth of case studies with other empirical evidence that makes *The Curriculum Redefined* such a worthwhile report. In this and in other co-ordinating and evaluative activities, CERI/OECD is a hugely rewarding source of ideas, good practice and vision. As with more normal forms of tourism and travel, an expanded knowledge base helps to clarify and put into a clearer and more robust frame the purposes, strengths and weaknesses of one's own system. Beyond this, of course, are the undoubted benefits which always accrue when we consciously reject the narrowness and paucity of parochialism and xenophobia.

REFERENCES

OECD/CERI (1994) *The Curriculum Redefined: Schooling for the 21st Century*, Paris: OECD.
OECD/CERI (1995) *Teachers and Curriculum Reform in Basic Schooling*, Paris: OECD.
Quotations from these documents are reproduced in this chapter by permission of the OECD.

6

CURRICULUM THEORY AND A CURRICULUM FOR THE 21ST CENTURY

Denis Lawton

Professor Denis Lawton is Professor of Education at the
Institute of Education, University of London. He was
Director of the Institute 1983–1989.

I had most interaction with John Tomlinson when I was a member of several
committees of the Schools Council and John was its Chair. It was a difficult
time for the Council – consensus was giving way to centralisation – but John
made many good things happen and we had several long discussions about
the curriculum – past, present and future. In this chapter I want to speculate
about the future curriculum, and my stance will be that there is something
called education theory and that it is useful to talk about curriculum in a
theoretical way.

The School Curriculum and Assessment Authority (SCAA) has recently
put out for consultation a document which proposes a framework for
reviewing the national curriculum. This will possibly give us an opportunity
to plan a curriculum more appropriate for the 21st century than the present
confused mixture of approaches and ideologies. Few would now claim that
the Baker curriculum of 1988 was a success; and the Dearing Review
1993–4 was no more than emergency surgery. What we need is a completely
new plan.

THE CURRICULUM NOW

I want to start by looking at the curriculum as it is now and by asking what –
from a theoretical point of view – is wrong with it. Traditionally there are four

approaches to curriculum design: curriculum based on content, objectives, process or assessment.

The content model comes in several forms but is well exemplified by a *traditional* A level syllabus (but not some of the reformed versions such as the London Geography 16–19). A content syllabus is seen simply as a list of topics to be covered, information (including arguments and theories) to be memorised, techniques to be mastered. A traditional history syllabus, for example, would expect students to know the relevant facts and to understand the views of historians about the Tudors and Stuarts and be able to write essays regurgitating their views. There is still plenty of the content approach in the national curriculum.

The objectives approach was partly an attempt to be more systematic than having lists of content to be covered by the teacher. The behavioural objectives theory said that a curriculum must be expressed in terms of output rather than input – in terms of items of student learning rather than of the expectations of the teacher. Objectives had to be precise, prespecified and measurable. This model has been very attractive to education planners from the 1920s in the USA to England in the 1980s. But there are very powerful philosophical, psychological and practical objections to it. In its pure, behaviouristic form it has all but disappeared from serious educational discourse, but some politicians are still very attracted by it. The word 'objective' is a useful term as long as we remember its limitations.

The process approach can be seen as a reaction against the content syllabus and behavioural objectives design. Psychologists such as Bruner (1960) argued that holistic understanding was more important than rote learning or reductionist mastery, and that the essence of good curriculum planning was better appreciation by the teacher of the structure of a subject – the key ideas, the concepts and the processes involved. This was a much more ambitious and more demanding view of curriculum knowledge for teachers. The curriculum planner had to have a much better insight into the structure of knowledge as well as how children learn (two kinds of process). Incidentally this is very different from the stereotype from a progressive classroom where children do whatever they like and discover everything for themselves.

The fourth approach – assessment-driven curriculum – is an attempt to revive a narrow view of objectives by focusing on assessment of outcomes. It is sometimes associated with high stakes assessment and accountability. It is a variant of the objectives model – and, at times, a very power-ful one.

I would like to make three general points. First, none of the four approaches really solves the problem of *what* to teach. They are design approaches rather than planning models. Second, it is essential to try to combine the complexity of knowledge (epistemology if you prefer) with the complexity of the learning process. Third, good assessment will then reinforce the curriculum-learning process rather than distort it. Having stated that, the question of what is wrong with the national curriculum may become a little clearer. The national curriculum has four elements:

1. Subjects (content)
2. Attainment targets (objectives)
3. Programmes of Study (detailed content with a little process)
4. An Assessment Scheme (the TGAT model).

I want to argue that the national curriculum is fundamentally flawed in several ways. The national curriculum is an ill-considered mixture of approaches. The result was a lack of coherence between content, objectives and process, but with assessment dominant – partly because it was necessary to provide market competition. The TGAT model was carefully thought out and some aspects of it received strong professional backing, but it was never accepted *in toto* and was gradually watered down to the point where it was barely recognisable to its authors.

Some Theoretical Issues

1. The *content* was a list of subjects – very traditional – with enormous gaps in coverage of what should have been required for a curriculum in the 1980s. I will spend a little time on this because it points the way forward to a better curriculum. The gaps in the ten-subject curriculum included many of the most important aspects of our culture: political, social and economic education; moral and health education; as well as being focused on content to be covered rather than skills and understanding.

The National Curriculum Council in 1990 tried to fill the gaps by supplementing the subjects with cross-curricular themes:

- Health Education
- Careers
- Economic and industrial understanding
- Environmental Education
- Citizenship.

The themes, however, were always a low priority compared with subjects because themes were 'non-statutory advice' rather than legal requirements. And successive Secretaries of State after Baker failed to understand the problem and vetoed further work of this kind. The gaps remain. Even as a content list it is inadequate and I suggest that we need to revive the cross-curricular themes or something better.

2. *The Programmes of Study* varied in interpretation from subject to subject (the Working Groups did not have time to confer). As time went on, process tended to get squeezed out in favour of facts and information.

3. *Attainment targets/objectives.* The objectives problem can be seen as a question of finding a place on a continuum stretching from very broad general aims to highly specific objectives. The national curriculum was never clear on this – hence more incoherence.

4. The related *assessment* problem can be seen in terms of sampling: do

you try to test everything or can you be satisfied with a small selection? The answer is, of course, a matter of fitness of purpose (for example, it is a good idea to assess every aspect of a pilot's training whereas we can be satisfied with a small number of questions for A level history). There should also be a match between decisions about curriculum and decisions about assessment/sampling: decisions about the curriculum should lead logically onto parallel decisions about assessment. There are advantages in having general aims and a low sample for some kinds of curriculum – you may be less interested in whether a candidate remembers every detail than in his ability to argue a good case. So in traditional examinations the whole set of questions may be looked at together, and a good paper on one part of the syllabus can compensate for a poor one elsewhere. This is regarded as fair and good examination practice; but we would not wish it to operate in the case of pilot training where we do not want compensation ('Excellent at take-off, poor at landing, but pass overall'). There are cases where the mastery model is essential. In the case of the national curriculum in 1988 this question was never seriously addressed. And a wrong decision was made in 1991 which led to the boycott in 1992–3. The decision was made to choose specific objectives with a high sampling rate and detailed reporting. Since large numbers of pupils were involved this presented the obvious problem of manageability. So Dearing shifted the pattern towards more general objectives (Level Descriptions instead of Statements of Attainment), but other fundamental problems remained.

5. I have noted the need to match curriculum and assessment; it is also important to plan the link between curriculum and pedagogy. In designing a curriculum it is important to make sure that there is a match between these two aspects of curriculum design – it is impossible to separate the two. Some politicians appear to want a modern curriculum whilst retaining traditional classroom teaching. But modern curricula require pupils not simply to memorise information but to think out issues for themselves – solving problems and sometimes working as a team. (Incidentally these are some of the requirements that employers specify for a reformed curriculum).

WHAT KIND OF CHANGE?

In the light of the above what changes are necessary for a curriculum for the 21st century? I have five suggestions.

1. *From content and objectives to skills and processes*

The Higginson Report (1988) complained that A level students spent too much time memorising and recalling facts and arguments rather than acquiring fundamental understanding of the knowledge. Similar comments have been made about the curriculum for younger pupils. And Charles Handy in his chapter in this volume has suggested that he would 'have more faith in a national curriculum if it were to be more concerned with process than with content.'

Robert Reich in *The Work of Nations: Preparing Ourselves for 21st Century Capitalism* (1993) has discussed the need for much higher levels of thinking skills in the computerised world of symbolic analysts who need skills of 'abstraction, system thinking, experimentation and collaboration'. Bruner (1960) also talked about process, structure and the need for children who were learning science to begin to think like scientists.

The Cognitive Acceleration through Science Education (CASE) project at Kings College, London has been very successful in improving learning in science for children aged 11–13. The aims of the project were broader than making science teaching more effective. It was concerned with the development of reasoning. The general assumption is that children develop their ability to think when they try to solve intellectual problems. Unfortunately in many schools teachers and pupils enter into an unconscious contract to avoid too much effort: teachers devise ways of keeping children busy on work that will not involve too much mental exertion.

The aim of the project was to raise expectations and standards. CASE lessons encourage discussion and critical appraisal of tentative ideas. Teachers are urged to encourage the learners to reflect on their own thinking processes: 'How did you solve that problem?' 'Explain it . . .' Another key word is bridging. Thinking skills do not automatically transfer to different situations – connections must be consciously made. Teachers and learners develop certain kinds of 'high level thinking': e.g. control of variables, probability, correlational reasoning. The researchers conclude that the way to raise academic standards is not investment in content-based technology, but on well-targeted programmes to improve intellectual ability or thinking scientifically. They recommended focusing on the 11–13 age group. The ESRC has recently invested in wider application of similar methods in other subjects such as maths and history. (The *Innovation and Change in Education* Programme coordinated by Professor Martin Hughes of Exeter University.)

2. From subjects and cognitive attainment to cross-curricular themes and the affective domain
Subjects may be useful up to a point, but they are limited – some of our most pressing problems are not conveniently packaged within a single subject. In real life we have to get beyond the subjects. The ten subject national curriculum encourages concentration on traditional cognitive learning, but young people grow up unable to cope with real-life problems involving an understanding of their own society, including its political structure, and unable to cope with questions of values and morality. A dramatic shift in the direction of social and moral education may be our most urgent need.

Recent work in psychology has shown that conventional intelligence tests have concentrated on one very limited form of ability and encouraged teachers to ignore many other kinds of intelligent behaviour. In the USA Howard Gardner's (1983) theory of 7 kinds of intelligence reinforces the view that we should think of a broader curriculum. The traditional grammar school curriculum was too academic and neglected personal and moral development. The Gardner theory suggests that not only is the traditional curriculum too narrow in terms of human abilities, but also that we should be looking for abilities and talents in all pupils. Professional teachers will have a richer concept of 'ability', and will try to adapt teaching to the intelligences of the learners; children do not all learn in the same way, and whilst it is not possible for all teaching to be individualised, it is possible for teachers to diagnose individual difficulties and take account of them. There is promising work in Canada and more recently in England (the Avon 'Learning to Learn' project).

3. *From didactic teaching to self-directed learning*

The National Commission on Education (NCE) Report (1993) drew attention to the need for older pupils to take responsibility for their own learning programmes. This does not mean that teachers should not continue to give direction (including some whole class teaching) but the emphasis should move, as students mature, in the direction of learning how to learn – learning how to become autonomous learners. Multiple intelligence theorising is related to the idea of self-directed learning. One of the greatest difficulties is for the teacher to encourage the whole class to move along in the same direction whilst recognising that the styles of learning and the range of achievement will be considerable.

Part of the task for the teacher is to plan carefully what kind of learning needs to be individual, what should be learned in a group, and when it would be better to have a whole class presentation by the teacher, always bearing in mind that pupils benefit from verbal interaction with the teacher. This is a very different picture from children simply engaging in 'activities' either as individuals or in groups. One of the hostile stereotypes of the 'progressive' classroom is that teachers never teach the class as a whole, but set work for groups or individuals, or simply leave them to 'discover'.

There is a further complication: part of the teacher's plan should be to cater for different levels of ability. This is very difficult and Neville Bennett (1987) has observed that: 'approximately 40% of tasks matched pupils' capabilities but there was a strong trend towards the over-estimation of low attaining pupils and the under-estimation of high attainers'. This is a finding supported by much HMI evidence (DES, 1978, 1983 and 1985).

One of the most sterile arguments in the last twenty years has been the debate about the advantages and disadvantages of setting and streaming by ability. This debate misses the point: it is not enough to have a class set for ability – what is needed is a much more complex pattern of organisation and pedagogy to cater for a range of individual differences. In 1993 the National Commission on Education (NCE) recognised this and devoted a whole chapter to 'Innovation in Learning'. It was particularly impressed by 'flexible learning', where pupils learn to take some responsibility for their own learning programmes.

The National Commission Report also recommended that by the age of about 14, pupils should be equipped to work independently in a flexible learning environment. It goes without saying that the flexible curriculum demands flexible assessment: it is also necessary to avoid age-related testing.

4. From academic **or** *vocational to integration of both aspects of experience*
We need to overcome the false and sterile opposition of academic and vocational (see Pring, 1995). Many outside education have complained about this characteristic of educational thinking. This is by no means an English phenomenon, but we have the problem intensified because our social structure is so dominated by class. Curricula should be designed with a view to eliminating the distinction between academic and vocational: young people need aspects of both traditions, as suggested by the IPPR (1990), the National Commission on Education (1993) and Richardson *et al.* (1995) *Learning for the Future.* We need a curriculum which gets beyond thinking in academic and vocational terms: this will not be easy because the two concepts are deeply embedded, and segregated, in our culture. All pupils need more social and moral education.

5. From a national curriculum 5–16 to life-long learning
We have at last reached the stage where most young people stay on in education beyond 16, but although much lip service is paid to the idea of life-long learning, very little thought has been given to relating the national curriculum 5–16, or education 14–19, to providing related opportunities throughout the whole of working life and beyond. Not only because most people will need to change jobs four or five times, but because they need to have opportunities to continue learning actively for the rest of their lives. These opportunities need to be planned – they are too important to be left to the market.

DANGERS

Failing to get the right balance.

1. I suggest that we need to talk more about process than content, but process must not drive out content completely. For example, it is important for young people learning history to begin to think like historians, weigh the evidence, and so on. But it would be an impoverished history curriculum if it did not provide access to the historical aspects of our cultural heritage – national, European and inter-continental. Cultural heritage is not a right-wing monopoly.
2. A modern curriculum needs more than subjects. But let us not make the mistake of the 1960s where, for the best of motives, some humanities courses resulted in good history teachers teaching geography – badly. The move should be to get beyond subjects without de-skilling the teachers and without losing what is valuable in the subjects.

3. From didactic teaching to self-direction – yes, but the practice of treating children as individuals can be taken too far. Teachers who simply set up tasks for individual children have a complex management problem which will take up all their energies (Simon, 1981). They are in danger of having no time left for teaching. Once again it is a question of balance – there is nothing wrong with whole class teaching at the right time. As for flexible learning, the NCE Report also pointed out its dangers. 'Flexible learning done badly can be disastrous . . . and pupils must be emotionally and intellectually ready to take some responsibility for their own learning . . . Self-directed learning does not work with non-self-motivated people' (p.90). Flexible learning is a very useful technique but not a panacea.

4. We must abolish the academic–vocational barrier without losing high academic standards.

5. Life-long education is a splendid goal but the basic curriculum 5–16 (or 3–16) is vitally important for the low achievers. Life-long education is not a problem for teachers or lecturers – but it is a problem for those who left education at 16 with no qualifications and little interest in learning.

CONCLUSIONS

We should be seeking a comprehensive solution to the curriculum: we need a better curriculum for all our young people – selection is a distraction from the main question of raising expectations and achievements for all. Our problem is not only to ensure that the most able are stretched; it is that we have two to three times as many low achievers as France and Germany.

We should also avoid being distracted by other fashionable obsessions, for example: by wasting money and energy on bolstering up the A level structure when we need a broader and better balanced curriculum 16–19 for all – including our most able young people. Or by league tables. Of course we need good assessment, and we need to be able to identify schools that are under-achieving, but the present obsession with making unfair comparisons of performance tables not only distorts the curriculum but also encourages the kind of market competition which is destructive of real quality. We must move on to planning a good comprehensive system for all young people, not allow many of them to be sold short in a very unfair market.

There is much wrong with our system in general and the curriculum in particular; in recent years education has been criticised – sometimes fairly, sometimes very unfairly. I remain optimistic about education but it is necessary to remember that education itself cannot solve the social problems.

REFERENCES

Adey P S (1988) Cognitive Acceleration – Review and Prospects, *International Journal of Science Education*, 10, 2, 121–134.

Adey P S & Shayer M (1990) Accelerating the Development of Formal Thinking in Middle and High School Students, *J. RES. Science Teaching*, 27, 3, 267–285.

Adey P S & Shayer M (1993) An Exploration of Long-Term Far-Transfer Effects Following an Extended Intervention Programme in the High School Science Curriculum, *Cognition and Instruction*, 11.

Bennett N (1987) Changing Perspectives on Teaching Learning Processes, *Oxford Review of Education*, 13, 1.

Bruner J (1960) *The Process of Education*, Boston: Harvard.

Department of Education and Science (1978) *Curriculum 11–16*, London: HMSO.

Department of Education and Science (1983a) *Curriculum 11–16: Towards a Statement of Entitlement*, London: HMSO.

Department of Education and Science (1983b) *Teaching Quality*, London: HMSO.

Department of Education and Science (1985) *Better Schools*, London: HMSO.

Galton M (1989) *Teaching in the Primary School*, London: Fulton.

Galton M (1995) *Crisis in the Primary Classroom*, London: Fulton.

Gardner H (1983) *Frames of Mind*, New York: Fontana.

Huff P, Snider R & Stephenson S (1986) *Teaching and Learning Styles*, Ontario Secondary School Teachers' Federation (OSSTF).

Hughes M (1993) *Flexible Learning Evidence Examined*, Network Ed Press.

Hunt D (1982) The Practical Value of Learning Styles Ideas. In J. W. Keefe (ed) *Student Learning Styles and Brain Behavior*, Vancouver: Reston.

Institute for Public Policy Research (IPPR) (1990) Education and Training Paper No. 1 *A British 'Baccalaureat'* Ending the Division Between Education and Training (David Finegold *et al*), London: IPPR.

National Commission on Education (1993) *Learning to Succeed*, London: Heinemann.

Pring, R. (1995) *Closing the Gap: liberal education and vocational preparation*, London: Hodder & Stoughton.

Reich R (1993) *The Work of Nations*, New York: Simon & Schuster.

Richardson W. *et al* (November 1995) *Learning for the Future – Initial Report*, London: Institute of Education Post-16 Education Centre and the University of Warwick Centre for Education and Industry.

Simon B (1981) Why No Pedagogy in England? In B. Simon & W. Taylor (eds) *Education in the Eighties: the central issue*, London: Batsford.

Yates C (1987) Teaching Correlational Reasoning to 11–13 Year-Olds, *Journal of Biological Education*, 21, 3, 197–202.

7

THE ARTS IN THE SCHOOL CURRICULUM

Eric Bolton

Professor Eric Bolton CB was the Senior Chief Inspector
HMI from 1983–1991. He was Professor of Education at
the Institute of Education from 1991–1996.

One of the many peculiarities of the English education scene is that the place of the arts in the school curriculum has always been somewhat precarious. There have been few out and out arguments opposed to the arts being in the curriculum at all, but the stance taken by Mr. Gradgrind in Dickens's *Hard Times* namely, 'Now what I want is Facts – Facts alone are what is wanted in life', is not an extreme exaggeration of the general thrust of much of the thinking that informed and drove along the growth of our public education system in the nineteenth century.

Despite Gradgrindery, past and present, we have never quite succeeded in excluding the arts from the curriculum totally, though they enter on sufferance, and persist by grace and favour. English, mathematics, science, history, foreign languages and, even geography are there because of what they are. The need to be numerate and literate rightly goes without question. Similarly, there is little argument about the need for children to have some understanding of how the physical world works through science and its ways of examining natural phenomena; nor about how things came to be as they are via some study of history, and, increasingly, the case for the necessity of foreign language learning, and grappling with the applications of science via technology, is being accepted.

Each of those subjects has one or more second-order arguments supporting its inclusion; many, but not all to do with individual career and vocational choices, and/or with national economic health and well-being. On the other hand, the inclusion of the arts seems, almost invariably, to require some secondary, contingent justification. The arts are 'good for you' provided they are not too raw, or questioning. They are: individually civilising and a necessary component of the civilised life and society; entertaining and their execution demands perseverance and discipline; important to the economy because they earn a lot of money abroad and attract visitors to this country.

The political rhetoric is wholly supportive of the general case for lively and viable arts, while that of education is equally supportive of their inclusion in the curriculum. But, when push comes to shove, action and rhetoric do not match – political or educational – if there is a distinction these days! Funding for the arts nationally, which has always bordered on the miserly, is cut pro rata with other demands on the public purse, and suffers disproportionately. Despite that, jingoism and, more respectably, national pride are supportive, in theory, of some of our orchestras and at least one opera house being 'world class' and of having, in our towns and cities, art galleries, theatres and concert halls that rank among the world's best. Equally importantly we want our authors, painters, sculptors, composers, actors, musicians, dancers, and singers to feature prominently, and perform well on the world scene.

To mitigate some of the adverse consequences of dwindling Treasury funding for the arts they were made one of the recipients of National Lottery money. There is much that can be said for and against that, but this chapter is not the place to examine that. My point in raising the matter is to show that even though it is national policy to fund parts of the arts through the lottery, there is huge public and political resentment about giving money to the arts. The grants to the Royal Opera House and to the English National Opera are attacked for encouraging elitist art forms and the entertainment of 'fat cats'. Money to the Tate Gallery is aligned by the tabloid press with Damien Hirst's dead cow in formaldehyde, Rachel Whiteread's 'House' and the now infamous, and mythopoeic 'pile of bricks at the Tate'. One could go on, sadly *ad nauseam* but, more worryingly, even when significant sums of lottery money go to charities there is a general belief, revealed time and again by both *vox pop* and more serious surveys of public opinion, that money spent on the arts would be better spent on 'good causes'.

As expressed by politicians, the press and various populist campaigns, we appear, nationally, to see the arts as an amalgam of expensive diversions for the rich; costly indulgences for idle/uncouth/untalented/effeminate people who call themselves 'artists'; unintelligible gibberish; subversive and difficult; comforting strokers of our prejudices and received opinion; only for the elite, pretentious few; and cosy and/or comforting leisure activities for senior citizens, women and children, and the mentally disturbed. Above all, the arts are seen as peripheral to life in earnest: to the serious business of living one's personal life and earning a living.

There are, of course, many thousands of exceptions to that over-simplified description of our national attitudes to the arts. Nonetheless, now, and historically, the position and treatment of the arts in the school curriculum relfect each and every one of those stereotypical views of the place and purposes of the arts in education, and education in the arts.

The school curricula's track record in respect of the arts is not good. It has not suddenly deteriorated, as a result of Government policies; or of recent neglect by schools, or LEAs. Until the National Curriculum came into being in 1988, art itself was the only arts subject that appeared in many schools. In the face of this reality a number of different arguments have been posited to justify a more thorough going coverage of the arts in future school curricula.

The first is that the arts should be in education, and particularly in the school curriculum, as some kind of counter-balance to the sciences. Put more pointedly, it is claimed that art, representing culture, decency, and civilised values, should be there to counter-balance the impersonal, utilitarian and functional worlds of mathematics, science and technology: William Blake versus Isaac Newton! In reality the two are not opposed, particularly if the comparison is set in the context of wider discussions about culture. In the Western cultural tradition in which we all stand, like it or not, science, and the interpretations of the world and natural phenomena to which it gives rise, are every bit as much a part of our culture, as are music, art and literature.

A close, analytical observation of natural phenomena and of human motivation and behaviour, are the basis of both science and art: empirical study, or observing the way things are. The distinction between the two lies in what they are able, and not able, to do with that evidence. It does not lie in basic differences in what interests artists and scientists, nor in the evidential base on which they operate. Stubb's anatomical studies of dead horses, and Leonardo da Vinci's close observation of Savanarola at the stake are examples in point.

An understanding of Western culture must acknowledge the individual and combined contributions of philosophy, arts and science. In fact, the separation of art and science is relatively recent in our history. What little I understand about what is happening at the frontiers of physics, suggests that the propensity of the arts to order phenomena into patterns that suit its purposes may be nearer to the truth than the classical, scientific belief that somewhere out there a pattern, or patterns exist, and that scientific enquiry will reveal it, or them, and hence the meaning of life, to the diligent searcher. It seems that advanced physics, and chaos theory, might well be indicating that there are no such patterns, or that they are so complex that the patterns we believe we see, are those that we impose. Tom Stoppard's recent play, *Arcadia* is, in part, a sustained analysis of that dilemma.

Second is the argument that the arts in education are a civilising force for good in human endeavour and that a liberal sprinkling of the arts in school curricula will bring an over-lay of decent and civilised behaviour to our lives. There must, however, be serious reservations about this claim. While it is difficult to envisage a civilised society that does not take the arts seriously, it is not self-evident from history that the greatest art is produced by the most civilised individuals and societies.

In general, positive attitudes towards, and encounters with, the arts have uplifting, sobering and civilising effects upon society and individuals. However, as Tippett said of that Berlin orchestral performance of Beethoven's 9th attended by Hitler and the hoi-poloi of the 3rd Reich, 'If music is sublime, then it is sublimely indifferent to the temporal affairs of men'.

Art is in a profound sense moral, but one of its central and important concerns is with thumbing its nose at conventional morality and attitudes. Hasek's *Good Soldier Schweik*; Straus's *Till Eulenspiegel*, and, most memorably, Shakespeare's Falstaff, are cases in point. Their irreverence is unavoidably softened by the passage of time and familiarity, but it is also needlessly de-barbed by approaches, performances and productions that emphasise the historical and quaint, while minimising the universality and contemporaneity of the central themes. Bach's *Saint Matthew Passion* reveals, fleetingly, the heights attainable by a humanity, built on compassion and unselfishness. But great art also explores, with similar insight and force, the darker sides of our nature. Richard Straus's *Salome* is a seductive exploration of the disturbing attractions of decadence and evil. Marlowe's *Tamburlaine the Great* uses beautifully poetic language to explore the complexity of the megalomaniac, child-slayer, sacker of cities, and slaughterer of men, women and children, who deeply loves and cherishes his wife, Zenocrate, and is loved in return despite her knowledge of the horrors. Far-fetched? Fictitious? Horror for horror's sake? Speaking of a world and human nature that have long gone? Before answering with a comforting yes to all of that, we should remember that the commandants and guards of Dachau, Belsen and Auschwitz went home to tea, to wives, and to children at the end of each shift and that Bosnia and Ruanda are still with us.

Education, if it is to deal effectively with the arts, has to take on both the dark and the light. Even in much that is included without question in the curriculum, teachers are faced with disturbing and difficult problems. How does today's teacher, in our culturally mixed society, handle the opening exchanges in *Othello*, when Iago tells Desdemona's father:

Even now, now, very now, an old black ram
Is tupping your white ewe.

or, Shylock, and how he is portrayed, in The Merchant of Venice; or Kate's final speech in *The Taming of the Shrew*:

Thy husband is thy Lord, thy life, thy keeper,
Thy head, thy Sovereign, . . . etc.

These issues cannot be ducked without sentimentalising and sanitising the arts. Nor can they be edited out, like an American version of Huck Finn that removed the word 'nigger' on grounds of ethnic and political correctness. Art of that calibre and importance is first-hand evidence of human concerns and endeavour at the time and more universally. As such, to edit and change it to conform with current perceptions, is as serious as burning the books. In effect, serious art goes about its own business. It is not concerned primarily with our personal comfort.

A third justification of the arts in education is that they are important for use in our leisure time. It is true that we engage variously with music, painting, plays and books in our leisure time unless, of course, we are professional composers, painters, actors, writers or academics. But to imply that the main purpose of the arts is, in some simple sense, to entertain us or to help us fill those blank hours between the serious business of earning our living and sleeping is surely wrong. That puts the arts in the same category as stamp collecting, Sunday football, rowing, or walking the dog. There is surely something of that perception of the arts in the Dearing reform of the National Curriculum that makes the arts optional after Key Stage 3 and proposes vocational courses for 14 year olds in the hope of better motivating them to learn.

There is much in the range and diversity of the arts that is relatively undemanding, geared to filling in our time in some more-or-less instructive and entertaining way. In the deepest and most complex sense, great art is entertaining: it must not; should not, be tedious and boring. Great art, even good art, makes demands of its audiences. It does not seek easy solutions, nor aim for easy gratification. We should never forget that however familiar works such as Picasso's *Guernica*, or Thomas Hardy's *Jude the Obscure* have become, they were inspired and driven along by deeply felt senses of pain and injustice. To lose sight of that, and to treat such works as cosy companions, is not only to do a serious injustice to their creators and authors but it is to fail to gather what is to be gathered from the works themselves. More seriously for the future, such a cosy treatment encourages us to expect contemporary art, and artists, to be strokers of our prejudices and supporters of received wisdom. Both stances are death to the arts.

In effect, the arts need no separate, external justification to be in education. They must be there. And be there in their own right not because of some useful but secondary justification for their presence. The arts constitute a particular way of explaining human motivation and experience in the world in which we live. They are a sustained, complex, palimpsestic analysis of the human condition – every bit as important and necessary as that carried out by the sciences. Seamus Heaney puts the case neatly in his collected Oxford lectures, *The Redress of Poetry*, when he states that the Czech poet, Miroslav Holub sees the functions of drama, poetry and the arts more generally as:

> analogous to that of the immunity system within the human body. Which is to say that the creative spirit remains positively recalcitrant in face of the negative evidence, reminding the indicative mood of history that it has been written in by force and written in over the good optative mode of human potential. (p. 24)

Despite, or because of that positive task, the arts do not exist to support, or bolster 'good taste'. The shifting and uncertain distinctions between high and low art do not run along the borderline between good and bad taste; cosiness and discomfort. There is no distinctive break between so-called high and so-called popular art and culture. High art of any value and worth has its feet in ordinary common-place experience. All art forms, periodically and frequently, have to return to those roots. Tony Harrison's play *The Trackers of Oxyrinchus* is a painful and entertaining contemporary exploration of that.

High art, from time to time, needs the vulgar, the common place and the immediacy of popular culture. And popular culture does things – important things – that high art cannot do. In direct, and indirect ways, high art feeds on popular, vulgar culture. The frequent use by great composers of folk song and melody ranging from Bartok and Dvorjak to Haydn, Mozart and Beethoven is just one example. There are many others in architecture, painting, poetry and, extensively in dance; an art form that is not open to vulgarity is no art form at all.

The arts, in that all-embracing sense, must be invited to sit at the curriculum table. But they must and will come as they are. We cannot expect them to have perfect table manners; nor to be unfailingly polite to authority and supportive of the way things have always been done. Nor will they be concerned to put us at our ease, or to do us good. They will be irreverent, and decidedly not politically correct. From time to time their jokes will become strained and their comments painfully personal – and they won't all be blonde, white and deferential. Some will be black or brown and have interests and tap roots into cultures that stretch across continents, religions and the divisions of the haves and the have nots.

The arts will do what they have to do, which is to push and worry at the frazzled edges of the human condition. In doing that they might, as Yeats said, 'Help ease the dreadful loneliness of man' or as Nietzsche put it 'Force us to gaze into the horror or existence, yet without being turned to stone by the vision'. They will, at times, be the Furies and at others the Kindly Ones. Like music, they will have 'charms to soothe the savage breast'. But their claws will only be sheathed, not removed.

How we cope with them, and with their wildness and wilfulness, in the school curriculum is for decision at particular times and in particular circumstances. Whatever good intentions they may set out with, politicians cannot resist attempting to tame, prettify, or distort the arts and artists. They simply cannot keep their hands off; and it has to be said that artists don't help. They will insist on being rude and unkempt and, like Pasternak, ultimately unreliable, concerned as they are with the way things really are as distinct from the way conventional morality, fashion, propaganda, and expediency would have us believe them to be. However we are to conduct the exciting and necessary relationship of education and the arts, it is imperative that political interests do not have the final, or the most influential, say. So, in Lenin's words, 'What's to be done?'

First we must return to curriculum breadth and balance throughout the whole period of compulsory schooling. All other developed nations achieve this and keep a larger proportion of the pupil cohort for longer than we do. Surely we are not dealing with a different form of human being in this country than is the case elsewhere? The arts, as of right, must be a part of such a curriculum for all. The analysis of our education service and the proposals for tackling weaknesses and building on strengths, contained in the Keith Joseph White Paper of 1987 *Better Schools* stands up to scrutiny today. We could achieve a workable and motivating broad and balanced curriculum for all if we had faith in the qualities of our children; trusted our teachers (with proper checks and balances) to devise and carry out course work and its formative assessment; and re-introduced an updated form of curriculum planning.

The decline in the power and influence of LEAs has had particularly damaging consequences for work supporting the arts in schools that, to be done well, needs to be done at a higher level than that of the individual school: music, drama, dance and art centres; teams of peripatetic artists and instrumental music teachers are cases in point. (That is not to denigrate the considerable gains in other aspects that have come via LMS.) New networks are needed to devise ways of maintaining and furthering those arts-in-schools supporting activities by ensuring funding, quality control and administrative efficiency. Many such partnerships are coming into being often involving new-style LEAs more concerned with facilitating than with bureaucratic, or political hegemony. Regional Arts Boards; newly autonomous schools; art agencies such as orchestras, theatres and dance companies; individual artists and, more rarely as yet, local and/or national businesses, and higher education institutions can also play their part. Nationally, however, the government of the day needs to have a vision for the public education service that includes a substantial and positive engagement with the arts for each and every pupil throughout compulsory schooling. This must not be seen as a luxury that can be sacrificed whenever the squeeze on time or resources makes broad curricula provision difficult, but as a necessary and vital component in the school curricula of a decent and aspiring public education service.

There are tentative, but promising moves on all these fronts not least the recently announced Government strategy for access to the arts by young people, *Setting the Scene, The Arts and Young People* (Department of National Heritage, 1996). Nonetheless, much of what has contributed to healthy and stimulating arts education in our schools remains precariously placed. While there is a constant need for new thought and endeavour in all things if they are to be vital, and avoid the debilitating effects of nostalgia, we must, over the next few years, be vigilant in seeking to keep alive in the arts in the education field that which has so successfully shown its value and quality in the past; survival will be the prime concern of the next decade. Perhaps we must emulate the characters at the end of Ray Bradbury's short novel *Fahrenheit 451* – who wander the wild woods beyond the city limits memorising the words of great literary texts in order to keep them alive for when the world turns round again and better days return – as we wait for, and work to influence the shape and nature, in education, of:

what rough beast, its hour come round at last, slouches towards Bethlehem to be born.

W.B. Yeats, *The Second Coming*

REFERENCES

Department of National Heritage (1996) *Setting the Scene, The Arts and Young People.*
Heaney, S (1995) *The Redress of Poetry*, London: Faber and Faber.

8
_____

CATCHING THEM YOUNG: THE JOY OF THE UNDER-FIVES

Tricia David

Professor Tricia David is Professor of Early Years
Education at Christ Church College Canterbury. She was a
Senior Lecturer at Warwick University from 1985–1995.

As we approach the millennium, we seem to be at a unique juncture in our country's attitude to and treatment of the youngest children in our society. More than ever before politicians of all parties are beginning to take an interest in educational provision for children in their earliest years. The cynics among us might question their reasons – has edu-care (daycare which engages children in appropriate learning opportunities) become a vote-catcher? Is it because of evidence that early learning promotes children's later achievements, including those assessed by the National Curriculum tasks and tests (eg. Ball, 1994; Shorrocks, 1992; Schweinhart and Weikart, 1993)? Or that criminal tendencies can be curbed by early intervention (Schweinhart and Weikart, ibid.)? Or have politicians woken up to the fact that the United Kingdom is being overtaken in economic terms by countries which are willing to invest in young children and that perhaps, after all, there may be something in what the advocates of nursery education have been saying for most of this century?

WHAT COUNTS AS NURSERY EDUCATION?

As a result of the neglect of under-fives' provision in this country by every successive government (David, 1990), we are currently trying to start from a place which is very different from that in some of our competitor and our partner countries (David, 1993). We continue with the muddle, lack of coherence and, in some areas, lack of provision and of choice, which has been detailed by Pugh (1988; 1992).

A decade ago, the only forms of provision which were deemed 'nursery education' were those settings overseen by a qualified teacher and inspected by HMI for Education. Thus nursery education was regarded as taking place in nursery schools, nursery classes and combined (Education and Social Services) provision, mainly in the public, ie. maintained, sector. In addition, other forms of provision ranging from private nurseries, local authority daycare and playgroups, to workplace creches and childminders, inspected by and accountable to social services departments were not recognised as nursery education.

Further, although many schools implemented policies of admitting children into primary school reception classes at the start of the year in which they would become five so that many four-year-olds began to attend Year R classes, these frequently had less favourable staffing ratios, equipment and/or space to that defined as nursery education. A 1989 HMI report pointed out the influences of these factors on the experiences of the children, suggesting that those in nursery education derived greater benefits from 'work that is well planned with suitable emphasis on purposeful play and exploratory behaviour' (DES, 1989 p. 5).

Although in earlier times many nursery schools and classes catering for 3 and 4 year olds were offering most children on roll the equivalent of the primary school whole day attendance, by the late 1980s nursery schools and classes tended to offer only sessional (morning or afternoon) attendance, thus making it impossible for an employed parent to use this form of provision even if it existed in their part of the country, unless the child's attendance at a series of different settings could be organised, so that it covered the working day. Such fragmented experience cannot be expected to promote continuity of relationships and learning. It would be rejected out of hand for older children, yet appears unquestioned for smaller and more vulnerable learners.

Further fragmentation, through the lack of coordination between different types of services, with different histories, philosophies and protagonists, creates both logistical and perceptual problems for everyone – not just for parents and politicians. In attempts to remedy the incoherence, some local authorities have, during the last ten years, and especially since the implementation of the Children Act of 1989 and the publishing of the Rumbold Report (DES, 1990), coordinated provision by placing all under-fives' services administratively under one department. Examples include Strathclyde, Sheffield and Leeds. What such coordination can mean is that, given the will and the funding, parents with different needs and interests may find appropriate provision for their children and themselves. Parents wanting facilities which would cover their working hours and provide their child with relevant learning opportunities welcomed such initiatives. Additionally, carefully planned coordination has meant that staff with different expertise and backgrounds can be brought together to learn from each other. However, in some areas provision of any kind is limited, so attempts to meet parental demands, to coordinate and share ideas remains a forlorn hope.

The lack of publicly-funded provision is most acute for children under 3 whose mothers are employed outside the home. The issue of care facilities, especially those embedding planned learning opportunities appropriate to individual children's needs, proves intractable in most areas of the country. While the UK now ranks second in the European Union by having 61 per cent employment among women and the proportion of mothers of children under 5 who work has risen from 32 to 46 per cent in only the last ten years (Linton, 1996), it ranks bottom of the list (with Germany, Ireland and Spain) in having public daycare services for only 2 per cent of children under three years (Moss, 1996). Provision for this age group is generally termed 'care' rather than 'education'. However, members of the recently-formed national umbrella group, the Early Childhood Education Forum, which represents parents, childminders, private and voluntary providers, as well as nursery teachers and trainers, repeatedly call for recognition for children's learning from birth rather than simply from the age of 3. While still maintaining the view that daycare provision is a private family matter, Junior Education and Employment Minister Cheryl Gillan announced the publication of a Government consultation paper inviting comment from child care agencies (Linton, 1996; DfEE, 1996). The intention is to review daycare availability and needs for children of all ages and to stimulate the development of increased levels of child care provision, of high quality, largely through the private sector. The Labour Party is promising action in this area too so it seems that whichever of the main political parties will form the next government there will finally be acceptance that the state has a part to play in stimulating services. But will those who work in newly-developed services be trained to a level sufficient to recognise babies' and toddlers' capacity for learning?

With the implementation of the Government's Nursery Voucher Scheme for all four-year-olds (Phase 1 having begun in Norfolk, Kensington and Chelsea, Westminster, and Wandsworth in 1996; Phase 2 country-wide from April 1997), nursery education is now deemed to be offered by any group setting which can satisfy the conditions laid down by the Department for Education and Employment (DfEE, 1996a). Meanwhile, there are anxieties concerning the possible impact of the scheme on provision currently catering for 3 year olds. This has arisen partly from the clawing back of nursery funding from LEAs to finance the vouchers. To be recognised as providing nursery education for 4 year olds means a unit has complied with the self-assessment schedule, applied to be a voucher-redeeming nursery, and is subsequently graded positively on inspection by a Registered Nursery Education Inspector, according to the Ofsted nursery inspection schedule. There is no guarantee that a qualified teacher will oversee the children's learning nor that staff will necessarily have had appropriate early years training, though the Children Act did provide local authorities with some influence over staff training and qualifications.

EARLY CHILDHOOD: PERCEPTIONS AND EXPECTATIONS

What happens to, or is thought to be 'right' for, young children in any society or subcultural group is related to the childhoods constructed by that society (Nunes, 1994; Tobin, Wu and Davidson, 1989). For many years babies and young children were not accorded the powers psychologists now acknowledge they have. For example, Deloache and Brown, 1987 and Singer, 1992 have documented the ways in which developmental psychology, because of its underlying assumptions and methods, failed to access these powers. Now Gardner (1983) has added a further dimension to this issue by proposing the idea of multiple intelligences, most of which we in the West appear unable to foster because we cannot 'see' and do not value many of the 'intelligences' Gardner identifies (see Charles Handy's chapter). As Gardner explains,

> The time has come to broaden our notion of the spectrum of talents. The single most important contribution education can make to a child's development is to help him toward a field where his talents suit him best, where he will be satisfied and competent. We've completely lost sight of that. Instead, we subject everyone to an education where, if you succeed, you will best suited to be a college professor. And we evaluate everyone along the way according to whether they meet that narrow standard of success. We should spend less time ranking children and more time helping them to identify their natural competencies and gifts, and cultivate those. There are hundreds and hundreds of ways to succeed, and many, many different abilities that will help you get there.
>
> (from an interview quoted in Goleman, 1996 p.37)

The dominant view of very young children in the United Kingdom tends to be based on limited and out-dated theories and beliefs. Ideas about maternal deprivation and children's emotional needs (Bowlby, 1953) have been used as arguments against the provision of nursery education in the past. Further, the idea that young children are active learners capable of constructing their own view of the world and of participating in the creation of knowledge is not informing a coherent policy for our youngest children. (See also the discussion in Stuart Maclure's chapter). It appears that in our United Kingdom society, it does not matter if children in this age-group experience numerous changes of settings during their first five years, some even spend time in two different edu-care settings within a single day, in order to cover their parents' work hours. Further, there is a notion that the learning achieved in the first five years is not 'real education' and that the purpose of nursery provision is simply to prepare children, to lick them into shape in a number of ways, so that 'the reception class can begin the proper process of education' (*The Times*, 1995 p.17).

Recent research indicates that babies and young children will live 'up or down' to societal and family expectations, that they will try to please the adults around them in order to be valued, loved and accepted (eg. Bruner and Haste, 1987; Trevarthen, 1992). So the curriculum we decide on for young children, both its content and its teaching approaches, may have crucial long term consequences for our society. We have to decide what kind of people we want our children to be and to become. We have to ask ourselves how they will cope with a world we will not be here to see and experience and, above all, we have to remember that while they may be small they are not our possessions. They are people who are actively trying to make sense of their world. And as the poet Kahlil Gibran writes:

> You may give them your love but not your thoughts,
> For they have their own thoughts . . .
> For life goes not backwards nor tarries with yesterday.
> You are the bows from which your children as living arrows are
>   sent forth.

> (Gibran, 1926, in the 1994 edition: 20)

LEARNING IN THE CULTURE: DEVELOPMENTALLY APPROPRIATE PRACTICE AND ITS CRITICS

Over the last two centuries, Western European advocates of an early years curriculum based on play and discovery learning have included Rousseau, Owen, Pestalozzi, Froebel, Montessori, McMillan and Isaacs. However, Sutton-Smith (1979) argues that play is used by societies to prepare children for life in that context and in some societies play may even be used to foster conformity.

In the UK, Jean Piaget has been a significant influence on practitioners' ideas about early learning and play. His work has been interpreted as indicating that children need time to play and investigate their environment free from the demands of adult intervention and that, in any case, Piaget's view of the fixed nature of cognitive stages meant that rushing children on, presenting inappropriate concepts would only result in confusion and later learning difficulties. So the idea of children being allowed to develop and learn 'naturally' by pursuing their own interests unimpeded grew out of the application of Piagetian theory to early childhood education.

This view reached its height in the USA in the 1980s, where Developmentally Appropriate Practice (DAP) was advocated by a powerful early childhood lobby (Bredekamp,1986). This advocacy of developmentalism occurred as an antidote to the growth in formal, academic preschool programmes. The National Association for the Education of the Young (NAEYC) argued

> Programs have changed in response to social, economic and political forces: however, these changes have not always taken into account the basic developmental needs of young children, which have remained constant. Programs should be tailored to meet the needs of the children, rather than expecting children to adjust to the demands of a specific program.

> (Bredekamp, 1986 p. 1)

However, research studies (for example, King, 1978; Tizard and Hughes, 1984) had already exposed the way in which some early years teachers did not adapt to the needs of individual children. Nor did the teachers recognise the fact that some children had learnt from their parents and other family members how to access an informal curriculum, with its invisible structure, while other parents lacked this knowledge and were thus unable to help their children understand the subtle meaning of learning through play in the nursery setting, despite being competent actors in their own home environments.

Furthermore, the reality had to be faced that even where the children have some choice, the equipment, toys and activities made available have been selected by adults. Children pick up messages about which activities and behaviours are regarded as most important by the adults and, although early years teachers have sometimes found it difficult to know how to have a direct input into children's learning under a Piagetian-inspired regime, they do in fact maintain invisible control over 'the selection, expression and direction of ideas and activities' (Edwards and Mercer, 1987 p.112).

More recently, Bredekamp (1993) has herself recognised that the DAP 'documents have been criticised as being naively Piagetian, not reflective of Vygotsky and not reflective of information processing theories of learning' (Bredekamp, 1993 p.1) and, further, that DAP did not take account of the needs of children who do not come from white, middle-class backgrounds.

The growing impact of contact with very different cultural beliefs about young children, together with evidence from research by the Post-Piagetians in the UK and Australia (for example, Donaldson, 1978), by Bruner in the USA and the UK (1977; 1990), together with Vygotsky's (1978) ideas from Russia and most recently Trevarthen's (1992) in Britain, has all given rise to greater recognition for the social nature of young children's learning and the cultural context in which that learning is accomplished.

Here in the UK, following the implementation of the National Curriculum, parents have put pressure on under-fives' educators, demanding that their four-year-olds engage in bouts of formal writing and number work. This has been due to parental anxieties about the long term impact of the assessments at the end of KS1 (David, 1992). Yet parents are not blind to ideas about learning through play, they stress their wish that their children could 'afford the time for play' but believe achievement in our education system requires serious, formal inputs even for four-year-olds.

So is a more formalised, didactic regime necessary or is there a way in which early years teachers and colleagues can operate by teaching through the children's play, using Vygotskian principles, 'scaffolding' the next steps in learning? Colleagues in early years professions in some of our European partner countries, whose children romp to achieve once they enter primary school at six or seven, believe we will destroy the joy of learning and teaching in early childhood if overly formal approaches are adopted (David, 1993). Further contributions to the debate come from the USA, where experts Katz (1995) and Zigler (1987) argue against such formalisation and curricular narrowness but they do not say that early education should be unchallenging, quite the contrary. Clyde (1995), an Australian expert, argues that learning can be seen as

> an interpretative network which spreads across domains, a meaningful network of core understandings that ultimately become a meaningful frame of reference for causal reasoning and problem solving. The process involves the development and enlargement of a dispositional framework, based on the child's motivation, cognitive receptivity, and ability. This disposition cognition theory, while acknowledging the influence of previously ignored variables, including culture and gender, implies that the early childhood teacher has to plan ways of joining these spheres of motivation, receptivity and ability together to make learning meaningful for each child. This is a giant leap from Piaget's stages theory and DAP's ages theory.   (Clyde, 1995 p.115)

JOY IN LEARNING

In suggesting that early years practitioners need to move on from an overly Piagetian model of young children's learning, engagement in play and exploratory activities is not negated. It is the development of the role of the teacher, in observing, intervening, scaffolding and direct teaching, sometimes during play, sometimes in other ways, that is demanded. Children in this age group also learn, for example, through observing, imitating, and following instructions in activities like baking, or group singing sessions.

However, during play children are free to make choices and follow interests, are self-motivated, engage in what is relevant to themselves and their lives, dare to take risks, learn from mistakes without any fear of failure, negotiate and set their own goals and challenges.

Expecting children in this age group to be capable of long periods of adult-directed, formal and passive learning, from workbooks for example, has been shown to have negative consequences (Katz, 1987; Zigler, 1987). Perhaps the desire for more formal approaches and less play is driven by the UK ethos of the Protestant work ethic. This has been exacerbated by the recession so that perhaps even the very young are not supposed to enjoy themselves. Education too is then subjected to the maxim 'If it isn't hurting it isn't working.' Play, because of its enjoyable qualities and control by the child/player is not seen as contributing to serious learning.

Yet according to Hutt *et al.* (1989), children under five learn through two types of play experience. The two types of play occur in phases. On first experiencing a new toy, material or situation, it is as if the child is asking the question 'What does this do?' This is the exploratory, or epistemic, phase, when the child's concentration will be intense, the general demeanor and facial expression serious. When the child has gathered some information, the second phase occurs. This is called the ludic phase, when the child appears to ask the question 'What can I do with this?' In this phase, behaviour has what Miller

(1973) called a 'galumphing' quality – frequently involving shared laughter and funny voices. Both phases promote learning, which can be visualised as a spiral, as Moyles (1989) suggests, allowing for appropriate adult intervention. Both phases are thought to be enjoyable because of their self-chosen nature – but in different ways. Anyone who has struggled to achieve, find out about or make something, will appreciate the exhilaration equivalent to that of the epistemic phase. The enjoyment of the ludic phase is perhaps more akin to the 'having a good laugh with friends'. Both types of enjoyment have an important place in fulfilled lives.

Both phases capitalise on the inborn curiosity and joy of valued young children, who seem to have come into this world to remind us that life and learning can be a very exciting collaborative adventure. Only recently has the powerful influence of the emotions on learning been acknowledged. The Age of Enlightment split between body and mind, emotion and reason has not always served us well and it is especially limited for those who work with young children. Early childhood involves so much more overtly the imperatives of the emotions and bodily functions. This is not to say young children and their educators cannot be rational but that 'pure' rationalists have behaved as if the tip of the iceberg were the iceberg. We have reaped many benefits as a result of the scientific and industrial advances which have come in the wake of the Age of Enlightenment but it has also been responsible for the erosion of people's contact with the land and the rhythms of the cycles and seasons of nature. We are slowly realising our responsibility to the earth and our need to live in harmony with nature rather than seeking domination. Perhaps as a nation, we may have to undergo an equivalent realisation with respect to babies and young children. The Warnock Report's (DES, 1978) view that education should foster an individual's capacities for their own sake and should develop the ability, ultimately, to contribute to society, as well as ensuring that subsequent learning is met with joy and enthusiasm, has been embraced by early childhood educators. To those of a Puritanical frame of mind the idea that anything as serious as learning about the world and how to live together could be best achieved by being enjoyable, largely self-directed and controlled by the learner, especially when that learner is a small child, may be something of a paradox. Learning is indeed a serious business but this does not preclude the possibility for the experience to be fun, as well as challenging. This attention to joy is a particularly crucial aspect of early learning.

THE CURRICULUM AND BELIEFS ABOUT EARLY CHILDHOOD

Our beliefs about early childhood and the place of young children in society impact upon policy and practice. Although we cannot know for certain what their lives in the 21st century will be like, we need to ask ourselves what, if anything, we hold as a vision of education which will equip these very young people for a post-industrial, 'high-tech' world, where environmental, health and other global concerns are likely to be even more acute than they are today (David, Curtis and Siraj-Blatchford, 1992).

Decisions about curriculum reflect the values, the ideology, underpinning a society. Two ways of thinking about the National Curriculum for children aged 5 to 16, firstly, as an entitlement in the present, and secondly, as a way of ensuring a literate, numerate and technologically equipped future workforce, have consequences for children under five. In the first, the idea of the National Curriculum as an entitlement might mean that an edu-care curriculum provides a foundation, education for 'now' for all children, as well as enabling access to that later entitlement. According to the second view, the compulsory phase of education is seen as merely utilitarian and under-fives' provision becomes a narrowly-focused preparation for this.

In her letter to Sir Ron Dearing (School Curriculum and Assessment Authority: SCAA, 1995), Gillian Shephard, the Secretary of State for Education and Employment, requested that SCAA define a set of 'desirable outcomes' for children's learning by the time they enter compulsory schooling. She then emphasised 'parents and taxpayers need assurance that education for under fives, funded with public money, is of high quality and provides a sound preparation for the National Curriculum . . . The Authority should give particular attention to the development of early literacy and numeracy' (SCAA, 1995 p.3).

In most of our EU partner countries the curriculum framework for this stage is based on areas of experience (David, 1993). Such a model has had a number of advocates in this country, including the Rumbold Committee (DES, 1990) which conducted an inquiry into the education of 3 and 4 year olds. It is claimed that the SCAA (1996) document outlining the 'desirable outcomes' does not define a curriculum: 'A number of common features of good practice are recognised, across the full range of pre-compulsory school provision, as being effective in supporting children's learning. These features do not prescribe a particular or preferred curriculum or teaching approach. Such matters are for educators to decide' (SCAA, 1996 p.6). The SCAA (1996) document uses areas of experience for which 'desirable outcomes' are described. These include personal and social development; language and literacy; mathematics; knowledge and understanding of the world; physical development; and creative development. The desirable outcomes publication also stresses the need of children to feel valued; effective liaison with parents, among team members and with professionals from other agencies; learning through play and talk; the place of observation, assessment, recording and reporting (sharing assessment with parents); the environment and equipment; and staff identification of their own training needs.

Anning's (1995) thoughtful evaluation of the draft version of the desirable outcomes document recognises the need for a debate about the under fives' curriculum and unlike the SCAA (1995; 1996) documents themselves, she acknowledges that a curriculum has been prescribed, despite the SCAA denials. Further, SCAA's reticence seems strange, since the documentation includes pages intended to be helpful, demonstrating the links between the desirable outcomes and the National Curriculum at Key Stage 1.

There are fears that the Desirable Outcomes (SCAA, 1996) and a narrow system of 'baseline' assessment at age five, which is also undergoing consultation, will result in an over-emphasis on literacy and numeracy at the expense of children's other powers. Although a statement reassuring nursery providers that their validation for redeeming vouchers will not be connected to the results of whatever baseline assessment system for 5 year olds is implemented, it is unlikely that the nursery sector will be able to withstand top-down pressure from both primary school head teachers wishing to do well in league tables and parents who will take their vouchers where they believe literacy and numeracy teaching will put their children ahead in tests at 5.

Already responses to the National Curriculum by those working with children under five years, to whom the National Curriculum does not apply, have been varied, depending to a great extent upon the levels of confidence, training and expertise of the staff involved (Sylva, Siraj-Blatchford and Johnson, 1992). In fact, it is training for those who work in under-fives' settings which is probably the most acute requirement for this sector, if the improvements in the standards of educational provision for four-year-olds (and one hopes ultimately for children from birth to four) are to be realised. The majority of the research on the impact of the National Curriculum on the nursery curriculum demonstrates time after time that training, or more importantly lack of training, is the key to any problems (David, in press).

The system of inspections for voucher-redeeming nurseries has been criticised and derided (Beckett, 1996) because it is defined as 'light touch' and is felt to lack rigour in relation to the quality of provision. While we cannot yet assess the veracity of these criticisms, because the inspections are at an early stage, and while the values underpinning the whole exercise and the expectations embedded in the desirable outcomes may be questionable, the thrust of the inspections is intended to ensure breadth and balance in curriculum content and processes; attention to equality of opportunity for bilingual children and those with special educational needs; partnership with parents; and staff with appropriate expertise. Further, the registered nursery inspectors who will carry out this work are expected to go beyond what is required of the teams inspecting statutory schooling for they must be able to advise nursery education head teachers on actions they might take to improve provision in their setting.

Much that is positive could ensue from SCAA's interest and from the nursery inspections but providing a high quality curriculum for young children is a complex task, not least because definitions of quality vary over time and according to who is doing the defining (Lally, 1991; McLean, 1991; Moss and Pence, 1994). Because children begin learning from the moment of birth (maybe even before), because we now know that they are 'programmed' to make sense of the cultural context in which they find themselves, and because we know that the first five years of life present an optimal learning period, the levels of education and training of the educators are crucial.

CONCLUSION: UNRESOLVED ISSUES FOR DEBATE

In Sweden, Dahlberg and Asen (1994) have instigated a democratic debate about the nature of early childhood and the form preschool education should take among parents, educators, politicians and local communities. Here in the UK there remain many unresolved issues in the under-fives field which require debate. Some of those issues have been raised in this chapter. However, it has not been possible to cover everything, for example, the gendered nature of the early years workforce and its implications (see Stewart Ranson's chapter for discussion of emerging patterns of local democracy).

Further, although training has been identified as a key issue, aspects such as the Government's claim that the voucher scheme will provide the funding for the necessary training – a claim refuted by providers – have not been included, nor has the question of the potential impact of changes to teacher training on the professionalisation of the early years sector. Additionally, those working with children under five must be able to engage in supportive partnerships with parents to a greater extent than any other educators in the system. This issue involves not only questions concerning the content of training but also questions of time. And in an age when some parents may have plenty of time but no resources and others no time and a sufficiency of resources (Handy, 1994), we need to debate the issues of working hours and social justice as they impact upon children. Further, the African proverb 'It takes a village to raise a child' urges us to take stock of who is responsible for children – only parents or the whole of society, and what are the responsibilities?

Probably the most important debates to be held concern our constructions of early childhood, the values exposed by those constructions, and the resulting lack of investment in the babies and young children who will be tomorrow's citizens. In his many lectures and publications concerning children, including those aged under five, John Tomlinson has acted as a loyal advocate in tune with the sentiments of the United Nations Convention on the Rights of the Child. As he states: 'When a society makes an educational policy it makes an image of itself and of its vision of the future.' (Tomlinson, 1986 p.1). So let us have policies which engender a communal respect for and nurturing of all our young children, for they come, bringing joy,

> To see a World in a Grain of Sand
> And a Heaven in a Wild Flower
> Hold Infinity in the palm of your hand
> And Eternity in an hour.
> (Blake: Auguries of Innocence: in Ackroyd, 1995)

REFERENCES

Ackroyd, P (1995) *The Poems of William Blake*, London: Sinclair-Stevenson.

Anning, A (1995) *The Key Stage Zero Curriculum: a response to the SCAA draft proposals on pre-school education*, London: ATL.

Ball, C (1994) *Start Right: the importance of early learning*, London: RSA.

Beckett, F (1996) Going back to Dotheboys Hall, *The Guardian*, Education Supplement 27.8.96 p.18.

Bowlby, J (1953) *Childcare and the Growth of Love*, Harmondsworth: Penguin.

Bredekamp, S (ed) (1986) *Developmentally Appropriate Practice in Early Childhood Programs Serving Children from Birth through Age 8*, Washington DC: NAEYC.

Bredekamp, S (1993) NAEYC to revise position statements on developmentally appropriate practice. Position statement presented at NAEYC Conference, Anaheim, November.

Bruner, J (1977) *The Process of Instruction*, Cambridge, Massachusetts: Harvard University Press.

Bruner, J (1990) *Acts of Meaning*, Cambridge, Massachusetts: Harvard University Press.

Bruner, J & Haste, H (eds) (1987) *Making Sense*, London: Methuen.

Clyde, M (1995) Concluding the debate. In M. Fleer (ed) *DAP centrism: challenging Developmentally Appropriate Practice*, Watson: Australia, Australian Early Childhood Association.

Dahlberg, G & Asen, G (1994) Evaluation and regulation: a question of empowerment. In Moss, P & Pence, A (eds) *Valuing Quality in the Early Years*, London: Paul Chapman.

David, T (1990) *Under Five – Under-educated?* Milton Keynes: Open University Press.

David, T (1992) What do parents want their children to learn in pre-school in Belgium and the UK? Paper presented at the XXth World Congress of OMEP, Arizona 1992.

David, T (ed) (1993) *Educating our Youngest Children: European Perspectives*, London: Paul Chapman.

David, T (in press) Nursery education and the National Curriculum. In T.Cox (ed) *The National Curriculum and the Early Years*, London: Falmer.

David, T, Curtis, A & Siraj-Blatchford, I (1992) *Effective Teaching in the Early Years*, Stoke-on-Trent: Trentham Books.

Deloache, J S & Brown, A L (1987) The early emergence of planning skills in children. In Bruner, J & Haste, H (eds) *Making Sense*, London: Methuen.

DES (1978) *Report of the Committee of Enquiry into the education of handicapped children and young people* (Warnock Report), London: HMSO.

DES (1989) *Aspects of Primary Education: The Education of Children Under Five*, London: HMSO.

DES (1990) *Starting with Quality* (Rumbold Report), London: HMSO.

DfEE (1996) *Work and family: ideas and options for childcare*, London: DfEE.

DfEE (1996a) *Nursery Education Scheme: The Next Steps*, London: DfEE.

Donaldson, M (1978) *Children's Minds*, Glasgow: Fontana.

Edwards, D & Mercer, N (1987) *Common Knowledge*, London: Methuen.

Gardner, H (1983) *Frames of Mind: the Theory of Multiple Intelligences*, New York: Basic Books.

Gibran, K (1926) *The Prophet*, London: William Heinemann.

Goleman, D (1996) *Emotional Intelligence*, London: Bloomsbury.

Handy, C (1994) *The Empty Raincoat*, London: Hutchinson.

Hutt, S J, Tyler, S, Hutt, C & Christopherson, H (1989) *Play, exploration and learning*, London: Routledge.

Katz, L. (1987) Quoted in 'Burnout by five', TES, 18 September.

Katz, L (1995) A global view: an agenda for tomorrow and the future. Paper presented at the RSA Start Right Conference, London, September.

King, R (1978) *All things bright and beautiful?* Chichester: Wiley.

Lally, M (1991) *The Nursery Teacher in Action*, London: Paul Chapman.

Linton, M (1996) Minister rue 'gaps' in child care, *The Guardian*, 29 August p.10.

McLean, V S (1991) *The Human Encounter*, London: Falmer.

Miller, S (1973) Ends, means and galumphing: some leitmotifs of play, *American Anthropologist*, 75, 87–98.

Moss, P (1996) Perspectives from Europe. In G.Pugh (ed) *Contemporary Issues in the Early Years*, London: Paul Chapman.

Moss, P & Pence, A (eds) (1994) *Valuing Quality in the Early Years*, London: Paul Chapman.

Moyles, J (1989) *Just Playing?* Buckingham: Open University Press.

Nunes, T (1994) The relationship between childhood and society. *Van Leer Foundation Newsletter*, Spring 1994, 16–17.

Pugh, G (1988) *Services for Under Fives: Developing a Coordinated Approach*, London: NCB.

Pugh, G (ed) (1992) *Contemporary Issues in the Early Years*, London: NCB/Paul Chapman.

SCAA (1995) *Draft proposals for desirable outcomes of preschool learning*, London: SCAA.

SCAA (1996) *Nursery Education Desirable Outcomes for Children's Learning on entering compulsory schooling*, London: SCAA.

Schweinhart, L J & Weikart, D P (1993) *A Summary of Significant Benefits: the High/Scope Perry Preschool Study through Age 27*, Ypsilanti MI: High/Scope Foundation.

Shorrocks, D (1992) Evaluating Key Stage 1 Assessments: the testing time of May 1991, *Early Years* 13, 1, 16–20.

Singer, E (1992) *Child development and daycare*, London: Routledge.

Sutton-Smith, B (ed) (1979) *Playing and Learning*, New York: Gardner Press.

Sylva, K, Siraj-Blatchford, I & Johnson, S (1992) The impact of the UK National Curriculum on pre-school practice: some top-down processes at work, *International Journal of Early Childhood*, 24, 1, 41–51.

The Times (1995) Three kind mice. (Editorial) *The Times*, 12 September.

Tizard, B & Hughes, M (1984) *Young Children Learning*, London, Fontana.

Tobin, D, Wu, D & Davidson, D (1989) *Preschool in three Cultures: Japan, China and the United States*, Yale University Press.

Trevarthen, C (1992) An infant's motives for speaking and thinking in the culture. In A. H. Wold (ed) *The Dialogical Alternative*, Oxford University Press.

Tomlinson, J R G (1986) Public education, public good. Inaugural Lecture, University of Warwick, 2 June.

Vygotsky, L (1978) *Mind in Society*, Cambridge, Massachusetts: Harvard University Press.

Zigler, E (1987) Formal schooling for four-year-olds? No. *American Psychologist*, 42, 3, 254–260.

ENDPIECE 2

Justice Shallow

Justice Shallow was a regular contributor to *Education*
until its demise in 1996.

My dear Silence

A secondary headmaster I know, rummaging in the archives of his school, came across a timetable for the year 1910, and, behold, he looked upon the 1988 National Curriculum. The words were slightly different – woodwork and metalwork, of course, took the place of technology – but the substance was there. It was as though Schliemann, digging on the windy plains of Troy, had unearthed, not Priam's treasure, but a refrigerator, thus proving, if proof were needed, the rightness of what scripture says about there being no new thing under the sun.

There was a difference, however, in that the 1910 version was no national curriculum, but one put together by the staff of that school, though influenced by such things as past practice, local job opportunities, the demands of the examination authorities, the frontiers of the teachers' knowledge and the cash available. So homespun an approach would be intolerable today when the search for the perfect curriculum has reached epic proportions, not unlike the quest for the Holy Grail, with knight after knight riding out from London or from York, fighting with giants or malevolent dwarves, and ending, as such quests invariably do, with the hero in rusting armour, alone and palely loitering.

Curriculum reform is a revolution which devours other people's children. Too much thinking about it has made of it one of Sherlock Holmes' three-pipe problems, whereas it is little more than a quick-puff-behind-the-bike-shed one, best resolved by locking up a handful of experienced teachers under the chairmanship of a good-natured middle-grade functionary from the

DfEE, denying them all sustenance save the department's finger buffet and a glass of Romanian chardonnay, and telling them to come up with answers by next Tuesday. Instead of which, the panjandrums kept poking the sleeping creature with sharp sticks, or bashing it over the head with MEP, LAPP, SACRE, discussion papers, consultation documents, bills and acts, aphorisms and *obiter dicta* until it must have felt like E M Forster set up to go sixteen rounds with Mike Tyson. The 1988 Act aimed to draw order from this chaos. Kenneth Baker, brooding on the vast abyss, told the schools what they must teach, and how pupils work was to be assessed. Such divine simplicity is always attractive on paper, but implementation, alas, is somewhat more problematical. Reform bred bureaucracy on a stupendous scale. Whole new empires sprang up overnight, with cloud-capped towers and gorgeous palaces, carpeted offices and earnest officers. Paper manufacturers and printers found that Christmas had come for them on three hundred and sixty-five days each year, as they sent out massive wodges of paper into every school in the land, where teachers soon began to feel that picking oakum and walking the tread-mill would be delightful pastimes compared with their daily thankless tasks. The wretched drudges exchanged teaching forms for filling out forms, and an elastic school programme for one cast in immovable concrete. Instead of going on courses, they went on nervous breakdowns, and early retirement became as sought after as the perfect beer and often proved just as elusive. No doubt the Secretary of State had benevolent motives, seeking to ensure that all children were given daily fare that was relevant to the lives they were leading, and had in it some hard tack to stiffen the flavourless blancmange offered to them by some dozy establishments. But then last state proved worse than the first.

Still, cometh the hour cometh the man. Very few had ever heard of Sir Ron Dearing, but suddenly he was employed everywhere in education by desperate and despairing ministers. He became the Arnold Goodman *de nos jours*, a Mr Fixit who could be relied upon to pour oil on troubled waters, and balm on wounds, to persuade lions to lie down with lambs, and, above all, to save the trembling aristos of the DfEE from being strung up on all the lampposts along Great Smith Street. Yet, what a waste of his talents. Sir Ron – I am sure that the diminutive is part reason for his success: he seems more one of us than one of them – should have been sent to unscramble the problem of Ulster, bring peace to a troubled Yugoslavia, or save the House of Windsor from its comical excesses. To yoke him to curriculum is like asking John Maynard Keynes to audit the tuck-shop accounts of a two-class primary school, or compelling Louis XIV to do the washing-up after a state banquet at Versailles. His success was, nevertheless, spectacular. The curriculum empire, like the Spanish Empire of the 18th century, was ripe for looting and Dearing was the boldest of privateers. He simply made a lot of turgid material walk the plank, and thereby reduced teaching and learning to manageable proportions. Soon, of course, his caravel moved on, leaving behind a dog or two barking at a few residual problems – should history lessons be about Marlborough or Mao Tse Tung, William the Conqueror or

William Clinton: are lists of prescribed texts for VIth formers wise to include Christopher Robin and exclude Christopher Marlowe; should French be taught to enable children to buy haddock in Dieppe or to understand when best to use the past-historic or future perfect.

The attention span of our masters is not very great, and as Sir Ron was sent off to cross blades with the deft swordsmen of Higher Education, so they turned from the swamps of what children should learn to the firmer ground of how. There the answers are simpler and more comforting. For years, schools have been wrong – or, perhaps, wrongly advised, for the poor, bewildered pedagogue is seen as the victim of trendy, nut-cutlet-eating, carrot-juice drinking college lecturers who poisoned professionalism with their advocacy of small classes, discovery methods and a focus on the individual child. Now, however, it seems that children will learn more effectively if the teacher ranges hundreds of the little beasts in front of him, and tells them all, at the same time what to know, understand and do, a situation beloved of the Guards sergeant-majors of a depot battalion. It is, so it seems, the way they do things in Thailand, Ulan Bator, Phrygia, Pamphylia and the parts of Libya about Cyrene. The education policies of the East are now fashionable, as once were those of poor Germany whose methods, since its economic miracle vanished like snowflakes in the river, are seen as frumpish and outmoded as a bombazine bustle. Apart from anything else, though, it is extremely foolish to think of importing such ideas from abroad. The English dislike foreigners – all garlic and incomprehensible lingo – even more than they dislike each other, and, rush as they do to buy French beer and Japanese video recorders, the thought of their children being subjected to the classroom practices of Tokyo, will bring them out onto the streets in their tens of thousands, baying for broken glass.

One day, I daresay, all this yeasty ferment will settle down, and Louis XVIII return in place of the Robespierres and Napoleons. History, in due course, will give its verdict, and that will be a qualified favourable one. The important thing about curriculum reform has not been the quart into pint-pot venture, the imperialism of Secretaries of State, nor yet the ignominious retreats, but the fact that the matter was discussed at all. The tension between political imperatives and professional concerns made everyone think about what schools really are at – no mean achievement in these unreflecting, superficial days.

PART III

Education and Industry Links

9

SCHOOLS FOR LIFE AND WORK

Charles Handy

Professor Charles Handy is a social philosopher, writer
and broadcaster.

I left school and university with my head packed full of knowledge; enough
of it, anyway, to pass all the examinations that were put in my path. It was,
naturally, a rather partial sort of knowledge, containing nothing at all of
the natural sciences, or of languages other than Latin and Greek, because
you could not, in those days, reach the standards required of you in your
chosen field, and be, at the same time, conversant with all the other fields
of study. I was, however, considered by my teachers and my parents to be
a well-educated young man.

Unusually for that time, I went into industry. 'You are the first member
of our family to go into trade' my great-aunt said, with a disapproving sniff.
But work was the stuff of life and 'industry', or the business of making
and selling useful things or services, was an important part of that. As a
well-educated young man I wanted to work there, whatever my relatives
might feel. As a well-educated young man, I rather expected my work to
be a piece of cake, something at which my intellect would allow me to excel
without undue effort. School and schooling were behind me, thank God, and
life could now begin.

It came as something of a shock, therefore, to encounter the world outside
for the first time, and to realise that I was woefully ill-equipped, not only for
the necessary business of earning a living but, more importantly, for coping
with all the new decisions which came my way, in both life and work. My
first employers put it rather well: 'you have a well-trained but empty mind',
they told me, 'which we will now try to fill with something useful, but don't
imagine that you will be of any real value to us for the first ten years'. I was

fortunate to have lighted upon an employer prepared to invest so much time in what was, in effect, my real education, and I shall always feel guilty that I left them when the ten years were up.

A well-trained mind is not to be sneezed at, but I was soon to discover that my mind had been trained to deal with closed problems, whereas most of what I now had to deal with were open-ended problems. 'What is the cost of sales?' is a closed problem, one with a right or a wrong answer. 'What should we do about it?' is an open problem, one with any number of possible answers. Trained in analysis, I had no experience of taking decisions which might or might not turn out to be good. Knowing the right answer to a question, I came to realise, was not the same as making a difference to a situation, which was what I was supposed to be paid for.

Worse, I had been educated in an individualist culture. My scores were mine. No-one else came into it, except as competitors in some imagined race. I was on my own in the learning game at school and university. Not so in my work, I soon realised. Nothing happens there unless other people co-operate. How to win friends and influence people was not a course in my curriculum. Unfortunately, it was to prove essential in my new life. Being an individual star would not help me much, if it was in a failing group. A group failure brought me down along with the group. Our destinies were linked, which meant that my classmates were now colleagues not competitors. Teams were something I had encountered on the sports field, not in the classroom. They were in the box marked 'fun' in my mind, not the one marked 'work'. My new challenge, I discovered, was to merge these two boxes. It was the start of my real education.

'So you're a university graduate are you?' said my new Sales Manager, 'classics is it? I don't think that is going to impress our Chinese salesmen! How do you propose to win their respect since you will be in charge of some of them very shortly?' Another open-ended problem! I had never before been thrust among people very different from me, with different values and assumptions about the way the world worked, or should work. I had not even met anyone more than two years older than me, except for parents and teachers. Cultural exploration was a process unknown to me, nor was I accustomed to being regarded as stupid and ignorant, which I undoubtedly was, in all the things that mattered in their world. It was my first realisation that there is more than one way of being intelligent.

My education, I decided then, had been positively disabling. So much of the content of what I had learnt was irrelevant, while the process of learning it had cultivated a set of attitudes and behaviours which were directly opposed to what seemed to be needed in real life. I had to discard all memories of that world and start afresh. It would be nice to think that this sort of experience could not happen now, that our schools, today, prepare people much better for life and for the work which is so crucial to a satisfactory life. But I doubt it. The subjects may appear to be a little more relevant, but we are still left to learn about work at work and about life, by living it. That will always be true but, we could, I believe do more to make sure that the *process of* education had more in common with the processes of life and work as they are to-day, so that the shock of reality is less cruel. I would have more faith in a National Curriculum if it were to be more concerned with process than with content.

Schools are charged by society with multiple functions, which is one of their problems, but they are the only safe practice grounds for life which we have. They are, for that reason, precious and protected places, but they need to be clear about the implications. A school for life and work should, I suggest, subscribe to the following propositions, which apply equally to life, work and learning.

1. THE DISCOVERY OF ONESELF IS MORE IMPORTANT THAN THE DISCOVERY OF THE WORLD

Both are important, of course, but the world will always be there. We need to build up a belief in our competence to deal with it. Too many people experience school as a failure experience, leaving with their self-esteem in tatters, believing that they are stupid, inadequate and incapable. This is the worst possible starting point from which to start looking for work, particularly when so much of that work will, in future, have to be created by ourselves. By the turn of the century, it is now clear, less than half of the British workforce will be in full-time long-term jobs. We can no longer rely on our work institutions to fill our empty minds with their skills.

'Look for customers, not jobs' I told my own children, on leaving college, because only if you can make or do something which other people will pay you money for will you ultimately be employable. But that requires self-confidence, a saleable skill or competence and social skills of quite a high order. It is not easy to sell one's own goods or services. It should be a guarantee to all children, as of right, that they will have these three components of survival, by the time they leave school. If they leave without them it is the school, not they, who will have failed. Nelson Mandela once said:

> Our deepest fear is not that we are inadequate, our deepest fear is that we are powerful beyond measure. We ask ourselves 'Who am I to be brilliant, gorgeous, talented and fabulous?' Actually, who are you not to be? You are a child of God. We are born to manifest the glory of God that is within us. It's not just in some of us, it's in everyone.

This sentiment, whether put in a religious context or not, should be one of the articles of belief of a school for life and work. We can do many things to bring it about. We can, for instance, look for ways to give every young person a success experience of some sort every year. That will be easier if the second proposition is adopted.

2. EVERYONE CAN BE ASSUMED TO BE INTELLIGENT, BECAUSE INTELLIGENCE COMES IN MANY FORMS

Howard Gardner's list of seven intelligences is but a starter (Bull and Gardner, 1984). To them we can add Daniel Goleman's important concept of emotional intelligence. But even without these academic aids we can all make our own list, from our own experience of life. This is mine, with the important proviso that the different intelligences need not, indeed usually do not, correlate with each other. You can have one or two but not the others. Fortunate are they who have more than three to any degree.

Factual Intelligence – the know-it-all facility that Mastermind addicts possess.
Analytic Intelligence – the ability to reason and to conceptualize.
Numerate Intelligence – being at ease with numbers of all sorts.

A combination of these first three intelligences will get you through most tests and examinations and entitle you to be called clever. But there is more to intelligence than these.

Linguistic Intelligence – a facility with language and languages, even if one talks nonsense in all of them, which can happen if this intelligence is not aligned with the others.
Spatial Intelligence – an ability to see patterns in things. Artists, entrepreneurs, and system analysts have this ability, but often do poorly in tests of the first three intelligences. They therefore fail at school but can prosper in later life if their self-esteem is not too dented.
Athletic Intelligence – although some might prefer to call it talent, the skill of athletes is a recognizable form of intelligence, still too easily dismissed as leisure activity. We mock some American Universities for offering athletic scholarships, but perhaps they are only extending the concept of education and intelligence as they, and we, should.
Intuitive Intelligence – an aptitude for sensing and seeing what is not immediately obvious. Often opposed to analytic intelligence, making it difficult for the two to communicate. 'You have won the argument, but I'm right' says my wife, on occasion, and she usually is, because her intuitive intelligence gets it right more often than my analytic approach.
Emotional Intelligence – Self-awareness and self-control, persistence, zeal and self-motivation, often more important in life than any of the others. Goleman quotes Aristotle: 'Anyone can become angry – that is easy. But to be angry with the right person, to the right degree, for the right purpose, at the right time, and in the right way – this is not easy'.
Practical Intelligence – Often called common-sense, the ability to recognize what needs to be done and what can be done. The person

who gets on with it, while everyone else is debating what should be done.

Interpersonal Intelligence – the ability to get things done with and through others. Sometimes called social intelligence, or elevated to leadership skills, this intelligence is crucial to success and survival at work.

Musical Intelligence – easy to recognize, whether in opera singers, pianists or pop groups, this intelligence seems pleasingly unrelated to age, which means that it is an important route to success experiences for the young.

The list could continue, because there may well be other categories of intelligence, nor do the precise names of the various intelligences matter. The point is that these many and varied intelligences or abilities are all resources which we can use to contribute to the world, to earn a living and to make a difference. It cannot be proved beyond doubt, but it is a reasonable assumption that everyone has some degree of at least one of these intelligences. Nor is it obvious, looking at people in later life, that any particular set of intelligences is more important than any other. Any one of them can be developed to be the basis of a successful life and useful work.

It should be the first duty of a school for life to help the young person identify which intelligences define them, to build up an 'intelligence profile', then to encourage them to develop their best intelligences, and to work out how best to employ them in their work. This will provide the basis for that self-confidence without which little learning can occur. Only when this has been done would it be useful to go on to try to develop the missing intelligences. A narrow focus on the first three intelligences in this list runs the risk of labelling as stupid those who do not shine in them but who have undoubted capacities in the other areas. That is to cheat them of a life.

It will be pointed out that the delivery of these first two propositions is very teacher intensive, focusing as they do on the unique qualities of each individual. That is true, but then we really do have our ratios in a mess. Instead of giving special attention to individuals in the early years of life we give it to them when they really should not need it at all. Thus we have 30 pupils or more to a teacher in a Primary School, but 10 or fewer in Higher Education. It ought to be reversed, in which case we would need, ultimately, no more teachers in total, and they would probably cost less.

Sir Christopher Ball has a neat formula for these ratios – take the age of the pupil and multiply by two. Five-year-olds then get one teacher for every ten, and 20–year-olds, 1 per 40, but by then they should be independent learners. There obviously can not be a straight swap of professors for primary teachers, so an initial investment will be needed at the lower end. We could start by cutting back on the cosmetic Youth Training Schemes which are supposed to equip our educationally-failed youth for work but are really rather poor social rescue schemes which don't work because their participants were let down at the very beginning of their educational career.

If we don't get it right at the beginning, it will cost much more to correct it later on.

3. LIFE IS A MARATHON, NOT A HORSE-RACE

In a horse-race only the first three count. The rest are also-rans. In a marathon everyone who completes the course is a winner. While some run faster than others and some compete with others up at the front, most of the runners are running against themselves, seeking to better the standards which they set themselves. Life is more like a marathon for most of us. We choose which races to enter, and what pace to run at, seeking, most of the time, to better ourselves. There is no winning and losing in the ultimate, only the taking part, and the getting better.

Compulsory tests at 7, 11, 14, and 16 turn education into a horse-race not a marathon, because the scores, however neutral they are intended to be, inevitably label the young person as below, or above, average. Comparative grading at set ages turns education into a sorting device, not a development process. Although some may respond creatively to the news that they are below average in some aspect of their work, most young people turn away immediately to find some other area where they might have better luck, preferably one outside the remit of their school.

If we ran our driving tests in this way, with compulsory once-only tests on everyone's 17th birthday, passing only those who were average or above, we should undoubtedly have safer roads with better and fewer drivers, but we would have disenfranchised, for life, nearly half the population. Yet that is what we are doing with our school examinations. It is, in that respect, immoral in a democratic society.

The odd thing is that we have a perfectly acceptable model in our midst, one with graded examinations, high standards, but almost universal pass rates. I refer to the system of music examinations which pupils take only when their teacher estimates that they have a good chance of passing. These examinations are not age dependent – you take them at any age when you are ready for them, they set high standards and are universally respected. They are the appropriate examinations for a marathon as opposed to a horse-race and replicate the sort of hurdles which people will encounter later in life, leaping them when they are ready for them, if they are wise.

Tim Brighouse calls these examinations 'Just-in-Time Examinations' (Brighouse, 1996). I prefer to think of them as Grades, as in the music world. A young person should always have something to aim at, but something attainable, something re-takeable, something which he or she can hold up as a mark of their achievement, irrespective of the age when they reached it. Adult life is not as ageist as schools are, where the actual date of one's birthday, let alone the year, can be of crucial importance. These kind of Grades ought to be the required model in a proper school for life.

4. KNOWING 'WHAT' IS NOT AS IMPORTANT AS KNOWING 'WHERE', 'HOW' and 'WHY'

Implicit in my education was the assumption that the objective of education and training was to fill my mind with as much stuff as possible, so that it would be there when I needed it. Of course, I forgot most of it. In life and in work, we learn things when we need them, not before we need them. Knowledge, for most people, has a very short sell-by date. Unless it is used very quickly it goes off. That is why it is very difficult to learn a foreign language in absentia, as it were. If the new words and phrases do not get used within days, they evaporate.

Knowledge, these days, is readily available, whether it be contained in books and manuals, on CD-ROMS or in cyberspace, or in other peoples' experience. The trick is not to try to transfer it all to ones own brain, but to know where to find it, how to access it and what to do with it when you have it. We need early practice in doing this. As part of their role as practice grounds for life, schools ought not to be force-feeding their students, but teaching them how to feed themselves. Original thought, I sometimes console myself, often goes with a bad memory. An overstuffed brain has less need to work things out for itself.

This, inevitably, changes the role of the teacher. Instead of being the sole repository of knowledge, which has traditionally been the source of their authority, teachers have to be prepared to watch their students seek out other authorities through their computers, or by interrogating other adults, calling up Einstein himself to explain his theories. The job of the teacher is to set the task which requires the search for the knowledge, to help the individual, or the group, to seek it out, and to realise how the knowledge can be used.

Some starting skills are needed, of course. A facility with Words, Numbers and Emotions are the real essentials. We may not need to write, or even to type, in a future where we will talk into a computer and watch the words be spelt out in any language we choose, on the screen, but we will have to read, speak, preferably in more than one language, and be able to answer a telephone. In a digital world, where much information will come in the form of numbers, it is crucial that we are all at ease with those numbers from an early stage, and can understand how numbers relate to each other. Most importantly, we need to learn how to manage our emotions, in Daniel Goleman's sense of the word, to develop self-awareness, self-control and empathy and the arts of listening, resolving conflicts, and co-operation (Goleman, 1996).

Those who have the appropriate native intelligences will have an easier start, but a good school can do a lot to develop these skills and abilities in all its students, starting at a very early age. Self Science, for instance, is a core curriculum subject at one San Francisco school, tailored to helping the young students understand their feelings and how they impact on other people. In a downtown school in New Haven the Social Competence Program tries to do the same for a student body that is mostly black and Hispanic. If, however, the students can learn social competence and the other skills by using them in their normal classes, using them to work on a task which they find fun and interesting, then the learning will be less likely to 'go off'.

In this respect, we should remember the arts, particularly the performing arts. Theatre, dance and music allow young people to experiment with their emotions in a safe context. Different roles bring out different aspects of our characters. Uncomfortable as an oil executive, I glowed with confidence as a teacher, but I was over thirty before I discovered how to be comfortable in my own skin. We should not need to wait that long to find a part in which we are at ease.

5. SCHOOL SHOULD BE LIKE WORK, AND VICE VERSA

Visiting a range of schools some years back, I would often start by asking how many people worked there. I always got a response in the tens, ten or twenty, maybe, or seventy, if it was a large school. They always left out the children in their counting. The children, I came to realise, were not seen as workers, but as the products of these human factories, taken in as raw material, processed, inspected and graded, before being placed on the market.

It was a depressing thought, but it provoked me to think about what would happen if we treated the children as the real workers in an enlightened factory of creativity, with the teachers as the consultants and senior managers. Work would be organised around tasks to be done. Most of the work would be organised in small teams or groups. There would be competition between groups but co-operation within them. The tasks would be as real as possible, but with opportunities for skill improvement and information gathering built into the timetable.

Accountability and responsibility would then become live concepts, with consequences, because it would be the students, as well as the teachers, who would have them. They would learn that if you turn up late for work, aren't properly prepared, or are too tired to give of your best, it isn't just yourself whom you are letting down, but the whole of your group. No man is an island, entire of itself, said John Donne, but you don't believe it until you experience it.

Learning would then be seen to be the necessary ingredient for better performance on the tasks. The students would learn that it is a combination of different talents that makes things happen, and the discovery and harnessing of these talents which is critical. Older students would work with younger ones, for part of the time at least, and would have responsibilities appropriate to their relative seniority and competencies.

Our young son had the gift of a beautiful treble voice. He joined a distinguished cathedral choir. What we did not realise at the time was that the one thing which grown men cannot do is to sing treble. Small boys like him had, therefore, to be treated as adults, full working members of the choir.

His performance in that choir was exemplary, while his work in the more traditional parts of the school syllabus was patchy. I asked his choirmaster what the secret was – how did he get such good results where others failed. 'It's simple', he said, 'What we do is work, what the others do is school. He takes work seriously because we take him seriously'.

The proposition that schools should be more like work organisations could and should be taken further. Work organisations now concentrate their own resources on their 'core task', bringing in other specialities to do what they can do better. Schools have gone down this route only to the extent of contracting out the catering and the maintenance. They could go much further, if they saw themselves, principally, as the designers and managers of a young person's development, not as the only teachers. Schools can't, and shouldn't, do everything. Practical skills such as word-processing and computing, driving, first aid, languages, home management, money management and presentation skills, could all be done, on contract, by specialist bodies, leaving the teachers free to concentrate on the more general education and development of the child.

Technical skills are best learnt, as in Germany, in the workplace, but this can be seen as an adjunct to the school and as part of education, to be monitored and arranged by the school. The work of society, and the values and norms of the world around us, can, again, be best learnt by working in and with the surrounding community, on assignments and secondments arranged by the school. Turning the workplace into a school for youngsters is not always a solution welcomed by those who run the workplace, but they will come to realise that early education is better and cheaper than later remedial education. If the skills and attitudes needed for work are best learnt at work, then the workplace will have to get involved, not as an ultimate destination, but as part of the learning process.

A better spread of responsibilities for schooling between work and school would allow the schools to concentrate on what they do best. Fewer core staff, better paid, achieving more is the formula for productivity in industry, achieved by getting others to do what they do better and more efficiently. If schools adopted the same formula, they could pay teachers better and see them regain the esteem which has been sometimes lacking in the recent past, because they would be doing what they alone could do – designing the development programmes of their students. It was once said of the Education Act of 1944 that it was the greatest confidence trick played on the British parent, in that it suggested that schools would be responsible for the full development of our children. That never was true, and never could be true, but it allowed everyone else to leave it to the school. It is time to reverse the assumption and to give the actual school a smaller but crucial role in the education of our young.

There has always been a lot of learning going on in society, but most of it has happened outside school. We ought not to regret that but to capitalise on it.

6. LIFE IS A JOURNEY, WHICH STARTS AT SCHOOL

Life, for most people, is a circular process of discovery – who we are, what we can do, and, ultimately, why we exist and what we believe. It is a circular process because, when we discover what we are capable of and work out why we exist, it changes the way we see ourselves, which can send us off in new directions, discovering new capacities and new reasons for our existence. This spiralling journey is the true meaning of lifelong learning, and it remains, for those who pursue it, an endlessly fascinating journey, one which enriches not only the individual but all those around. Those who have tired of the journey, have tired of life. They come across as dull and boring, and can soon infect their friends and colleagues with their apathy.

The best way to learn how to travel is to start travelling, with experienced travellers to advise and help. The development of one's emotional intelligence, followed by the discovery of one's full intelligence profile, is the start of that journey, but even young people should be encouraged to take the next step, the exploration of belief about the purpose of life, because this will start them on the second round of the circle. The natural curiosity of the young is the only fuel which is needed, provided that it is not damped down. Learning how to learn is, in its essentials, a process of discovering, and then stretching, oneself.

This process, like most of the important things in life, cannot be taught, only encouraged. The lessons learnt cannot be graded because each of our journeys is unique to ourselves. It does not, therefore, fit easily into a formal curriculum, only into the enveloping culture of the school. I once complained to my son's headmaster about what I saw as the excessively academic slant of the school. He replied that, because society, and his pupils' parents in particular, regarded examination results as important, he was determined to meet their wishes as efficiently as possible, 'but, that done', he said, 'we get on with the real education, the individual search for identity and meaning. We all know that is what we are really about, but we need to get the numbers right first in order to be free to do it.'

The underlying lesson was that real life, and work, has its constraints. We have, most of the time, to operate within those constraints but move beyond them. The challenge for the school is to make up its mind where it wants to go when the constraints have been met. The journey of life is as relevant to the institutions of education as it is to their participants. It is not enough to survive.

We are fortunate to live within the British tradition. Change in Britain traditionally comes not by edict but by case law made fashion. It was only because the case law failed to advance that edicts made their appearance in the educational world. If we want to hold further edicts at bay, we must make our own case law, our own ways of translating these propositions into practical action. There are no sure recipes, only an invitation to create new schools for life and work that are appropriate for a new kind of world. It is a world where, more than ever before, we shall each be responsible for our own destiny, our own definition of success, our own journey of discovery.

The danger is that our schools will lag behind, designed by people from a world that used to be, for a world that will be no more, rather like our armies which were always well-trained for the last war. If we fail, this time, to leap beyond our own experience, we will fail our youth. It is indeed a time for bold imaginings, a time to bring life and work into our schools, so that our schools may more truly be part of life and work.

REFERENCES

Brighouse, T (1996) The Need to Go Beyond the National Curriculum, *RSA Journal*, CXLIV, 5470, June.

Bull, C & Gardner, H (1984) *Frames of Mind: The Theory of Multiple Intelligences*, London: Heinemann.

Goleman, D (1996) *Emotional Intelligence, Why it can matter more than IQ*, London: Bloomsbury.

10

RAISING ACHIEVEMENT

Geoffrey Holland

Sir Geoffrey Holland KCB is Vice Chancellor of the
University of Exeter. He was Permanent Secretary
of the Department for Education from 1993 to 1994;
Department of Employment 1988–1993.

Will you walk a little faster said a whiting to a snail.
There's a porpoise close behind us and he's treading on my tail.
(Lewis Carroll)

There could be no more relevant theme this year than 'raising achievement'.
It is vital and urgent that we should. For some time now the porpoise has
been treading on our tail and, indeed, overtaking us. Last year's World
Competitiveness Report from the World Economic Forum shows the United
Kingdom in 18th place in global competitiveness terms, down from 14th place
a year earlier. We come behind the United States, just about every country in
Northern Europe, and some of the rapidly developing countries of the Pacific
Rim – Singapore, Japan, New Zealand, Taiwan and Australia. There are many
things going for this country. The World Economic Forum considers us the
second most competitive country in terms of both foreign direct investment
into this country by overseas companies and overseas investment by UK
companies. But it is the quality of our workforce and the quality of our
education system that let us down. The workforce this year slipped to 24th
place in the world in terms of skills – down from 21st place a year earlier.
And what the Forum describes as our 'inadequate educational system' ranks
35th in the world despite our being at mid-table point (considerably above
35th) in terms both of funding for education and class size in schools.
  During 1995 the National Institute of Economic and Social Research

produced a slim volume entitled *Productivity, Education and Training* whose author was S J Prais. It brought together in summary form the main findings of more than a decade of detailed research studies. Those findings make sobering reading. They address themselves to the outcomes of education as they manifest themselves in economic terms.

First, the proportion of the workforce having a university degree is about the same in Britain, France, Germany, The Netherlands and Switzerland but the proportion holding intermediate level qualifications tells a very different story. In France it is 40 per cent; in Germany 63 per cent; in The Netherlands 57 per cent; in Switzerland 66 per cent. In this country the figure is 25 per cent. The proportion of the workforce having no vocational qualifications is the obverse of that coin: in France 53 per cent; in Germany 26 per cent; in The Netherlands 35 per cent; in Switzerland 23 per cent. In this country the figure is 64 per cent. All this shows through in productivity – and thus in competitiveness. Sooner or later that shows through in jobs, in unemployment, in the economic and social well-being of the country.

The National Institute series of studies took matched organisations in different European countries and looked in detail at the way in which work was organised and the results. The Institute did not take exotic new jobs or firms but rather everyday products and activities. It did not take large companies, but more typical medium-sized companies. It did not take the obvious leaders or the obvious laggards. All that makes the results even more disturbing.

Take engineering. The firms compared more relatively simple straight-forward products: springs, valves, drill-bits, screws. Average productivity for these four engineering products was 63 per cent higher in Germany than in British plants and 36 per cent higher in The Netherlands. In the manufacture of wood furniture, output per employee in Germany was about 2.3 times higher than that in Britain. Manning levels on similar machine lines were over twice as high in Britain as in Germany. In the manufacture of clothing German organisations produced roughly twice as many garments per employee house as in Britain. In Germany there was one additional direct or indirect worker for every two machinists; in Britain it was one additional worker for every machinist. In The Netherlands, plants manufacturing biscuits produced 15 per cent higher quality content per unit of weight than the average British biscuit plants. The French average was 30 per cent higher than the British and the German average was between 2 and 3 times that figure. The real value of the average biscuit produced in The Netherlands was 10 per cent higher than in Britain, in France the figure was 20 per cent ahead of us and in Germany the figure was 80 per cent ahead of us.

And what about the service sector? Here the study was of hotels – not international, luxury hotels but middle-grade 'good average' hotels. To produce the same outcomes, German hotels needed only half the number of employees of British hotels. A parallel study to Dutch hotels produced much the same results.

Why were there these differences? The National Institute was clear that the major determining factor was the qualifications and education and training of the workforce. Thus, in engineering, 80 per cent of turners and millers on the continent had craft qualifications compared with only 40 per cent of employees in this country. In woodworking some 90 per cent of those engaged in shop-floor production had attained craft level qualifications in the German sample compared with only 10 per cent in Britain.

In the manufacture of women's outer wear, 80 per cent of German machinists had acquired examined vocational qualifications following a systematic traineeship, whereas in Britain not a single machinist had attained a qualification at a similar level. In the hotels, three-quarters of all 'housekeepers' in Germany had attained recognised qualifications following a three-year apprenticeship course covering the full range of hotel functions. In Britain, not a single housekeeper had attended any external courses in hotel work.

You may say, what has this to do with schools? Is not all this a reflection of a poor and unreliable vocational training system after compulsory school age? In part it is. But I have reminded us of these figures for two reasons. First, in order to begin this conference as I hope we shall continue – with a focus on outcomes. And secondly, because the outcomes I have described have their origins in what has happened before.

And here once again there is no doubt that we must raise achievement and do better. In the United Kingdom some 75 per cent of our 16 year olds are enrolled full-time in education. The comparable figure in France is 92 per cent and in Germany 95 per cent. And our young people so enrolled do not stay long. The figure for enrolments of 17 year olds drops to 55 per cent in our country, compared with 87 per cent in France and 93 per cent in Germany.

Comparisons of attainment are also instructive – and dispiriting. The proportion of 16 year olds reaching the equivalent of GCSE grades A–C in mathematics, the national language and one science is 27 per cent in our country, compared with 62 per cent in Germany and 66 per cent in France. At the upper secondary level (18+) the proportion of young people obtaining a comparable upper secondary qualification from school is 29 per cent in our country, compared with 68 per cent in Germany and 48 per cent in France.

The classic ground for detailed study of achievement, as many in this audience will know, is mathematics. The bottom 40 per cent of 13 year olds in English schools were set the following test:

$$2.6-4.12+6.3-0.44$$

Only 4 per cent answered correctly.

The bottom 40 per cent in Germany were set a rather more complex test question:

$$5634.3-3194.02+4571.6+378.98-856.75$$

In Germany 76 per cent of the bottom 40 per cent in schools answered correctly.

In general, 13 year olds in English schools lag two years behind their continental equivalents and never catch up later. A recurrent theme of comparative studies – whether by the National Institute or others – is that of the excellence of the best in our country but the under-achievement of the many.

To depress us still further (and I promise I shall soon get more positive and more cheerful), let us not lose from sight one of the most damaging but constant statistics relating to our schools. Time and time again, over the years, Her Majesty's Inspectors and now OFSTED find that 30 per cent of the lessons they observe in schools are unsatisfactory. To put it another way, young people have learned nothing during those lessons and are, if anything, worse off at the end than at the beginning.

From all of this it will be abundantly clear that, for all the £27 billion of public money we spend annually on education in this country and for all the £35 billion a year that employers spend on training, our achievements are not competitive internationally and are, if anything, slipping. Yet we are hurtling now towards a 21st century in which the jobs available will be jobs that robots cannot do; and where our survival, both economically and socially, depends on applied intelligence, enterprise, initiative, flexibility and ability to survive rapid change. We are not well-equipped and it is time for a national crusade to raise achievement all round.

There are some areas where we know we should be doing better and which we are now addressing. I have no doubt that the Secretary of State will remind us of these when she speaks. They include nursery education (where again provision here lags behind our continental rivals), the curriculum and achievements of 14–19 year olds, and the financing of further and higher education. In all these areas the jury is still out, and the question remains whether we will be bold enough and whether we will act quickly and decisively enough?

The underlying issue we need to address, however, is that of public expenditure. When I was in Whitehall, it took me all too long to realise that the popular image of the public expenditure round is a fiction. It is not the case that there is rational, open-ended discussion about each programme, each Department's concerns and needs. The fact of the matter is that there is one Department and only one which is the overwhelming concern of Ministers – the Department of Social Security. Social security expenditure is now so large – two out of every three public expenditure pounds – and so rapidly growing (as a result of a population which is living longer and of high and continuing unemployment) and the Treasury's over-riding concern is to control and settle that budget. Every other public expenditure programme (roads, housing, defence, law and order, yes – and education) is a residual. Each is fighting, as it were, for the scraps that fall from the DSS table.

That is the fact of life – and it is a fact of life that will not quickly change. Thus, when we are discussing and tackling the issue of raising achievements in our schools – or more generally in the education service – the central fact of life is that there will not be great additional resources for education available from the public purse. That will be true whatever Government is in power. There will be no additional money – or if there is any additional money, there will not be much of it.

So the issue for us and the country in raising achievement in education is how to secure a bigger return – a much bigger return – for the expenditure that we already have. To quantify that, we have to get at least 30 per cent greater added value from the pounds we already spend. That is what we need to address at this conference. If we address our theme from any other starting point, we are in cloud-cuckoo land.

Can it be done? My answer is that it can. And it can through a fourfold programme:

- we must cut out waste and get a bigger return from every house and every pound
- we must innovate much more
- we must include rather than exclude
- we must develop and exercise leadership at all levels.

In the remainder of this address I shall say something about each of these in turn. I shall conclude by outlining a ten-year strategic development programme to take us to where we need to be.

First, I said, we must cut out waste and get a bigger return. I suggest five action points here. The first is to tackle head on the 30 per cent of lessons which are unsatisfactory. We must not tolerate poor performance by teachers. And we must not tolerate poor initial teacher training. We should expect more of teachers, pay them better, value them more highly in terms of status whether within organisations or in the community; but simply not be prepared to tolerate poor and incompetent performance. Such incompetent performers are damaging young people, damaging the profession, damaging our future.

Next, we often neglect the fact that time is the most precious resource of all. Far too much time of teachers, head teachers and governing bodies is taken up with administration rather than what they and they alone contribute and add by way of value. We are drowning in paperwork. We are drowning in over-regulation. Too little thought has been given within many institutions to spending some of the precious budget on administrative support, thus freeing up the time of our most precious resource, qualified teachers and failing to make the best use of the time of our precious external supporters, governing bodies. Overall we need a crusade from Government and quangos downwards to reduce administration paperwork by 50 per cent.

We shall get a much bigger return in our schools and colleges if we realise that what we are about is learning, not teaching. This requires a fundamental reappraisal of the role of the teacher. That in turn begins in our teacher training programmes and must continue in our whole approach within the schools, to the curriculum and to organisation. Qualified staff must be about helping and supporting learners to achieve individually, collectively and successfully.

Providers of educational opportunities in any community need to get together. A visitor from another planet descending on any part of our country would be astonished by the huge educational investment there is in any community: nursery provision, primary and secondary schools, colleges, universities, private educational and training establishments, employers' establishments, voluntary organisations. Yet the most striking feature of each and every one of those is the under-utilisation of equipment, premises and people. And the second most striking feature is that they do not combine forces as they might to enrich programmes and enhance achievement and results. We need to devise ways of doing that, perhaps through new institutions locally, perhaps through informal but effective networks.

And as part of this every individual school needs to see itself as a community centre of learning, openly accessible to all – and openly accessible throughout the year for every working day of every working week. The best schools, we know, are doing this. But what is true of the few is not of all.

My second action heading was innovation. The education service suffers from exactly the same weakness as every other part of our economy and society. There is plenty of research and plenty of experimentation, but there seem to be invisible barriers between the research findings and their widespread application or between experimentation and generalisation.

We must work hard at bringing those barriers down. For example, a vast amount of research has been undertaken into how people learn, the speeds at which they learn, the settings in which individuals learn most swiftly or effectively, the differences that produce more or less success in learning for individual people. We do not see that knowledge reflected in our schools. We need a sustained programme of dissemination and application of research and its results – a programme that could well mean, over time, a restructuring of the school day, the learning environment in schools, the way that students are supported.

A particular case is that of the new technologies. Whatever anyone says or writes about the impact of those new technologies on learning, their effect is almost certainly profoundly under-estimated. You can tell that the world has changed when it is suggested that some of the greatest innovators in learning and education are and will be the Microsofts and IBMs. In my view, we have not begun to grasp the full potential and implications of IT and other new technologies in our schools. Yet many of our young students have grasped that potential and are more familiar with CD-ROMs, with the Internet and the Worldwide Web than we are. In many ways now the home is better equipped for learning than the school – and if that is not quite true everywhere yet, it soon will be. The new technologies are not a marginal add-on. They will transform the learning process and the opportunity that time at school presents. All too often, however, they are approached from the point of view of the technology and its wizardry, rather than the point of view of the learner.

Within each school, we need to think what we are doing and how we are doing it for a technology age. It is not a case of adding a computer here or there (however desirable some of that may be short term). It is a case of a complete rethink from the point of view of the learner and the potential. Access is immeasurably increasing. Unit cost is rapidly decreasing. Learning is becoming fun. And the potential for joint learning with others, not just in this country but overseas, is there for the taking. Every learner will soon have access to the very best learning resources and the very best teachers in the world. Already anyone with the right equipment (and it is not dear) can browse through the library of Congress, have access to colour reproductions of every painting in our National Gallery or take a journey to the moon.

My third action point was inclusion rather than exclusion. The plain fact is that we do well by the elite and the top 10 or 15 per cent of the population. Where we are failing in achievement is with the rest. Both as a country and as individual schools and organisations, we need to take to heart those facts. Of course the elite, the top 15 per cent continue to matter and we must not let their achievement backslide; but the focus needs to be on the many, not the few.

That, too, should call for a rethink. For example, if we are serious about raising achievement of the many, we need to get away from an age-related examination system in schools. We know that not all people learn at the same rate: some are faster and some find more difficulty. Yet we have major hurdles at age 16 and 18+: hurdles at which so many fall or fail.

Yet, at the same time, we have invested a huge national effort in a Vocational Qualification system which is not about age, nor time spent learning, nor whether the student is full-time or part-time. The NVQ and GNVQ systems turn on demonstrated competence, no matter when or whether that competence many be demonstrated. They are based on criteria, not norms. It is my firm view that, over the next few years, we need to adopt that approach throughout our school system and for all learners. Such a system implies, of course, a unified qualification system after the age of 14. It implies waiving goodbye to A level which has served us well in its day but is no longer relevant to the future. But it also implies injecting into the new unified qualification system a rigour of assessment and testing and a professionalism in application which are not yet present in the NVQ and GNVQ structures.

My fourth action point was that of leadership. I distinguish leadership from management and I distinguish both from administration. At the moment, as I have said, too many of us are bogged down in administration. And too many of us think that the task stops with management which I define as control, as system, and as evaluation of performance and results. I define leadership as vision, longer term strategy, aligning people and organisations with longer term priorities, communication, encouragement and visibility.

We are not developing leaders in our schools as we should. We need to understand that there is no one leader in a school – or at least in a school which is raising achievement. We need to develop leaders at every level: in the governing body, in the head teacher, in heads of departments, in individual units. The preparation, selection and development of people for these positions in our schools is, to put if mildly, haphazard. We have an *ad hoc* system for identifying potential leaders and developing them; haphazard practices in the selection of people; too little commitment to continuing professional development; too little opportunity for sharing leadership issues and problems with others; and too little support for teachers. All these issues need to be addressed urgently. I believe that leadership skills can be developed.

I do not believe that you are born a leader or never will be a leader. Leadership can be learned, can be fostered and can be developed. We need badly to develop systems for doing so.

My themes in the course of this address have been the urgent need to raise achievement and, in doing so, to focus on outcomes rather than the detail of processes; the likelihood (I would say certainty) that there will be no great additional resources (if any) for education as a whole no matter which government is in power; the need, therefore, to take matters into our own hands and focus on cutting out waste and getting a bigger return for the money we spend; the need to innovate more readily and rapidly; the need to include rather than exclude learners of all ages, all stages and all abilities; and the need to develop leadership qualities and leadership at all levels in our school system.

All this implies a new vision of where we are going. We need to take time at all levels to develop that vision. In what is a long term investment business, we are much too focused on short term, on crisis management, on this year's and this term's objectives. If we go on like that, we shall lurch on without direction and above all without any real raising of achievement.

In 1982, the then Manpower Services Commission, working with employers, trade unions, the education service and voluntary organisations, put forward a short document called *A New Training Initiative*. It was a dark moment in vocational education and training. The Industry Training Boards were being abolished. Funding for training was being reduced. Apprenticeship was collapsing. Unemployment was rising. The New Training Initiative proposed three objectives for the next decade. These objectives were that all young people up to the age of 18 should have access to good quality education or training, full or part-time; that our vocational education and training system should be based on standards of competence rather than time-serving or the age of the learner; and that we should seek to open up many wider opportunities for adults.

Those objectives were all highly controversial at the time of their promotion. In general, employers did not believe that all young people needed broad-based education and training programmes. We had no structures of standards of competence. Adult learners were still very much the poor relations (as arguably they often remain today). Yet within the decade huge progress was made on all three fronts. I do not need to rehearse it again now. The first two objectives were achieved and the third saw a real advance. Moreover, because the New Training Initiative was put together by a partnership of all involved, everybody could relate to it. Even those who held differing political views could unite behind recognised and agreed banners.

I suggest that the time has come for something similar in education. We have national education and training targets. What about national objectives for the next decade in education? The overall objective would be clearly stated: to secure at least a 30 per cent improvement in achievement at all levels and in all organisations in the education service and to do so within present resources. Within that there would be five other clearly stated objectives:

a)	to redistribute present resources so as to ensure that the greatest investment would go to the parts of the system in greatest need. This would mean:

- introducing a new funding structure for further and higher education which would treat all students, full or part-time, alike after the age of 18, which abolished the binary line between further and higher education and which enabled all students of further and higher education to have access to loans and to pay back the cost of post 18 education over a lifetime through a student graduate tax;
- redistributing some of the money thereby saved to nursery education and to primary and secondary schools in inner city areas;
- thereby securing a marked increase in unit expenditure on primary education and a reduction in primary education of class size;
- and thereby also securing access to nursery education for all;

b)	introducing at the earliest date a unified qualification system which would bring together in one overarching system all kinds of qualifications, thereby abolishing and debilitating the now outdated divide between academic and vocational. This would mean:

- creating at the earliest date one overarching qualification authority from the School Curriculum Assessment Authority and the National Council for Vocational Qualifications;
- unhooking the resulting qualification system from age-related examination dates;
- enabling any student, young or old, to proceed at her or his pace;
- allowing every student the opportunity to demonstrate that she or he could, in shorter or longer time, reach the recognised standard of performance;
- securing the establishment of a rigorous, recognised and credible professional assessment and performance measurement capacity capable of applying the new qualification system openly and incontrovertibly;

c)	carrying through, throughout the whole of the education system a major innovation programme, focused on rethinking the design of learning in every educational establishment, particularly schools, through the comprehensive and integral use of the new technologies and their potential;

d)	rethinking the role, training and professional development of teachers so that they become supporters of learners and turn their backs on now outdated practices, systems and methods. This would also imply:

- introducing and applying rigorously a system of appraisal, performance targets and performance monitoring for individual teachers which would be intolerant of failure, whilst recognising and rewarding success;

- developing and introducing an entirely new and reliable system for the selection, preparation and development of teachers, headteachers and governors;

e) establishing new local bodies at sub-regional level charged with overseeing the quantity and quality of provision for education of people of all ages in the local community, thereby making more effective use of resources and enriching learning experience at all ages and stages.

Who might draw up such a document? Not, I hope, politicians. Political time horizons are too short. We are not in sound bite territory. We have had enough of every Secretary of State wanting her or his own new initiative. We have had enough of short-term wheezes, schemes and initiatives. What we are about is far too important for it to be a child of Government alone though, as I shall say in a minute, Government is a critical partner.

Answering my question becomes slightly easier because we already have a blueprint: the outline is all there in the reports of the National Commission on Education. We also have an interesting ready-made body which might be developed to take on the task – the National Advisory Council on Education and Training targets.

I would remodel and develop that National Advisory Council. I would extend its membership to include the professional bodies, the lead qualification bodies (in particular, SCAA and NCVQ), the Funding Councils for both further and higher education and representatives from all parts of the education system. That need not be cumbersome. As the experience of the Manpower Services Commission showed, it is quite possible to mould together a nationwide alliance in a cause in which all believe and to which all are committed.

But what of the role of Government? In my view, we have again a clear model. I believe that one of the most effective and cost effective programmes for raising educational achievement in this country was the Technical and Vocational Education Initiative – TVEI. It was a programme in which, eventually all parts of the country were involved. Born initially in controversy, it ended by transforming the curriculum, the equipment and facilities of many schools, and the training and development of many teachers. It was a ten-year development programme. In total it cost £1 billion. It operated through contracts – in that case with Local Education Authorities and schools and colleges within those Authorities. It operated on the basis of bids which were made against a framework of stipulated outcomes sought. I believe that we can and should launch another such major programme called, what else?, 'Raising Achievement'. We should dedicate to it £1 billion of additional public expenditure spread over the years between now and 2005.

The programme would fund projects, locally based and locally designed, whose clear objective was to raise achievement by at least 30 per cent and which also addressed themselves to the achievement of the national objectives I have just set out. Schools, colleges, universities, employers, private education and training providers would be invited to combine locally with clear plans and projects to achieve those ends. They would be invited to show their commitment by setting out the resources they themselves intended to dedicate to the achievement of the objectives. Government would add money as it did in TVEI for a limited period of time – no more than five years per project. The outcome sought would be to secure a step improvement in achievement by the end of each project.

As I said, TVEI cost £1 billion spread over ten years – the money was not dispensed evenly in each of those years because projects started slowly and rose to peaks of activity. But because different projects came from different parts of the country at different times and because there was, in each year, a limit to the number of new projects that could be afforded and started, the annual expenditure was never more than about £300 million and in most of the ten years it was a great deal less than that. Not much, compared with the £27 billion expended annually now (and planned for the foreseeable future) on education at all levels.

This, I suggest, should be Government's part in the new national enterprise – an investment well worth making, one which would give a great return and hugely improved value for money for present expenditures. It would not break the Treasury bank or public sector borrowing requirement. If the country cannot afford this in its present and future state, there is something seriously and very sadly wrong. In the highly competitive world of the 21st century, investment in our people and in their continuing education throughout their lives is the most important investment that the country or any of us can make.

I am clear about two things. First, we must not look for alibis that prevent us from getting started. We need to raise achievement. We need to tackle the task vigorously and urgently. We must put behind us the temptation to say that we could do whatever it is that has to be done if only somebody else did something else first. Raising achievement does not depend on someone else. It is the responsibility of each of us and we need to get on with it with the large resources of money and time we currently have.

Secondly, time is most emphatically not on our side. A few weeks ago, I was asked to address another conference on the education of 14 to 19 year olds. Within ten days I found myself before the Select Committee on Education of the House of Commons giving evidence on precisely the same subject. I calculated that these were the 249th and 250th occasions on which I had been asked to speak on this subject in the last fifteen years. Some of you will have been present at or will have spoken at many more such occasions than I. It was Harold Macmillan who, paraphrasing Winston Churchill, produced the phrase 'Jaw jaw is better than war.' When it comes to the necessity to raise achievement that is emphatically not the case. We have had enough of 'jaw jaw' and now need to get down to serious action everywhere.

Francis Bacon, that great English statesman, scientist, writer and Renaissance man wrote, as you will recall, an essay entitled *The Advancement of Learning*. In that essay occurs the following sentence:

In this theatre of man's life it is reserved only for God and angels to be lookers on.

If you remember nothing else of this Presidential Address, I urge you to remember that sentence. When it comes to raising achievement, none of us is or can be a looker on. It is a task for all of us. We are capable of that task. But only if we roll up our sleeves.

NOTE

This chapter was originally given as an address to the North of England Education Conference on January 3rd, 1996.

11

EDUCATION AND INDUSTRIAL PERFORMANCE

Kenneth Adams and Eric Bates

Kenneth Adams CVO, CBE is Honorary Industry Fellow, Comino Foundation and Honorary Fellow, St. George's House, Windsor Castle. Dr. Eric B Bates CBE is Education Fellow, Comino Foundation.

In the early 1970s, it was clear to any objective observer that British industrial performance was in steep decline. Our share of the international market for the export of manufactured goods was rapidly declining. The bad relationships between management and workforce in our industries was internationally notorious. We were tormented weekly by strikes in industry. We were failing to meet completion dates for contracts or for the delivery of orders. We suffered a period when we were reduced to working a three-day week and our troubles were referred to on the Continent as the British disease.

Behind this extremely worrying situation, a small group of people meeting in a series of consultations at St. George's House, Windsor Castle, from 1974 discerned a fundamental problem which was not being, and could not be, addressed by Government or political parties working on their own. For a variety of reasons, Britain had developed, from the late nineteenth century, an anti-industrial culture. This culture permeated all parts of our society – Government, civil service, education, church, broadcasting, journalism, the arts, and indeed industry itself. We had become an industrial nation bedevilled and frustrated by an anti-industrial culture.

Many people believed that one of the factors contributing to this situation was the style of education in our schools. In 1975, Lord Bowden, then Principal of the Manchester Institute of Science and Technology, had powerfully drawn attention to the effect of that education on our universities when, in an address to his Court of Governors, he said:

> What effect are our universities having on society as a whole; what effect, either direct or indirect have the universities and their graduates had on British industry and the gross domestic product? In the last four or five years, most of our efforts seem to have been in vain. The English no longer want to study any discipline which will fit them for a career in productive industry. They have deserted university schools of science and technology in droves. The places they left vacant have been filled by a multitude of eager foreign students, who have come here to learn how to make their native countries prosperous. The change in the composition of some of our classes has become alarming in the extreme. This year, the Master's course in Textile Technology has twenty-eight foreign students and none from this country. The corresponding course for Polymer and Fibre Science has ten foreign students and two Englishmen. We used to have the biggest undergraduate school of Chemical Engineering in Europe. For a decade or more, it recruited ninety Englishmen and half a dozen foreigners every year. This year, it admitted twenty-three Englishmen and twenty-five foreigners. Our post-graduate School of Production Engineering used to admit a couple of dozen Englishmen and a few foreigners every year. Today it has four times as many foreigners as Englishmen. Our Master's course for Hydrocarbon Chemistry, upon which the oil industry depends, was mounted by the great oil firms and the Science Research Council. We had forty-six students in the class last year of whom two were English and this year we have forty-three students of whom one is English.

This particular anxiety was given vigorous expression as a public concern in an important and well-reported speech by the Prime Minister of the time, Mr. Jim (now Lord) Callaghan, at Ruskin College, Oxford, in 1976. He made a powerful plea for radical new thinking on the style of education provided for our children, urging that it should be more closely related to the way in which we, as a nation, earned our living.

The adverse effect on our industrial performance of lack of understanding among teachers of the key role of industry in our society was well illustrated in a memorable speech by Sir Alex Smith, then Chairman of the Schools Council, to the National Union of Teachers at Bath University in January '77, in which he said:

> I want to talk now about the deeper longer term problem of the relationship between education and the well-being of the nation. There is a divergence between education and the means whereby we, as a nation, earn our living and it increases as the education reaches its higher levels. Many educators dislike, to the point of contempt, the activities and the values of the industrial sector. They see it as having little respect for human values, little recognition of human attributes, committed only

to rising production, heedless of value, unconcerned about the extent
to which people are dehumanised or the earth's resources are ransacked
in the process. They see it as dependent for its success upon pandering
to the baser human emotions of greed and envy.

INDUSTRY, EDUCATION AND MANAGEMENT

In July 1977, the Department of Industry published a very influential discussion paper entitled *Industry, Education and Management* and this also called for a review of what was taking place in our schools. Among other things, the paper posed this question: 'What specific steps can be taken to improve the relative status and prestige of a career in industry and to get across to the country at large the role of industry as the major creator of wealth for the benefit of the economy and the whole community and the excitement and challenge of working in it?'

Behind this public acknowledgement of the disastrous effect of an adverse cultural attitude to industry on our industrial performance and national welfare, lay a series of residential consultations starting in 1975 at St. George's House, Windsor Castle, devoted to exposing and addressing this problem, in which John Tomlinson played a very important part. People from all areas of influence in our society were drawn into these consultations with the aim of encouraging widespread understanding of the character of the problem, discerning its causes and encouraging those attending to take such action as was possible in their own circumstances to effect a change.

It was clear that the problem lay deeper than the fiscal, financial, legal or administrative concerns of Government. There was a profound cultural factor which was at work and The Windsor studies discerned five causes. These were: ignorance regarding the way in which we, as a nation, earned our living, disappointment with our industrial performance, disenchantment with some of the ways of industry, a moral ambivalence to the virtue of the wealth-creating activity of industry and an educational style which elevated theoretical learning above its practical application and so encouraged a snobbish attitude to industry and trade. It had long been considered morally better for a young person in Britain to make a career in the public service or the professions, than to enter industry or commerce.

The influence of this adverse cultural attitude was pervasive because no society can perform well in an activity which is held in low esteem within that community. There was, therefore, a moral issue to be faced. The moral worth of the wealth-creating activity had to be re-asserted and everyone brought to realise that the wealth-creating activity of industry and commerce is the prime social service in any community anywhere, because all other activities depend on it.

By 1977, it had come to be recognised that one of the principal causes of this adverse cultural attitude to industry was the character of education provided in our schools and it was to addressing this particular part of the problem that John Tomlinson was to make a leading and most significant contribution. It spanned his work as the Director of Education for Cheshire County Council and Professor of Education at the University of Warwick, which included periods of Chairmanship of the Schools Council 1978–81 and of the Council of the Royal Society for the Encouragement of Arts, Manufactures and Commerce (RSA) 1989–91.

John Tomlinson played a leading part in the initiation of a series of well-directed activities, all designed in different ways to improve the relationship between education and industry. He served on many influential committees working in this area and he pursued vigorously the work of the Schools Council Industry Project which was designed to encourage greater economic awareness within the curriculum. Some of the other most important projects in which he played a part included the establishment by the CBI of the Understanding British Industry Movement, designed to provide teachers with work experience in industry, and the establishment at the Department of Industry of an Industry/Education Unit (IEU) whose task was to encourage all activities designed to relate education in schools more closely to the way in which we, as a nation earned our living.

A driving force for the establishment of the IEU was the cultural shock one of us felt returning after five years on the continent, of realising the lack of esteem for (manufacturing) industry, and those who worked in it, compared with the rest of Europe, and the gap between leaders in industry and in education in the understanding of the vital importance of industry to national well-being. It seemed logical that the Department of Industry should have an input to education thinking, since all who enter industry must pass through the education provision.

However, the suggestion was not universally accepted within government, and it was difficult to know how one could begin to have a dialogue with those responsible for educational provision, especially as one's efforts could be construed as unwelcome interference. It was here that John Tomlinson lubricated the process. Through his chairmanship of the Schools Council he made it possible for specific projects to be undertaken. Through his contacts with his fellow Chief Education Officers he opened channels of communication that helped to start an ongoing dialogue, and through his Presidency of the Society of Education Officers in 1982 he was able to reach a wider audience to even greater effect.

Lord Seebohm, at Investors in Industry, encouraged the establishment by the Industrial Training Foundation of a movement entitled *Understanding Industry* which provides well-planned courses for first-year Sixth formers on the ways in which industry operates. The Industrial Society initiated a new Common Purpose Campaign led by Julia Cleverdon, which encouraged in schools and among parents, and perhaps especially women, a greater understanding of the key role of industry in the welfare of our society. The Standing Conference on Schools, Science and Technology expanded its work to encourage greater technological literacy in schools. There were many other exciting developments of a similar kind.

INDUSTRY YEAR 1986

By the early 1980s, these initiatives in education were being supported by work in other fields to develop an affirmative cultural attitude to industry in Britain. Working with others, John Tomlinson saw the value of a national event which would draw the attention of the whole nation to the key role of industry in our society and the excitement and challenge of industry as a career. So the idea of an Industry Year emerged and, with the support of the CBI, the TUC, the Institute of Directors, the Industrial Society and the Government, the RSA took on the task of mounting Industry Year 1986.

All the work being done in education played a prominent part in this event. Regional committees were formed to develop the activities of the Year covering the whole of the United Kingdom. A prominent part of this work in each region was that devoted to exposing the changes which were taking place in education and to encourage all involved to see the relationship between a well-educated society and a society which was successful in its industry and commerce. Strongly supporting all this work at the RSA and through educational structures, was John Tomlinson. During the work leading up to the initiation of the Industry Year, at a consultation chaired by Sir William Taylor, then Principal of the University of London, the need for greater professionalism in teaching was stressed and it was recognised that there was no central authoritative professional body to which teachers belonged. John Tomlinson vigorously engaged in this discussion and played a key part in drawing national attention to the fact that the future well-being of our community depended entirely on developing an educated and trained society. This required a national strategy for education and the encouragement of greater professionalism in teaching by the creation of a professional institution to which all teachers would belong. After further discussion, a memorandum recommending such action was sent to the Prime Minister. John Tomlinson has continued to work to establish a professional body for teachers through the General Teaching Council initiative.

When he became Director of the Institute of Education at Warwick University, John Tomlinson established the Centre for Education and Industry. This was a bold move to create a focal point and major resource for industry/education links, which operates through a number of inter-related divisions. It was the first institution to offer a post graduate course in education and industry; it provides the home for the National Westminster Financial Literary Centre, and for Research, and was the headquarters for Schools' Council Industry Project (SCIP). It has also established an International Division, with contacts world wide.

Amongst his many other activities, John Tomlinson is a Trustee of the Comino Foundation, which was established twenty five years ago by Demetri Comino. As a Trustee he plays his part in helping it to achieve its two main aims. One is to encourage a culture that affirms and celebrates both achievement and responsible practice in industry and commerce, and the other is to enable and empower young people through their education, to develop their potential for the benefit of themselves and others. The Foundation seeks to show them how to succeed, to set themselves and achieve ever higher objectives, and to be creative in their thinking and decision making.

These early moves contributed heavily to the success of several IEU initiatives. The Chief Education Officers had considerable power to 'make things happen', and since there were only 112 of them in England and Wales (and about a dozen or so key people in Scotland) each could be contacted individually. It would have been impossible to deal with more than 30,000 schools and Further Education Colleges separately. Local Education Authorities helped immensely by being the contacts to the maintained schools. (One consequence of the reorganisation which has reduced the power of Local Education Authorities is that it would now be exceedingly difficult to mount similar initiatives.)

THE LESSONS OF THE INNOVATION

Looking back over almost two decades what have such links achieved? What benefit have they been to our country, and what lessons might we learn?

It is not possible to answer such questions quantitatively, any more than we can do so in respect of the effects of education generally, nor is it possible in one chapter to encapsulate the efforts of all those individuals and groups who have contributed to the development of industry/education links. However we can make sensible observations on the nature and extent of changes that have taken place.

The main aim of the movement was to achieve a much better mutual understanding between two important areas of national life. The need for this had become increasingly important, as we have argued. On the one hand the emphasis on 'academic' education and lack of esteem for 'vocational' was contributing adversely to our national wealth-creating functions. In this respect we were unique amongst major industrial societies, where those educated and trained to promote manufacturing and engineering were and still are highly regarded. On the other hand industry was inarticulate in expressing what qualities and educational achievements it sought in prospective employees. Those responsible in industry frequently were not involved in education, certainly at school level, and had an imperfect understanding of how schools or 'the education system' operated. The major changes beginning to take place in education added to the complexity.

In our judgement there is now a far better mutual understanding and respect, a marked change in attitudes compared with twenty years ago. In

1985, less than ten years after industry/education links had begun to be taken seriously, a senior industrialist commented:

> My preconceived notion that teachers are people who simply work a five-hour day and get 14 weeks holiday have taken a severe dent. I was greatly impressed by the commitment of the people I spoke to, and their single minded determination to work at it and get it right.

That demonstrates a remarkable change in attitude within a relatively short time. Now ten years later it would be difficult to find a senior industrialist who would even claim to have held such 'preconceived notions'.

Teachers' attitudes have similarly changed. Industrialists are now openly welcomed in schools and on governing bodies. Links between schools and local industry and commerce are common place. Help is appreciated with the curriculum, in administration or managerial training for school staff. Many of the activities that formerly took place as 'optional extras' are now encapsulated in the life of the school.

One of the early successful IEU projects was th 'Young Engineer for Britain' competition which we ran for several years before handing it over to the Engineering Council. Another was the 'Micros in Schools' scheme, followed by the 'Micros in Primary Schools' scheme, as a result of which we were the first country in the world to equip every school with a computer. Within ten years the average number of computers in secondary schools has risen to one to every eight pupils and a recent report concluded that our young people have more access to Information Technology than those in any major competing country.

For so many years technology was a Cinderella of the curriculum, considered by teachers and parents to be suitable only for the 'less able' students. The Young Engineers Competition had helped to broaden an understanding of Technology and Engineering but the subject still traditionally was associated with woodwork and metalwork in dingy basements and definitely not for girls!

The 'Mini-enterprise in Schools' scheme followed, and was taken over with enthusiasm by National Westminster Bank as its main contribution to Industry Year. It enabled every school to have its own 'mini enterprise' and for many pupils was their first experience of business operations and working together in teams. Nat West continued the project until recently, replacing it in 1994 with their latest project 'Face 2 Face with Finance'. Both projects have given pupils an understanding of business and finance which otherwise they would have been unlikely to experience. 'Young Enterprise' adopts a format which involves students operating their own small business activities in teams and has enabled students to acquire an understanding of a wide range of business skills.

Another IEU initiative was the encouragement to schools to incorporate Business Studies into the curriculum, helped by companies. This has proved immensely popular with students, who gain so much self assurance and see it as 'their' subject in which teachers participate as facilitators.

The IEU launched British School Technology (BST) which sought to change perceptions of teachers and students, and to encourage more young people, including girls, to study engineering and technology. The project started with two second-hand red London double-decker buses equipped with specially designed British equipment and loaned to Bedfordshire LEA. Within two years the uptake of A level candidates in Technology in that county had rocketed and with the help of Peter Browning, the CEO, permanent premises were provided to modify more buses. Trent Polytechnic provided additional teacher training courses, the Manpower Services Commission shared initial funding equally with the IEU and BST was born. In time every LEA had at least one mobile classroom, and one was provided for 'Women into Science and Engineering' (WISE). BST later became a charitable trust and was finally disbanded in 1994 because it had achieved its purpose. Technology was by then established in the curriculum, and now an increasing number of schools have become Technology Colleges.

One of the long standing organisations dedicated to improving science and technology provision in schools, by forging links with industrial companies, is the Standing Conference on Science and Technology (SCSST). It is responsible for administering the Science and Technology Regional Organisation (SATRO) originally launched by the Department of Industry. Largely supported by industry, but with valuable help from the Office of Science and Technology, the SATROs represent a network of over 40 regional centres, acting as reference points for schools and colleges and responsible for overseeing regional competitions in technology and engineering. Their influence continues to grow and they make their unique contribution to resource provision for the national curriculum and vocational courses.

These achievements in technology have been helped significantly by several other initiatives most of which demand voluntary effort by engineers and teachers. It is impossible in a short space to detail them all, but those that continue to play a vital role include the Young Engineer Clubs, the Neighbourhood Engineers, and the CREST awards scheme operated through the SCSST. There are also many schools who do not enter any of the award schemes and competitions, but who benefit from the advice of technologists and engineers, employed by local companies, who give freely of their time.

The Royal College of Arts has also taken up the challenge, and through its Technology Project has produced technology course material designed to meet the needs of the curriculum. It also contributes to the aim of 'parity of esteem' by promoting the development of GNVQ's especially in Design and Technology, and Manufacturing.

These initiatives serve two purposes. They aim to increase the number of engineers and technologists and to increase understanding by other students of the importance to the community of these subjects. It is hoped that a more technologically literate society will foster more favourable attitudes to industry.

A number of projects are in operation designed to increase public awareness of science and technology. The Royal Society is currently developing its

Community Science Project. The Parliamentary Scientific Committee seeks to increase the understanding of its members from both Houses of Parliament. The media now have regular feature programmes, well produced and informative, which help to change perceptions of industry. There have also been projects designed to extend understanding of the nature and purpose of industry beyond the spheres of technology and engineering and to try to foster positive attitudes.

As a consequence of the industry/education movement, education is becoming progressively more community linked. This broadens the experiences of students, helping them better to understand the world around them and hence to accommodate more easily to it when they leave full time education.

UNDERSTANDING BRITISH INDUSTRY

One of the early organisations linking industry and education is Understanding British Industry (UBI), founded in 1976 as an activity of the CBI Education Foundation and now a nationwide organisation with a regional network; it is increasingly effective. Over the last six years it has successfully established and expanded the Teacher Placement Service, having delivered 200,000 placements, and annually reaching 8.5 per cent of serving teachers, close to the Government's target of 10 per cent. Careful planning and debriefing of each placement ensures they achieve the highest quality and provide first-hand experience of the role of business. The Government supports the work of Training and Enterprise councils (TECs) in this field, and UBI in monitoring and support services.

The increasing autonomy of schools demands ever increasing managerial expertise and UBI offers management training with an industrial perspective for some 1,000 Headteachers and senior educationalists. The training programmes are arranged in conjunction with leading companies who provide both expertise and financial support. The need is being addressed also by the Teacher Training Agency which administers the Headlamp scheme. The agency has introduced the 'National Professional Qualification for Headteachers'. A recent development to assist British Industry in its constant efforts to improve the competitiveness is the 'Investors in People' initiative. Already it is proving its worth in industry and UBI has pioneered its introduction into schools, where it is already showing benefits.

Another organisation early in the field is Understanding Industry (UI) launched by the 3i Group and supported by industry. It concentrates on 16–19 year old students, seeking to give them knowledge, enhance their skills, and improve their attitudes towards industry and commerce. Its courses cover the whole range of business activities and independent surveys have confirmed that its success rate is high.

Business in the Community (BITC) has the campaign slogan 'Aim High' to encourage Education Business Partnerships with the clear purpose of raising levels of educational achievement towards the National Targets of Education and Training, and has set itself a number of criteria by which success can be judged. These Partnerships help also with career guidance, were heavily involved in the TVEI (Technical Vocation and Education Initiative) and continue to be involved in local Schools' Curriculum Industry Partnerships. They involve other organisations such as local Chambers of Commerce and work closely with LEAs and TECS. They are increasingly involved in Teacher Placements.

The promotion of the 'compact' between local schools and local employers, governing such aspects as attendance, punctuality, homework and course work deadlines aimed to ease the transition of young people from school to adult and working life. They improved motivation and helped to raise self esteem and standards.

It is commonplace for companies with available resources to contribute either to one or more of the regional or national industry/education organisations or to assist local schools and colleges. Many large companies support both approaches and have also developed more strongly their links with Higher Education. Major international companies naturally feel a responsibility for and an affinity with schools within striking distance of their UK based operations. It is often simpler and easier to offer the support of local personnel and other resources. However, additionally they support national initiatives in large measure, and without their help the main Charitable Trusts that depend on external funding would collapse. Thus major national competitions including the Young Engineers, CREST, UBI, UI rely heavily on industrial support. The total contribution by industry to the development of local links cannot be estimated. It continues to grow and was given added impetus by the impact of Industry Year 1986.

One example of the impact of Industry Year is the continuing work of the 'Merseyside Industry and Commerce Awards for Education' (MICA). This offers an opportunity for 17–18 year old students to work as members of teams to tackle a real life business problem with the support of a major employer on Merseyside. The dozen or so companies work together with others including the local TEC and the Comino Centre based at Liverpool University. MICA is not a competition, it is about 'developing teamwork and initiative, and furthering the interaction between education and business'. Its relevance to the issues facing a city such as Liverpool is obvious and because of its success it continues to flourish. The students gain in self esteem and confidence.

But how do employers view industry/education links? Do they consider that they achieve much? Judging by their continuing support they must consider them worth while. A recent survey showed that 84 per cent of employers believed there should be such links. Almost two-thirds of companies employing over 100 people have links and over one-third of all employers have links with the local Education Business Partnership. Of the companies involved, over 80 per cent have links with secondary schools, 61 per cent with Further Education colleges, 30 per cent with primary schools, and 47 per cent with universities. Larger companies tend to be involved with all types of educational institutions and are more likely to be involved with universities. They are also more likely to have formal policies towards education links and to evaluate their effectiveness. Their reasons for getting involved can cover a wide range. On balance most employers see the relationship is more about giving than receiving. Offering work experience is the most common activity, and undertaken with the aims of influencing young people in their attitudes to work and their career choices. Most companies that provide teacher placements do so to help teachers gain a better understanding of the world of work and to influence the curriculum to make it more 'business friendly'. The placements help to improve employer contacts with schools and colleges, and are seen as providing a service to education. Although sometimes links are seen as means to recruitment, this is not a major company purpose. Of greater interest is the development of a culture which better understands business and how companies operate. The continuing business support for such links and the willingness to remain or become more closely involved even in times of recession, bear witness to the fact that they are regarded as achieving worthwhile objectives.

As the momentum for developing links grows, large numbers of initiatives continue to spring up. Indeed they were encouraged by the slogan 'let a thousand flowers bloom'. Companies are concerned at the plethora of requests for help from different organisations with apparently similar objectives. With limited funds at their disposal they sometimes have difficulty in deciding which to support and would welcome a higher degree of rationalisation. Several years ago attempts were made to bring national initiatives closer together but met with little success. The Industrial Society made a bold move by offering accommodation to half a dozen organisations in one building and through 'One front door'. This allowed sharing of services without affecting individuality. It worked well for a time but never commanded universal support and was finally abandoned.

Nevertheless the desire for a major focal point continues, and as in other areas the concept of a 'One stop shop' is often discussed. Business in the Community has successfully brought a number of activities closer together under its wing; a major advantage of such an arrangement is the far greater strength the organisation has in dealing with government departments and transnational organisations. In future we may see the strengthening of organisations such as BITC and a constant bubbling up of fresh local initiatives, some of which will be temporal, whilst others will survive and grow.

Still looking ahead, because support – from whatever sources – will continue to be limited, pressures to search for more cost effective ways of developing meaningful links will continue. Objectives will need to be clear and attainable, relevant and responsive to changing educational needs, and seen to be mutually beneficial in the longer term. It will remain a high priority to ensure high standards are maintained and to disseminate good practice, which means adequate monitoring and control procedures are vital. Perhaps we need also to examine whether there is a particular contribution that very small companies have to offer, for example in entrepreneurship helping trigger creative talent in schools.

One of the greatest achievements of the whole link movement has been the increase in mutual understanding and respect. The idea of links between industry and commerce and education at all levels in education is now accepted as the norm. It has moved from being an optional extra, to be bolted on when required, into the blood stream of education and accepted as an integral part of the responsibility of major companies.

CONCLUSIONS

There is a wider recognition in education of the importance of 'wealth creation' and the vital contribution that industry, including manufacturing industry, plays in the life of the country. Engineers and technologists are held in greater esteem, although we still have some way to go before they are generally as highly regarded as some other professions.

The issue of parity between academic and vocational education has surfaced dramatically. The pressures induced by new technologies have contributed to this. Technology is now firmly established in the curriculum. A major challenge is to establish GNVQ's as qualifications acceptable by the outside world and higher education.

One consequence, perhaps not generally anticipated, has been the far greater interest in education displayed by the general public. Many more adults are prepared to offer their expertise, and to serve as governors. There has been an opening up of education generally, and a greater appreciation of the importance of the changing role of teachers.

As a nation we tend to be reluctant to celebrate success in any sphere, and education is no exception. Indeed there are those who make a profession of cynicism. I believe there is great merit on occasion to look back, rejoice in what so many people have achieved, and see such achievements as a spring board for further effort and further success. Industry/education links fall into this category and John Tomlinson deserves much credit for his part in its development.

REFERENCE

Department of Industry (1977) *Industry, education and management*, Discussion Paper.

12

WORK AS A SCHOOL SUBJECT

John Eggleston

Professor John Eggleston is Emeritus Professor of
Education at University of Warwick. He was previously
Professor of Education and Chairman of the Education
Department from 1985–1992.

John Tomlinson is one of the few educators who can be credited with introducing a new subject to the curriculum. The subject is work. In his years as
chairman of the Schools Council, then as Chairman of the Further Education
Council and finally as one of the founders of the Centre for Education and
Industry at the University of Warwick he has played a major role in defining
and establishing this new component which now characterises much of the
secondary school curriculum and significant aspects of the primary school
curriculum.

Most subjects have been added to the school curriculum only when informal
education by family, church or community became unable to ensure the
learning needed for adult roles. The history of the '3 Rs', school science,
physical education, environmental studies and sex education show that all
these subjects have 'arrived' in this way. Vocational education and industrial
training became part of the curriculum when pre-occupational training was
unavailable informally. Work itself, now the newest subject in the curriculum,
has a similar history – though recent demographic and economic events across
the world speeded the historical process.

In the recent past the experience of work was indivisible from the experience
of family, community and society. Only during the past century and a half has
work, for most citizens, been taken apart from the day-to-day life of family
and community and transferred to separate institutions – factories, shops,
offices, workshops and warehouses. Such institutions are increasingly 'closed':

for reasons of complex technology, security, privacy, hygiene or hazard they are only accessible to those who work therein and within their prescribed working hours.

Yet the twentieth century has seen a further development in the nature of the experience of work. Not only is it a separable part of human experience, but it is also one that is not being made available to all human beings. When modern societies first experienced mass unemployment it was believed that it was but a temporary phenomenon caused by short-term 'malfunctioning' of the economic mechanism such as depression or recession. Now it is realised that unless effective alternative strategies are identified and adopted, such 'malfunctioning' may become a permanent feature: unemployment becomes structural.

YOUNG PEOPLE AND WORK

In this new situation major problems arose for young people thus giving much concern to John Tomlinson's Schools Council and Further Education Unit. By far the majority are beyond the reach of any school or college 'remedy' and it is misleading and dangerous to imply otherwise. But some have considerable relevance for the work of schools. One is that in many countries unemployment, especially for the young, co-exists with unfilled vacancies in the areas of work which require skills, understandings and attributes not generally possessed by school leavers. Thus there are shortages of young people for vacancies in the 'servicing trades' responsible for the maintenance of motor cars, television sets and other domestic appliances, building maintenance and even gardening and window cleaning. There are also recurring shortages of candidates for higher level work in computing, electronics and a range of scientific and creative occupations. Of course, not all of these shortages are 'real', some are 'technical', but there is little doubt that many do exist.

A second problem is that young people who leave school and do not experience work seem to find it increasingly difficult to obtain it. Potential employers believe that some kind of atrophy develops; just as the muscles in a broken leg lose their power, so a total lack of work experience is believed to diminish the capacity to satisfy the very requirements of work such as industry, responsibility and punctuality.

A third, and perhaps the most fundamental, problem is closely associated with the second; it is that work experience provides the basic contexts for 'normal life'. These contexts include the use of time and the achievement of social 'standing' with its rights and duties and many of the attitudes and values that underpin participation in all the other human contexts offered by society. We may express the situation in two ways. One is that vocational identity is the key to social identity. The other is that work is the central instrument of social control in modern societies. Without the experience of work how can the individual develop an adequate social identity and how can the society exercise the social control over its members necessary to achieve stability and continuity?

THE EXPERIENCE OF WORK

We have now come to the crucial nature of work experience which the Further Education Unit saw clearly. Like most human experiences, it has been taken for granted while its existence seemed assured. We have come to see its importance more clearly when its availability is at risk. It is necessary to notice, however, that work experience involves a dual context. One is the context of the specific job being done – with its skills, expectations, norms and values. The other is the context of the labour market with its organisations of labour and management, its norms of production, payment and security. Both these aspects will be examined in the consideration of work experience provided by the schools.

Almost all young people see work as the key to the achievement of full masculinity or femininity. Willis's study of working-class boys in an English comprehensive school in an inner-city area depicts the social pressures on the boys to take their place on the shop floor and so earn the acceptance of the community to which they belong (1978). These boys needed to prove themselves amongst their workmates as capable of facing and surviving the realities of the factory floor with its 'hard and brutalising' conditions. Willis writes:

> The lads are not choosing careers or particular jobs, they are committing themselves to a future of generalised labour. Most work – or the 'grafting' they accept they will face – is equilibrated by the overwhelming need for instant money, the assumption that all work is unpleasant and that what really matters is the potential particular work situations hold for self and particularly masculine expression, diversions and 'laffs' as learnt creatively in the counter-school culture. These things are quite separate from the intrinsic nature of any task. This view does not contradict, for the moment, the overwhelming feeling that work is something to look forward to . . . the lure of the prospect of money and cultural membership amongst 'real men' beckons very seductively as refracted through their own culture.

But as the 'lads' attitudes clearly show, of even greater importance than specific occupational role is the set of understandings and the self-image that the individual brings to his roles. This identity with which the individual imbues his roles is crucial to the way he plays them, modifies them and develops them, and to his own personal future within them. A label, such as the lathe operator, is but an incomplete guide to human behaviour in work – the identity with which the incumbent fills the role is the key component. How does he perceive himself as a lathe operator? He has chosen the work or is it a forced decision? If the former, what are his alternatives? Are they realistic or only based on fantasy? How does he adjust to the role in the absence of alternatives? What are the implications for his other social behaviour? Fundamentally, is the vocational identity, with all its consequences, compatible with his ego and his self-image? If it is not, how may greater compatibility develop within the role?

The development of vocational identities is complex in modern society. In early, labour-intensive industrialisation, when large numbers of workers were required to perform routine and repetitive tasks, individual identity seldom came to exercise a dominant influence on production. Their self-image was of relatively little consequence to most employers. Young people were fitted into their roles in conditions which Durkheim described as 'mechanical solidarity'; the role transcendent, the individual subordinate.

The concept of identity alerts us to an alternative process which has major implications for schools and colleges. It is one in which young people may prefer to 'contract in' to both the specific job and the labour market generally rather than to accept them passively. This new approach is highly relevant to some aspects of contemporary social conditions. It is compatible with the expressed views of young people who wish to 'count for something' in society rather than to be 'on the receiving end' of 'the system'. But it is also appropriate for the needs of some sectors of modern industry which calls for human beings not to act as 'machines', but to use their capacity to adapt, adjust and initiate. For such occupational roles an active vocational identity rather than a passive vocational role is highly preferable.

Unless an acceptable vocational identity can be achieved, then life for the individual is likely to be at best incomplete or compartmentalised; at worst, frustrating, enervating and incompatible. Problems are likely to arise not only for the individual, but also for society – which is likely to experience widespread alienation or disruptive behaviour if vocational identities are generally felt to be unsatisfactory. And if work is not available the problems are likely to occur in an even more serious form.

THE ACHIEVEMENT OF WORK IDENTITY

We have already noted that, until recently, most vocational identities were acquired by predominantly informal means. The learning of occupational roles literally began in the cradle as the child saw his parents at work in homes, farms and workshops. The phrase 'like father like son' epitomised not only the informality of learning but also the predictability of the vocational role that awaited most young people. The circumstances of the parents determined the future role of the young and the learning appropriate to it. Such identities were strongly reinforced by the norms of the community which defined, often with great precision, such things as woman's work and man's work; noble work and base work. Definitions of this kind were sometimes strongly reinforced by initiation ceremonies as a prelude to entry to adult vocational roles and still feature in some apprenticeship schemes.

Informal mechanisms for achieving vocational identities are, however, not always appropriate in modern dynamic societies, where occupational structures are changing rapidly and in which it may not be possible for young people to have sufficient knowledge of the available roles in sufficient time to learn them and identify with them in anticipation. A characteristic problem of all advanced industrial societies is the rapid growth of new occupational groups such as electronics engineers, motor car repairers and salesmen, advertising and sales personnel, which has meant that many young people enter work to undertake roles for which they have been able to achieve little or no preliminary identification. New generations of vocational identity may commence with each new initiative in technology and commerce.

SCHOOL AND VOCATIONAL IDENTITY

Until recent initiatives, most associated with organisations linked with John Tomlinson's, schools have usually played only a small part in helping young people to achieve vocational identity. Though in the past half-century they have come to exercise a major role in helping to identify talent through the examination and accreditation systems, there had been little attempt to assist the young in achieving the identities to accompany the examination qualifications. There has been even less success in helping those without examination qualifications to achieve such identities. Not only have many young people lacked an adequate identity for work, but also they have lacked it for the other aspects of life that are linked to work.

Gintis (Bowles and Gintis, 1976) came to see the growing potential importance of school as a transition institution into the labour force; an institution which 'accredits' young people with the various needs of the labour market (including unemployment) and achieves the necessary correspondence between supply and demand. Grubb and Lazerson (1981) demonstrate ways in which even new strategies of career education have, in practice, been used to stratify the school system, and to separate lower-class and ethnic minority youth from their white and middle-class peers.

PROVIDING WORK EXPERIENCE IN THE SCHOOLS

John Tomlinson recognised clearly that present-day economic and social systems compel schools to take an active role in the achievement of work identity and the provision of experience in which it may occur as did Watts (1981) who wrote:

> The world of work is central to our society, and to the generation and distribution of wealth within it. For schools to neglect the world of work behind rhetoric like 'concern for the whole person' – as though the role of worker was not an important *part* of the whole person – is abjectly

to neglect a critical part of their educational responsibilities . . . The
need for schools to address the world of work, but to do so in a critical
and dynamic way, is all the more important because of the crisis that
is taking place in relation to the place of work in our society.

The new planned work experience schemes in schools take many forms.
Essentially, they are interventionist strategies designed to provide a substitute
experience of work when the 'normal' social forces fail to deliver 'the real
thing'. Work experience is, of course, a long way from the real thing: it can
offer work tasks in work environments, but it cannot offer normal pay and
tenure – essential adjuncts to identity as a worker.

There have always been some educators who have believed that work
experience is too important to leave to chance – or just to be talked about in
the schools. J.S. Mill, J. Dewey and Kurt Hahn advocated this view strongly
and in different ways it is embodied in the curricula of the German Technical
High Schools. But in present conditions, when work experience cannot be
relied upon 'just to happen' for the majority of young people, its provision
becomes an urgent social need. In some countries it has become a major focus
of national politics. Australia provided a typical example. In November 1979
the Commonwealth and States announced a series of initiatives known as the
Schools-to-Work Transition Programme Aus. Two hundred and fifty-nine
million dollars was spent over five years on a range of technical courses,
student counselling and special programmes for young people. The reason
for the government's action was obvious. Already one young Australian
in five was out of work, and another 50,000 were due to enter the labour
market with little or no hope of a job.

Variations in practice are widespread as befits a developing field. The
categorisation of process is presented in some detail in the forthcoming
pages. The categories used are: infusion, work experience courses, work
creation schemes, link courses and work simulation schemes.

Infusion

The oldest form of work experience is that in which it is infused into the
total curriculum rather than constituting a separate additional activity. Only
recently has this total approach been labelled as infusion – a term now
widely used in the United States. Yet for centuries schools have provided
work experience exactly relevant for the needs of their elite students – those
who are entering the learned and academic professions. Such students have
experienced working in the academic library, acting as teachers with titles
such as monitor or prefect, conducting religious worship and much else. More
recently, however, a conscious strategy of infusion has brought work experience into the whole curriculum for more students. Science has concerned itself
with the practice of science in industry, mathematics with its commercial and
business utilisation, linguistics with careers in communication at all levels. In

particular, work in design and technology has been closely linked with the experience of industrial production. In all these activities, argument for such infusions is that preparation for work is not just another subject – it is what school is all about.

A specific attempt to infuse work into the curriculum was the Schools Council Industry Project in which John Tomlinson played a major part. Jamieson and Lightfoot (1981), both members of the project team, note that:

> The most common way of including teaching about work was by incorporating the topic into a generic that already existed in the school for the fourth and/or fifth years. The majority of these courses are based round the theme of 'living in a modern industrial society'. Such courses are very often designed, or at least used, by schools to accommodate a variety of 'demands' made by those outside the school (for example, parents, industry, or the LEA) for the inclusion of subject matter which is thought to be necessary for a child's education, but which does not easily fit into an existing curriculum slot. Examples of these topics include health education, moral education, political education, economic education, occasionally careers education, and 'the world of work'.

One can immediately see the potential difficulties of such courses. The treatment of each issue is likely to be relatively superficial because of the large amount of ground to be covered. The course is likely to lack conceptual coherence, particularly if it is taught by teachers from a variety of subject backgrounds, which is commonly the case.

They draw particular attention to the problem we have noticed already: that work experience tends to be offered more fully for precisely those children whose prospects in the labour market are most limited. In most secondary schools these are the 'non-examination' students. 'If there are omissions, then it is usually the top ability band which does not take the course, being left to concentrate on its examination courses.'

This is, of course, not essential, as Jamieson and Lightfoot (1981) recognise. But there are certainly difficulties:

> The main source of the difficulty can be well illustrated by the case of pupil work experience, where the control of the experience which is to be examined passes out the hands of the teacher. It is difficult to examine what pupils have learned about work from work experience placements which have all been markedly different from one another. Such problems can only be partly ameliorated by the use of a suitably designed GCSE where course-work makes an important contribution to the final results.

Though compellingly straightforward in principle, the practice of infusion is difficult. Quite apart from the problems of examination, even when coherently planned as in the Schools Curriculum Industry Project, generations of tradition and academic teacher selection and training make it difficult for both schools and teachers to make the radical change across the board, whilst its very diffusion makes it difficult to evaluate. The objectives are easy to list, the achievements are distinctly harder to identify. The way forward was to develop work experience as a well-established activity of the school system first and then to integrate if effectively in the whole curriculum. Certainly, the 'additive' courses seem to be able to offer more identifiable results.

Work experience courses

These are perhaps one of the best established of the 'additive' solution within the schools. In such courses pupils visit one or more vocational locations where they have the opportunity, over a period, to mix with workers at a variety of levels and to learn something of the formal and the informal culture of the workplace – the ways in which life is experienced by those who work therein. In some situations it is possible for pupils actually to experience work with its productive rhythms, its rewards and constraints, but unfortunately problems of employer and union restrictions, insurance hazard and many other administrative difficulties generally restrict such opportunities to casual work and certain kinds of agricultural situations. (Though in England and Wales some enabling legislation exists – such as the Education Work Experience Act of 1973.)

Such courses are well-known, although some variations – such as 'shadowing' (where a pupil shadows an adult throughout his working day) – are less familiar. They fit happily into the contemporary orientation of many secondary schools where renewed emphases are being placed upon initiation into the life of the community.

Such emphases have followed a recognition in that although children spend most of their life outside the school, they none the less have surprisingly few entrées into the adult world that exists beyond their homes and in the immediate neighbourhood. Whereas, in the past, children encountered working adults in many contexts and had many opportunities to identify with them, they may now seldom see a working adult other than the postman and the dustman. Work experience courses attempt to fill this dearth of first-hand experience.

The development of work experience schemes and their evaluation has been a particular focus of the Warwick University Centre for Education and Industry working though the schools curriculum industry Partnership which has enjoyed major business and government funding. A vast range of reports and curriculum materials has been generated (e.g. Lawlor and McKay, 1993; Forrest, 1996); there has been a major involvement in the European Work Experience Project (Griffiths, 1995) an extensive range of in-service teacher education and a large number of doctoral and master's theses.

Work creation schemes

Closely linked with the provision of work experience – and a logical extension from it – is the creation or identification of work not currently being undertaken by existing paid labour. Here the school is not only able to provide work experience, but also to provide necessary services for the community. The report of the CERES project in Brunswick, Melbourne describes an urban environment field station project involving the reconstitution of ten acres of degraded urban land with community gardens, city farm, environmental displays, low energy building, low energy display and a community meeting place for community use and community support, public environmental education and training, school and tertiary projects, energy research and development, educational recreation and developing employment opportunities. The genesis of the project lay in the liaison of the seven local secondary schools in a joint body, the Brunswick Secondary Education Council (BRUSEC) and its work with a range of statutory and voluntary bodies.

A notable work creation scheme at a school is the Study Work Programme at Marion High School, South Australia. Here young people beyond minimum school leaving age work in an industrial setting within the school grounds. Working a thirty-five hour week, which includes three units of study related to their desired job, twenty-five participants undertake a range of work such as furniture repairing, printing, book-binding, landscape gardening and the like. They received a salary moderately in excess of the basic unemployment rate. The work is sought at commercial rates from the local education authority and other bodies and the programme covered its costs including salaries and the running and maintenance of the factory specially built in the school grounds. The average stay was less than two months – many participants obtained jobs in three or four weeks.

Much the same strategy was being explored in some English schools and youth groups where community skills are learned and undertaken and young people are subsequently helped to set themselves up as 'self-employed' window-cleaners, gardeners, etc, and are taught business and marketing skills to assist them. Grants or loans towards the purchase of tools and equipment may also be made available. In this way, unemployable young people can become employed and services needed by the community remain available. The Tiverton Youth Employment Support Group in the Devon Education Service was a typical example of such a scheme.

Link courses

A less well-known form of school programme is that of the link course which bring together John Tomlinson's concern to link schools and colleges. In such courses, senior school pupils spend part of their time out of school in the community and vocational colleges and factory schools which are attended by young people already at work. Here the opportunity to work alongside workers and to learn and understand their views is seen to have many advantages, even though it is taking place within a college rather than a work situation. Skinner (1970), writing about such a link course, commented:

By a 'Link Course' I mean, not isolated visits to a college, or a purely college organised class, but a fully integrated course between school and college, involving a truly joint approach, whereby the staffs of both institutions not only co-operate together in their approach, but are seen by the students consciously to do so, in such a way that each teacher is capitalising on the work of the other within an integrated whole.

Apart from the various specific aims of each course, 'Link Courses' have, in general, four main aims:

1. To bridge a gulf between school and work by giving students a more realistic atmosphere for their studies of the 'real world'. The 'outward-looking' emphasis can be developed in ways which are not always possible in school workshops.
2. To give students knowledge of employment conditions with particular reference to their environment. Consequently, they should be better able to assess their own employment potential by assimilating various means of self assessment which practice in college workshops makes possible.
3. To make students familiar with the variety of Further Education courses available, to which many will subsequently enrol on either a full-time or part-time basis. They also come to realise the various 'safety valves' that exist in Further Education for those who thought they should change their career aims because they had failed school leaving examinations.
4. Introduce students to the diagnostic and problem-solving situations that occur increasingly in the changing commercial and industrial environment.

There are limits to what can be achieved under these aims, but certainly there is evidence that the courses have become an attractive and desirable part of the school curriculum, ranging from year 10 practical and commercial courses, to sharing IVth form A level courses. The youngsters themselves feel this is giving them worthwhile advantages. Recent developments in GNVQ opportunities for 16–18 year olds relate very effectively with 'Link Course' schemes.

Work simulation schemes

Yet another form of programme is the work simulation scheme. Such schemes involve the creation of work situations in school. For example, school workshops may by used to set up a production line system in which a basic object – a Christmas card, a coat hook or a toy may be 'mass produced' and in which all aspects of production – product design, market research, trial production, quantity production, quality control, marketing, accounting and much else, may be incorporated. A wide range of experience can be concentrated in well-designed schemes, and many of the determinants of modern vocational identities – the economies of scale, the concept of labour intensity, cost-benefit analyses, and so on, can be incorporated. Such understandings are all too commonly incompletely held by many working adults – even at senior levels.

Douglas (1975) investigated a number of these projects and reports:

> The investigation found that school-based factory projects embraced a wide area of activity, ability and experience, involving greater scope than had, at first, been anticipated. For example, two mixed secondary schools in Lincolnshire undertook experimental programmes involving production line projects and demonstrated that the approach was feasible for both boys and girls, while in North Wales a low ability schools leavers' class in one school became motivated and industrious for the first time when given the opportunity to produce articles as a viable commercial undertaking.

He identified some of the main objectives of these projects as:

1. To widen the pupils' understanding of the world of industry.
2. To increase the pupils' awareness of the career potential in different parts of industry.
3. To involve pupils in problem selection and solution related to product and organisational design of an industrial nature.
4. To introduce pupils to the planning techniques and methods required for efficient quantity production.
5. To provide the opportunity for increased achievement and social interaction through group or team methods of working.

THE TECHNICAL AND VOCATIONAL EDUCATION INITIATIVE

All the forms of school and industry programmes described came together in the Technical and Vocational Education Initiative (TVEI). Launched in 1985 it poured in its various stages millions of pounds worth of staffing and resources into virtually all secondary schools and most further education colleges for programmes for 14–18 year old students. The analysis of TVEI would require a further chapter. It is sufficient here to say that though John Tomlinson was not specifically involved in its germination (it is from DTI not DOE) his ideas were crucial in its implementation.

The TVEI and the various forms of school programme have three aims in common. The first is to increase the possibility of employment and to ensure a more effective linkage between the role of the student and the role of the worker and to facilitate the transition between school and work so that dissonance and disturbance to the young person, his fellow workers, his employers, his family and his community is reduced.

The second feature of all such projects is that they embody a knowledge content. All identify a body of understandings, skills, values and orientations which, it is believed, are valuable components of vocational identity. All too often, however, this knowledge content is determined largely, if not wholly so, by the adult participants. Yet we are increasingly aware that the understandings of the young people themselves provide a crucial component of their vocational identity and that, unless they are taken into account in devising such programmes, it is likely that the achievement will fall far short of what might have been possible. The incomplete recognition of the understandings of young people is clearly to be seen in the quotation from Willis's work that has already been used.

Yet a third issue of school-based schemes is the range of adult participants' understanding and experience. Unquestionably, teachers must play an important, if not central, part in their organisation. Teachers who have previous experience in adult occupations other than teaching are likely to have a particularly valuable contribution to make (though much depends on the perceptions of work held by such teachers). But in addition to teachers, it is important that adults, who are themselves working in industry, participate: it is even more important that these include people who are doing the jobs to which pupils are immediately aspiring. Only in this way is effective and acceptable communication likely to be achieved.

In reporting the issues and achievements of the years of John Tomlinson's direct involvement it is important to remember that debate over policies and practice has never ceased and, indeed, it is as active in the mid 90s as it was in the 70s and 80s. *The British Journal of Education and Work* was launched in 1987 with Ian Jamieson as Editor and John Tomlinson as an associate editor and from its first issue plunged into the debate with Baxter's probing examination of the link between work and schooling (1987). By 1993 Gleeson was lamenting the missed opportunities in the Further and Higher Education Act of 1992 on which John Tomlinson had been consulted (Gleeson, 1993) and a few months later Ashton was calling for a new conception of the changing youth labour market (1993).

Even more fundamentally Hamner and Furlong (1996) went on to question the advantages of any kind of continuing education for 17–19 year olds from lower socio-economic groups. Wolf in her inaugural lecture at the London Institute of Education made a similar analysis claiming that work related training for the young had been an 'abject failure' (reported by Pyke, 1996). The debate has been closely linked to that concerning the role, status and efficiency of the qualifications offered by the National Council for Vocational Qualifications (shortly to be merged with the Schools Curriculum and Assessment Authority). The many publications on this topic have been brought together effectively by Robinson's (1996) analysis.

These issues and many more, including the crucial problems of evaluation have been followed up assiduously by the Centre for Education and Industry at Warwick University under the leadership of John Woolhouse and the inspiration of John Tomlinson – at first in the Department of Education chaired by the present writer and, in the past two years within John Tomlinson's Institute of Education.

CONCLUSION

Building upon the early initiatives of John Tomlinson's Schools Council and Further Education Unit and an ever widening range of educational and industrial bodies, the movement to establish work as a key school subject for all pupils has now become not only a British initiative but one that is worldwide. John Tomlinson's part in this constitutes one of his most significant contributions to educational development.

REFERENCES

Ashton, D (1993) Understanding Change in Youth Labour Markets – A Conceptual Framework, *British Journal of Education and Work*, 6, 3, 5–24.

Baxter, A (1987) Job Designs, progressive education and the correspondence between work and schooling, *British Journal of Education and Work*, 1, 1, 33–44.

Bowles, S & Gintis, H (1976) *Schooling in Capitalist America*, London: Routledge & Kegan Paul.

Careers Research and Advisory Centre (1979) *Schools and Industry*, Cambridge: CRAC.

Department of Industry (1980) *Industry/Education Liaison*, Industry/Education Unit: Department of Industry.

Douglas, M H (1975) Industrial Design and Production Projects in Secondary Schools, *Studies in Design Education and Craft*, 8.1.

Forrest, G (ed) (1996) *Experiences of Work: Current Issues and Developments*, Warwick: SCIP.

Gleeson, D (1993) Legislation for Change: Missed Opportunities in the Further and Higher Education Act, *British Journal of Education and Work*, 6, 2, 29–41.

Griffiths, T (1995) *European Partnerships: European Work Experience*, Warwick: SCIP.

Grubb, W and Lazerson M (1981) Vocational Solutions to Youth Problems: the Persistent Frustrations of the American Experience, *Educational Analysis*, Vol. 3, no. 2, pp. 91–104.

Hamner, T & Furlong, A (1996) Staying on: the effects of recent changes in educational participation for 17–19 year olds in Norway and Scotland, *Sociological Review*, 44, 4, 675–691.

Jamieson, I & Lightfoot, M (1981) Learning about Work, *Educational Analysis*, 3, 2.

Lawlor, S & McKay, F (1993) *English and Work Experience: An active learning resource for schools*, Warwick: SCIP.

Lazerson, M (1971) *Origins of the Urban School*, Cambridge, Massachusetts: Harvard University Press.

Manpower Services Commission (1981) *A New Training Initiative*, London: Manpower Services Commission.

Pyke, N (1996) Vocational Training Rejected, *Times Educational Supplement*, 18 October.

Rees, T L & Gregory, D (1981) Youth Employment and Unemployment: A Decade of Decline, *Educational Analysis*, 3, 2.

Robinson, P (1996) Rhetoric and Reality, *Britain's New Vocational Qualifications*, London: Routledge.

Skinner, W G (1970) Link Courses in Colleges of Further Education, Part 1, *Survey 4*, Staffordshire, Keele University (for Schools Council) April.

Watts, A G (1981) Schools Work and Youth: An Introduction, *Educational Analysis* 3, 2.

Willis, P (1978) *Learning to Labour*, London: Saxon House.

ENDPIECE 3

Justice Shallow

Justice Shallow was a regular contributor to *Education*
until its demise in 1996.

My dear Silence

In *'1066 and All That'* terms, it is, I suppose, a Good Thing to remind educators that many of their charges will end up in the world of work, and that it would, therefore, be sensible to vary their accustomed diet of social theory, poetry, truanting and New Age insightful experiences with compensating dollops of lessons based on the 'what it's like to get your hands dirty in the university of life' curriculum model. Where all this started is not easy to discover. Fragments of the impulse might be discovered in John Ruskin's attempts to persuade soppy undergraduates to forsake Aristophanes, and, instead, help him to build a useless road to nowhere just outside Oxford. And there are echoes of it in all those pale novels of the thirties in which decadent young men are sent down from Oxford for nameless offences, and told by their apoplectic, mill-owner fathers that they will have to seek redemption in the family firm, starting at the very lowest point, sorting out the tops from the noils under the pitiless eye of charge-hands with names like Seth Blatherthwaite and Herbert Oakenshaw.

By the late seventies, however, the subject had become too serious for idealism and romantic fiction. Cerebral men and women, with names like Gertrude Blatherthwaite and Giles Oakenshaw, poured out theses to show that members of the educated classes were congenitally hostile to trade, and much preferred to send their young to schools where discussion of the public sector borrowing requirement would be as repugnant as wearing a brown suit in the City. Governments became alarmed. Inflation, strikes and falling exports were crippling the country, and competitors, dastardly foreigners, were moving in to capture all our markets. The response was swift and decisive. Speeches were made. One Prime Minister said that education was grievously at fault, turning out only parasites – I suppose he meant lawyers, accountants, consultants, professors of education and members of parliament – instead of horny-handed sons of toil. He gave that speech, as I remember, at Ruskin College, but stopped short of encouraging his audience to rush from the hall and finish off old John's crumbling, grass-covered road, making thereby an appropriately practical interpretation of his argument. One junior minister, of a different party, later started his climb up the greasy pole by advocating that every school in the land should have a computer, and, thus, in place of the squeak of chalk on blackboard, and the scratch of pen on paper, a soothing electronic hum would hold children in thrall as they clicked along the keyboard to find out how the futures market was performing.

So, in the quick forge and working house of thought, perhaps in the deep cellars of Number 10, or along the dismal corridors of Elizabeth House a strategy was evolved. The forts, redoubts, salients, redans, lunets and bastions, built so cunningly by the education establishment, were to be stormed, sapped and mined by the shock-troops of industry. At education conferences, their captains, with chalk-stripe suits and baritone voices, leapt from podium to podium to tell us just where we were going wrong – deliciously ironic considering there was scant evidence of much going right in their own business ventures. One – and I have longed for most of my adult life to hear someone do this – actually advised us to read Samuel Smiles, but to my great disappointment did not go on to call for a repeal of the 1833 Factory Act. Thankfully, most of them stayed more or less in contemporary Britain, plying us with modish phrases about there now being windows of opportunity through which, as a matter of urgency, we should all pass – though, in my experience, such windows are usually twenty-seven floors up.

Government also pressed our friends to take their messages deep into the heartland of education management, and become members of the governing bodies of polytechnics, colleges and schools, there to show the political hacks, placemen, and the remote and ineffectual academics how the businesses really could be run. Some of them, to their eternal credit, stood wide-eyed with amazement that the business could be run at all from so miserable a financial base, and made no bones about letting their views be known. Others were placed at the advisory rather than effective end of education, and were asked to sit on national boards and committees. Royal Commissions had gone out of favour, seen to be as full of delays as the law, and no more productive than mules, so, like the huddled masses from Eastern Europe crossing to America, the tycoons sailed in to colonize the new-sprung quangos which ruled the smaller principalities and fiefdoms of education. I believe they found all that a drudgery. These highly intelligent men and women, used in their own boardrooms to vigorous command and speedy decision, suddenly came up against the subalterns of academia whose whole training had taught them that there are not two, but forty-two sides to every question, and who wore circumlocution and obfuscation as badges of pride. In a few places, however, like the Training and Enterprise Councils, they worked mainly with like-minded colleagues, and passed many a happy hour looking at balance sheets, devising mission statements, and learning, perhaps for the first time, what it is like to be caught in the twisting eddies and rip-tides of government policy, constant in nothing save inconstancy.

Above all, the government had initiatives. At the sound of that word, a minister's eyes sparkle, and his step becomes as light as a lover's in May, for it carries suggestions of imagination and resourcefulness and new beginnings. Alas, no sooner are these bold ships launched than they are sunk, forgotten or replaced – MSC, *fons et origo*: CPVE: YTS: TVEI, all now worm-eaten hulks rotting in scattered creeks and inlets, or lost beneath the sands as though they had never been.

Yet the thrust was a right one, and continues to be so. Educationalists usually do construct a world out of their own heads, and look to their pupils to inhabit it with them.

What's the word I'm looking for, Jeeves?
I think it might be 'solipsistic', sir.
That's the chap!

So it made sense to send in capable people from industry and business to attempt the task of deconstruction and reconstruction. Some failed, some became disillusioned, and yet others succeeded – not unlike the record of most human endeavour. Balance is all, for the important thing as far as education is concerned is to harry the zealots and the fanatics wherever they come from, and follow the wisdom of the old Church of England in keeping the means between extremes.

PART IV

Professional Concerns

13

EDUCATION, LEADERSHIP AND THE GLOBAL PARADOX

Michael Barber

Professor Michael Barber is Professor of Education and
Dean of New Initiatives at the Institute of Education.

The notion of 'the global paradox' comes from John Naisbitt's book of that
name. He defines this paradox as: 'The bigger the world economy, the more
powerful its smallest players' (Naisbitt, 1994). His underlying argument is
that, as the communications revolution transforms the global economy,
the smaller players – people and companies – become, paradoxically, a
great deal more powerful. 'Small' is not only beautiful, as Schumacher
argued a generation ago, but also more efficient and powerful. Hence large
companies are breaking themselves up into smaller business units, head offices
are being 'downsized' and increasing numbers of people are operating as
consultants and/or working from home. Hence too the 'democracy' of the
Internet.

It is not necessary to buy the whole of John Naisbitt's vision of a world
of consumers communicating with each other on their mobile telephones in
a global market place to recognise that the global paradox has tremendous
implications for education and therefore for educational leadership. Indeed,
the trend, noticeable in many countries, towards delegated budgets, site-based
management and self-managing schools demonstrates the impact that global
paradox thinking is already making. Less clear is what further impact it
will make in the future and what it implies for education early in the next
century.

This chapter is an attempt to explore that question. In the first section
it looks at the aims of education in the next decade. The second section
examines possible developments of the idea of self-management and 'the

power of the small.' The third section suggests what this might mean for educational leadership. In the conclusion it is argued that there is indeed an educational version of the global paradox which we need collectively to reflect on in the years ahead. The chapter draws extensively on British examples and it is admitted at the outset that this qualifies the extent to which generalisation is possible.

SECTION 1: THE AIMS OF EDUCATION IN THE NEXT MILLENNIUM

Across the globe, governments are attaching ever more importance to the success of national education systems. If there is one policy shared by every government it is that education should be given priority. The terminology varies from country to country but the underlying argument is the same everywhere. In Britain it tends to be put in terms of competitiveness. Hence in a recent White Paper (*Competitiveness: Helping Business to Win*, 1994), the Prime Minister, John Major, argues:

> We must prepare this country for the changing world of the next century. My aim is to create a climate in which our companies can beat the best . . . I believe we must give our young people the highest standards of education and training. Their skills will be the key to our future.   (DTI, 1994)

Tony Blair, Leader of the Opposition, argues in similar terms: 'I am convinced that the new challenges of the new century will demand that we tap the talents of every individual. Education is not just the basis of a healthy economy, but also of a healthy society' (Tony Blair speech, July 1994). The argument is international and crosses traditional party political lines. The argument is no doubt right too. I want to suggest, however, that the case for improving the quality of education across the globe is both wider and deeper than this, not least because in global terms the argument that education reform is aimed at national economic salvation is evidently inadequate.

Tony Blair's comment hints at an extension of the case for improving education: the quality of life in 21st century society will depend upon it. There is a link – not direct or simple but nevertheless powerful – between education and levels of crime, certainly in western societies. On the day after the trial of the two boys who were convicted of killing three year old James Bulger, one British newspaper commented chillingly that the two had nothing in common 'except a pact in underachievement.' This is one devastating example of the link between educational failure and other social problems including crime, family breakdown and poverty.

Improved education alone will not solve these social problems but it must surely be part of the solution. As the influence of the church has receded and the family as an institution diversified, so the importance of the school in facing these challenges has grown. Certainly there is no benefit in waiting

– as much of the social policy analysis of the 1960s suggested – until these social problems are solved before working for improvements in education.

Nor is educational progress necessary solely for economic and social reasons. It is surely increasingly important for the quality of democracy. Citizens of the late 20th century need to be literate in the broadest sense of the term. They need to be capable of understanding and sometimes criticising messages that come to them through a variety of media, electronic and otherwise. They need to be capable of seeking information from a huge range of possible sources. And they need the confidence to put their case when and where it needs to be put. This last ability, which is still in the possession of only a minority in even the most educated societies, is becoming ever more important as the pace of change, and hence decision-making, accelerates.

Beyond even these broad imperatives to improve the quality of education lies another more fundamental still. George Walker, Director-General of the International School in Geneva, expresses it thus:

> Why should [students] worry about the 90 million annual increase in the world's population, the half million who sought asylum in Western Europe in 1991, the 19 million refugees supported today by the UN High Commission for Refugees, the 400 million unemployed in the 'South', the annual global per capita expenditure on the UN of $1.90 compared to an arms expenditure of $150, ozone depletion, drought, famine and poverty?
>
> There is of course one very obvious reason . . . Anyone . . . over the age of 50, given reasonably good luck, can expect life to go on much as it is now until we achieve our generous life expectancy. Those of you between 20 and 50 will need unusually good luck for that to happen and anyone under 20 . . . has no chance at all. Something is going to have to change and this creates what a distinguished United States Ambassador to the UN in Geneva recently described as 'the culture of necessity'.
>
> (Walker, 1995)

In other words, the generation currently attending schools across the globe will be required to solve many problems which this generation and its predecessors have failed to solve. If that is not an overwhelming argument for improving education, then what is?

Moreover, it is an argument for an education with an international perspective. As George Walker explains:

> An international education does not imply the rejection of an individual's cultural roots, but it does mean educating young people to recognise and accept the global nature of the major issues that confront societies today . . . Yet until now in many societies the education system has been consciously designed and used by national governments to inculcate an awareness of national identity and often of nationalistic identity.
>
> (Walker, 1995)

It is in resolving this potential conflict of interest between the national and international that the educational equivalent of the global paradox may be helpful. For it seems that at the same moment that these global imperatives are coming to the fore, public education systems are increasingly delegating responsibility from national, regional or local levels of governments to the schools themselves. Precisely how, varies from place to place but the trend is unmistakable.

SECTION 2: THE FUTURE OF SELF-MANAGEMENT

The trend towards self-management in many parts of the world has been analysed by many researchers and commentators. Perhaps the most perceptive examinations have come from Brian Caldwell and Jim Spinks (1988, 1992). In their book *Leading the Self-Managing School* they argue that ten megatrends in education can be identified in the 1990s.

1. There will be a powerful but sharply focused role for central authorities, especially in respect of formulating goals, setting priorities and building frameworks for accountability.
2. National and global considerations will become increasingly important, especially in respect of curriculum and an education system that is responsive to national needs within a global economy.
3. Within centrally determined frameworks, government schools will become largely self-managing, and distinctions between government and non-government schools will narrow.
4. There will be unparalleled concern for the provision of a quality education for each individual.
5. There will be a dispersion of the educative function, with telecommunications and computer technology ensuring that much learning which currently occurs in schools . . . will occur at home and in the workplace.
6. The basics in education will be expanded to include problem-solving, creativity and a capacity for life-long learning and re-learning.
7. There will be an expanded role for the arts and spirituality, defined broadly in each instance; there will be a high level of 'connectedness' in curriculum.
8. Women will claim their place among the ranks of leaders in education, including those at the most senior levels.
9. The parent and community role in education will be claimed or reclaimed.
(Caldwell and Spinks, 1992, pp.7–8)

Certainly in support of my argument up to this point, the first three of these megatrends are of critical importance. In speculating about the British education scene, I have tried to develop an overall framework to examine the paradox implied in these megatrends whereby the growing concern of national governments to improve education uniformly across a whole population appears to involve delegating power to school level and thus encouraging diversity. The speculation resulted in Figure 13.1 which uses a categorisation from that light-hearted study of British history called *1066 And All That*. Sellars and Yeatman, its authors, define the Cavaliers as 'wrong but romantic' and the Roundheads as 'right but repulsive.'

	INEQUALITY	EQUALITY
DIVERSITY	WRONG BUT ROMANTIC	RIGHT AND ROMANTIC
UNIFORMITY	WRONG AND REPULSIVE	RIGHT BUT REPULSIVE

Figure 13.1 Categorisation of educational megatrends

In Britain over the last fifty years – generalising ruthlessly – the debate has been between a Conservative Party which favours diversity and tolerates inequality and a Labour Party which promises equality but accepts that uniformity is a consequence.

In the 1990s the polarity of this debate is beginning to break down and not before time. As if to make the point, Labour's recent education policy document was entitled *Diversity and Excellence* (Labour Party, 1995). The Conservative Government, meanwhile, is increasingly concerned to improve education for those who have traditionally failed in the system and recently announced a package of measures designed to promote school improvement, particularly for schools which are struggling (DfE, 1995). In other words, Labour is beginning to link its traditional concern for equality with a new recognition of diversity while the Conservative Party is beginning to recognise the threat posed both socially and economically by excessive educational inequality. Both parties are recognising not only the importance of equality in the sense of everyone in education reaching high standards but also of the huge growth of diversity in terms of race, religion, lifestyle and aspiration which has characterised the last fifty years.

Hence, increasingly, the chief question to ask about any issue of educational policy is what is the maximum amount of diversity consistent with equality? Or put more simply, how can we become the first generation in history to be both right and romantic?

This is where some of the other megatrends identified by Caldwell and Spinks become relevant. In the past the conflict between uniformity and diversity has tended to play itself out at the institutional level. Within a large bureaucracy – the education system – any diversity that has existed has been planned. Thus in Britain after the second world war there were to be grammar schools for 'the academic', technical schools for 'the technical' and secondary modern schools for everyone else. In Germany, similar divisions were planned. More recently in the United States, magnet school systems were established in large conurbations as a planned response to the need to promote racial integration in education. Similary, the British City Technology College programme is a planned central government intervention.

But in the 1990s, as Caldwell and Spinks identify, bureaucracies are collapsing, governments are increasingly controlling not through bureaucratic direction but through pulling financial levers and the imposition of various accountability models focused on outcomes. Meanwhile, institutions are being encouraged to take greater control of their own destinies. For example in England and Wales, where self-management was originally accompanied by a highly prescriptive National Curriculum, schools are now being urged to use their 'professional judgement' in making the curriculum work for them.

However, diversity at the level of the individual institution will always be limited. In order to play the social role expected of them by most governments, all publicly funded schools, regardless of how they choose to develop, will be expected to teach the basics of numeracy, literacy and technological competence, to develop among students the habits and skills of learning, to establish certain moral codes relating to living in communities and in demo- cratic society, and to provide students with some broad understanding of their place in time and space. We might call these the basics of the 21st century.

This leaves room for only limited diversity and many societies support, for example, religious schools, schools that specialise in a curriculum area or have a particular educational philosophy. The question is whether this is sufficient to solve the equality–diversity paradox, particularly given the fourth megatrend identified by Caldwell and Spinks, which suggests that 'There will be unparalleled concern for the provision of a quality education for each individual.' No amount of sorting, sifting and selecting is likely to fit each individual into precisely the institution that meets her or his needs. As one commentator remarked ironically about the model of education designed for post-war Britain: 'The suggestion of the Committee seems to be that the Almighty has benevolently created three types of child in just those proportions which would gratify education administrators' (Curtis, quoted in Barber, 1994). In any case, in rural or small town parts of the world, economics is likely to demand that one secondary school serves all the students and potential students in the area.

The equality–diversity paradox requires therefore that we do not continue to regard education and schooling as synonymous. Caldwell and Spinks' fifth megatrend makes the point: 'There will be a dispersion of the educative function, with telecommunications and computer technology ensuring that much learning which currently occurs in schools or institutions . . . will occur at home and in the workplace.' With this perspective in mind, the potential for diversity becomes vast. We need over the next decade to begin to think of a young person's learning happening in three strands. The first would be learning at school. Here the focus would be on the basics of the 21st century. School would also be the place in which educational advice, guidance and support was provided.

The second would be learning that might take place in a range of out-of-school settings: evenings, weekends and school holidays; camps, outdoor activity centres, music schools, dance schools, churches, sports centres or schools being used out of hours. In this strand, the focus would be on providing a rich diversity of opportunities in which enthusiastic expert teachers were matched with enthusiastic learners who had chosen to achieve in that discipline. These kinds of opportunities are currently extensively available to children whose parents can afford them. They would need to be made available to all if equality as well as diversity were to be provided.

Means would also need to be found of accrediting such provisions and controlling its quality. Tim Brighouse, Chief Education Officer in Birmingham, is developing proposals for a University of the First Age which would accredit learning of this kind as an extension of Britain's distance learning university, the Open University. It is an idea with immense potential. The third strand would be learning at home. Already many young people have access to unprecedented quantities of information and learning opportunities at home through technology. This information is often provided in ways which make it easily accessible and highly entertaining to use. The Microsoft Encarta programme alone – one CD – would represent a huge improvement on the information available in most homes across the globe.

Research undertaken at Keele University confirms that information technology not only helps to motivate students, it also assists them to understand better, to learn more quickly and to carry on learning in the absence of a teacher (Denning, 1995). If its potential is to be exploited, then young people must be able to make use of it at home so that the amount of time they spend on structured learning is extended and the quality of their homework assignments and assessed course work is improved. Again this raises a major issue of equality. As information technology becomes more pervasive and unit costs fall it should, however, become perfectly possible for every student to have access at home to unimaginable learning opportunities. Where, through poverty, the homes themselves are the problem, education systems may need to structure out-of-school study support systems based in community locations.

All of this is now well within the realms of possibility. Indeed, every aspect of it is already happening somewhere. The next question is what it implies for educational leadership.

SECTION 3: LEADERSHIP, EQUALITY AND DIVERSITY

A study published in 1995 by the British National Commission on Education examines schools which have succeeded in disadvantaged circumstances: hence its title, *Success Against the Odds* (Maden and Hillman, 1995). Each of the eleven schools covered by the study was evaluated by a team consisting of a leading educationist, a business person and a representative of the local community. Looking at the eleven together provides many fascinating insights. Perhaps most fascinating of all is the insight it provides into the nature of successful educational leadership. Of course, eleven schools in one country hardly provides a firm foundation for generalisation. Nevertheless, the results of the study are important and indicative of a trend.

The leaders of those eleven schools are not in the Lee Iacocca heroic mould. Nor are they axe-wielding barbarians demanding that their staff are either for them or against them. They are people with a vision. It is a vision of a school as a learning community, an organisation which, whatever the pressures, be they financial, political or social, always ensures that teaching and learning are given the highest priority.

The vision is communicated not so much through rhetoric as through living it. It infuses their daily activity; the questions they ask the pupils, the conversations they have with staff, the choices they make about their use of time. Margaret Maden and Josh Hillman, who edited the study, describe this, brilliantly, as 'omnipresence.' They write of one of the heads in the study:

> Each Monday morning, she spends a couple of hours in a different class, observing the teacher and talking to the children about their work and she follows this up with a feedback discussion with the teacher.

Of another head, they say:

> She knows the name and family circumstances and progress of every child [and] is a frequent visitor to all classrooms.
>
> (Maden and Hillman, 1995)

Some of the heads go further and communicate their vision on a wider local or national stage. In spite of the demands this makes, it often reinforces rather than detracts from the communication of the vision within the school since it helps to enhance the respect the staff has for the head. What comes through in most of the case studies is a firm and quiet effectiveness rather than charisma. At one of the schools, the head is described as giving the impression of 'irresistible cheerfulness in a low key and understated way.'

The study confirms the findings of many others. The evidence of both the business management and the education literature is that effective leaders encourage and foster leadership throughout the organisation. It is a characteristic of many improving schools that staff at all levels are encouraged to take responsibility and to take risks and expect the support of the head teacher when an idea fails. In short, they are encouraged, in Michael Fullan's memorable phrase, to 'practise fearlessness' (Fullan, 1991).

Many effective leaders of schools also emphasise the extent to which they themselves are learners as well as educators. They may not go as far as Roland Barth's suggestion and call themselves 'Head Learner' (Barth, 1990) but the concept captures the spirit of their attitude. Pat Collarbone, former head teacher of the rapidly improving Haggerston school in Hackney described herself as the 'lead learner' of her school, where the idea of everyone – including all staff – being considered a learner is constantly promoted. This attitude helps to ensure that the school is a learning organisation which not only encourages the formal involvement of all staff in professional development, but also involves turning many aspects of the school routine – staff meetings, budget decisions and daily briefings, for example – into learning events.

Underpinning this kind of approach, which has an increasing currency, is an emphasis on monitoring, evaluation and review. Evidence of the schools' effect is collected systematically, debated openly among the staff and used continuously in decision-making. Both consequence and cause of collecting and using evidence is a questioning of all practice. The idea that 'we do things this way because that is how we've always done them' ceases to be influential. Instead, change is assumed, welcomed and shaped. I have described this process, to be observed in many improving schools, as restless self-evaluation (Barber, 1996).

Achieving this approach to leadership is demanding and requires people of exceptional talent. This makes it all the more remarkable that it is becoming increasingly widespread. If this is the cutting edge now, what changes or extensions to the patterns of leadership might be anticipated as the implications of the equality–diversity paradox become clear?

One is that schools are likely to need to become increasingly effective at providing advice and guidance to young people about their educational progress and the choices that are available to them. If more options become available through out-of-school learning and home learning then good advice and guidance will be more necessary than ever and at a younger age. This would be a substantial extension of the role of the school with major implications for teachers and Headteachers.

In addition, advice and guidance of a personal and social as well as educational nature may become increasingly necessary. The pace of change in the world, the uncertainty of the job market, the break-up of traditional models of the family and increased secularisation are all likely to cause young people to seek security and advice from teachers and schools. The same social forces are also likely to increase the importance of school as the social institution which establishes for young people the moral codes which govern democratic societies. Thus creating in school a positive ethos, in which young people are respected as future citizens, is likely to become an increasingly important task for school leaders.

Another area of leadership likely to increase in importance is networking. In the increasingly diverse educational world, school leaders will be more part of an ever changing network of contacts and less part of hierarchical bureaucracies. Their ability to function through and build influence in a network will become skills of the greatest importance. The networks, furthermore, will, as a result of the impact of technology, be less geographically defined and more interest defined. It is, for example, becoming perfectly possible to be part of a very close international network committed to promoting a particular philosophy or aspect of school leadership. The Institute of Education here in London has responded to this trend by establishing a Leadership Centre for London which will not only provide a network of support, training and development for head teachers in the London region, but also unite them to a growing international network of school leaders.

CONCLUSIONS

Finally and perhaps most daunting of all, as the range of international challenges (which create 'the culture of necessity' referred to earlier) becomes more obviously apparent, school leaders will need to be able to promote, above and beyond local and national understanding, a genuine international perspective among children and young people. Governments may or may not promote this role but, whether they do or do not, in the unfolding sequence of the next decade, it seems to me that school leaders will need to see themselves increasingly as citizens of the world. This in turn has major implications for the professional development of the school leaders of the present and the future.

If that sounds implausible, unrealistic or naïve, it is worth noting that in the world financial markets and many areas of business, it has already occurred. How else could a 'rogue trader' in Singapore, dealing in Japanese futures bring down a London bank and end up being arrested in Frankfurt? How else can the defining moment of the Major government – Black Wednesday – be interpreted? The global markets destroyed in an afternoon both the policy of the British government and its relations with the European Union. These markets are beyond the regulation of individual government. Perhaps the best hope is that they operate within some global respect for democratic values. If the global market place is to operate within any such framework of morality based on notions of democratic society and focused on solving the huge range of global challenges ahead, then the time left for schools and their leaders to catch up is limited.

We need to develop and refine our own concept – as educators world-wide – of the global paradox. For the purposes of starting an international conversation on the theme I would frame it thus:

> As the significance of education's smallest players – schools, teachers and learners – increases, adherence to a vision of global education and world citizenship will become ever more important.

This paper is loosely argued in places and based on a range of evidence which is too limited. It seeks to reach out in the dark for solutions rather to find them. Its conclusions are therefore tentative. Its aim is not to end an argument but to begin one.

REFERENCES

Barber, M (1994) *The Making of the 1944 Education Act*, London: Cassell.

Barber, M (1996) *The Learning Game: Arguments for an Education Revolution,* London: Gollancz.

Barth, R (1990) *Improving Schools from Within,* San Francisco: Jossey Bass.

Blair, A (1994) Speech to conference in Manchester (unpublished).

Caldwell, B & Spinks J (1988) *Leading the Self-Managing School,* Lewis: Falmer.

Caldwell, B J and Spinks, J M (1992) *Leading the Self-Managing School,* Lewes: Falmer.

Denning, T (1995) *Information Technology and Pupil Motivation,* Keele: Keele University.

Department for Education (1995) *Improving Schools Initiative,* London: HMSO.

Dept. of Trade & Industry (1994) *Competitiveness: Helping Business to Win,* Government White Paper, London: HMSO.

Fullan, M (1991) *The New Meaning of Educational Change,* London: Cassell.

Labour Party (1995) *Diversity and Excellence,* London: Labour Party.

Maden, M & Hillman, J (1995) Lessons in Success in National Commission on Education in *Success Against the Odds,* London: Routledge.

Naisbitt, J (1994) *The Global Paradox,* London: Nicholas Brealey Publishing.

Walker, G (1995) To Educate the Nations, Harry Ree Lecture, Settle, UK (unpublished).

14

POLITICS AND EDUCATION

A. H. Halsey

Professor A. H. Halsey is Emeritus Professiorial Fellow
of Nuffield College, Oxford. He was Professor of Social
and Administrative Studies at University of Oxford from
1978–1990.

The idea of improving upbringing by political action has been a theme
throughout my life. I wrote in my autobiography (Halsey, 1996), and it
is true, that my experiences with the politics of education deserve another
book. But perhaps this chapter will serve: I have published several other
books written primarily from a sociological point of view. One truth, or at
least partial truth, would be that my big chance for action came in 1965 when
Anthony Crosland asked me to join him at the Department of Education (then
in Curzon Street) to advise on the sociological side of educational reform.
He told Maurice Kogan (Kogan, 1971) that the 'mind of Whitehall' had
been much impressed in the 1950s by the reappraisal of latent talent in the
population and the powerful potential of schools in alliance with popular
ambition to enlarge the flow of able youngstcrs, malc and female, from
secondary schools into colleges. The *Early Leaving Report* of 1956, I was
often told, exactly reflected my and Mrs Floud's impact on policy thinking
in this broad respect. I had, for example, 'proved' in a *British Journal of
Sociology* article (1956) that an untapped reservoir of working-class talent
was going to waste, and that genetic determinants of intelligence in no way
explain the middle-class bias of educational selection. The sociological tide
was powerful, and also powerfully backed by psychologists who criticised the
11+ procedure and, later, the alleged fraudulence of Cyril Burt's hereditarian
data. At Kungalv in Sweden in 1961 the story was extended over all the OECD

countries and I was able to formulate the summary that, in the modern world, economic growth created popular ability and also supplied the resources to pay for the deserved opportunities of working-class children.

All this clearly fitted Crosland's own policy analysis in his *Future of Socialism* (Crosland, 1956). We really did have an alternative to nationalisation as the means for creating a socialist society (and incidentally one based on liberal rather than Marxist ideas). No wonder Edward Boyle, his conservative opposite number, could in effect advocate a bipartisan educational policy. Oddly however, one massive implication – the expansion of higher education – though not ignored, was rather neglected by Crosland in that, unlike Harold Wilson, he failed to recognise the great significance of another practical policy, the founding and the expansion of the Open University (what Wilson was calling the University of the Air).

A major deficiency in my own capacity to advise was my woeful ignorance of the anthropology of the civil service – a strange tribe with more affinity to the adjutant and the bureaucracy of the RAF than I appreciated and with a more theoretical, less urgent, drive to get things done than I had learned as a sanitary inspector's boy in my local authority.

One learns, but slowly. I wrote to Tony Crosland afterwards in 1968, referred to Saul Bellow's *Henderson the Rain King* and wished that we could try the wrestling match in Curzon Street again only this time 'for real'. Tony, I knew, read Bellow and would enjoy the analogy in that he was the tribal chief while the visitor was the hired practitioner of a dubious expertise – rain-making in Henderson's case, ignorance-dispelling in mine. At that time I had yet to learn the esoteric habits of the Civil Servants and the distinctive self-conception of the education ministry. Quite innocently I reviewed a book edited by Hugh Thomas, *Crisis in the Civil Service* (Thomas, 1968) – an appraisal of ministers, civil servants and special advisers and, by and large, agreed with the authors in their criticisms of civil servants as less than perfect instruments for the attainment of socialism.

A debate began at the end of the fifties with the prospective possibility of Labour's return to power. The Civil Service had had no serious overhaul since the 1870s when it was effectively fashioned to the purpose of a night-watchman state. The underlying theme of the book was that such a Civil Service could never serve as an engine for the establishment of socialism and indeed, while it remained unreformed, was a major liability in the business of keeping the Island afloat in a complex, dangerous, changing and ungentlemanly world.

The three main contributors, Thomas Balogh, Roger Opie and Dudley Seers were all economists and all outsiders who were brought into Whitehall by Labour. They joined the 'stampede' for the 8.52 from Oxford to Paddington on 16 October, 1964. It was part of their argument that the stampede was much exaggerated, that too few professional economists worked in Whitehall. Their contention was that the Civil Service is fatally weak in its structure 'favouring centralization and this dilettantism' (Balogh). 'The Treasury knights are . . . the most powerful politicians in Britain today (Seers). 'The relative power of ministers and officials . . . is heavily and increasingly in the hands of officials' (Opie). There was not enough 'expert knowledge in the policy-making machine' (Balogh). 'The archetypal entrant to the Service has, after all, a First in Modern History from Oxford, indicating not only that he can pass exams but as a bonus will be very well-mannered and know next to nothing of the modern world' (Opie). 'Lack of any education or even systematic reading on economic questions, for example, does not prevent them from expressing strong, even if imprecise, views on subjects such as international liquidity, or commodity policy, views often based on the fashionable journalism of a few years previously' (Seers).

And the remedies proposed were to reduce the power of the hierarchy. Here the suggestions included putting the job of the head of the Civil Service into commission, the creation of a 'cabinet' and an economic section to advise all important ministers (i.e. the minister should bring his own immediate advisers with him when he takes office), the setting up of parliamentary committees in each ministerial field with power to question not only ministers but also senior civil servants on the reasons for policy. The redrawing of the Official Secrets Act so as to cover protection against espionage alone was proposed by Hugh Thomas on the grounds that publicity is in fact the sole means by which ministers can keep control of their civil servants and that 'any serious study of the present times or any serious sociological analysis based on up-to-date data', is impossible under the Act as at present worded.

The authors also wanted to increase the expertise of the Civil Service by recruiting trained economists, developing the Civil staff college, providing for a wider occupational experience within the Civil Service by exchanges with the universities, industry and international organisations and by encouraging the retirement of the elderly and ineducable.

The book as a whole was an outspoken contribution to a vital debate. It was, I thought, a pity that our present rules excluded the permanent professional civil servants from joining in. In consequence I received a letter from Herbert Andrew, the permanent secretary to the Department complaining that I had perpetrated 'a McCarthyite smear' on the integrity of my Curzon Street colleagues. I was astounded as well as angry, not having yet understood that the tacit rules of Whitehall were totally different from those of academia with respect to the discussion of values and attitudes in a seminar. My fault of course, but I had failed to see that the distinction between the seminar and the pulpit invented and maintained by the medieval university was, or at least was not yet, recognised by civil servants. I spoke to Tony about it. He grinned and assumed a pompous posture at the same time and insisted that 'these attacks on me (i.e. him) must immediately stop'. We then went on as before. But I have always regretted Andrew's misunderstanding. He eventually became ordained as an Anglican priest after retirement and was a thoroughly decent man.

My interest in advising Crosland was preceded by my admiration of his declared intentions for education as set out in *The Future of Socialism*. These Labour policies could simply be inferred from my own experience as working-class learner in my family, my village, my church, my schools and the night school. The route to a better society had to encompass equal opportunity, the best public services that the country could afford, no private privilege, and resources distributed to the weak as well as the intellectually strong. I knew we didn't know enough about the conditions of learning so I was happy enough to be taken on ostensibly to manage the research budget of the DES, having Tony's assurance that he would be accessible to me and would ask my opinion before deciding on anything at all central to the socialist programme of educational reform.

The whole thing was less successful in practice than in theory. I understood the sociology of learning, he was the master of the politics of education and, of course, he made the decisions. It was all too rushed and I didn't have nearly enough time with him though he worked hard at it, and his wife Susan was as helpful as she could be. In retrospect I realise that I spent too little time in Curzon Street and at the Crosland house in Landsdowne Road, and it was all precipitously brought to an end by Tony's translation to the Board of Trade.

One hugely important thing did go on – the Educational Priority Areas project. EPA was an exceptional educational crusade. Crosland, Young (then chairman of the SSRC) and I were devotedly in favour of comprehensive, neighbourhood, responsive schools at the nursery, primary and secondary stages of education. We recognised the tradition of 'missionary' school teaching. We wanted to carry out some local educational anthropology to identify what would work most effectively in raising levels of aspiration and interest among families in slum school districts. We were appalled by the so-called Black paper opposition. My friend and colleague Eric Midwinter dubbed them the Ku Klux Klan in mortar boards. The Right in general and Mrs Thatcher and Rhodes Boyson in particular supported them. Nevertheless we did get circular 10/65, and a neighbourhood school movement did find enthusiasts throughout Britain. The arguments still go on. The time necessary for amnesia to set in has now passed in a country feebly wedded to political arithmetic: so there is much talk about bringing back the selective apparatus of 11+ and even the antiquated prejudice that the IQ test will sort out the sheep from the goats. What is missing is a sophisticated sociology of the partnership between family and school from which would now follow a recognition that parental functions have to be undertaken by schools in a democracy of employed and lone mothers (as they once were for upper-class boys from families serving the empire overseas).

In a way it all goes back to my own schooling from which I derived two convictions. First schooling in the wide sense of upbringing is a total process involving the family, the community, the church and the mass media (what we then called the papers and the wireless) as well as the school itself. We still do not pay enough attention to the interactions between these social agencies. The current fashion is to attack local public education authorities and to 'empower' parents. But, whatever the fashion, the interventions are politics.

Second, I became convinced that the country needed more education and that all its children deserved what was given to me – a free place in a grammar school – but if possible without the conflict between school and home that such an education entailed; without social snobbery; and with the technical school element that was sadly neglected in the drive towards larger grammar school provision. In short we needed comprehensive schools. Yet all the present political signs are in the opposite direction. Education must be put into the market and there should be a rapid return to selection wherever possible.

Accordingly I want to put forward a personal defence of the educational and social cause to which I have devoted a lot of my life, my research, and my leisure. All my five children have attended comprehensive schools. I have been a comprehensive governor and have written books and articles galore on behalf of comprehensive reform.

One element in all this is the declining, almost disappearing, tradition of 'missionary' administration which depended in large measure on dedicated teachers. Management is no substitute. Alec Clegg was for me the doyen with a fabulous record in the West Riding. He knew his schools and turned up in them as if he never had anything else to do. He understood the teachers and the children: knew what made them laugh and cry, and was proud of their every achievement.

There was a fire brigade competition once, centred on Wakefield, and the schoolboys were clocking in the crews from other towns who raced in to the County Hall. One boy said to the driver of the first tender, 'And where 'ave you come from then?' 'Kingston, Jamaica', said the driver. 'That's champion' said the lad, 'Barnsley's not 'ere yet'. Some Americans, hired to fight for Lyndon Johnson's war on poverty with a 'head start' programme, came to seek British wisdom at Ditchley Park. Alec Clegg insisted that they come immediately to the West Riding to disabuse themselves of any idea that the worst schools were slum schools. He knew exactly where to take them. It was a bit like the advertisement I once saw on the side of a van in Birmingham:

> I. PATEL & DAUGHTER, PLUMBERS
> You've had the Cowboys,
> Now try the Indians.

Among teachers Harry Rée was similarly a hero, and a charismatic one too, with his gallant war record supporting the Maquis in France, and his conversion to popular education in the fifties and sixties. He was the headmaster of Watford Grammar School where I did my doctoral field work in 1950–52. He took the chair of education in York when Eric James was the Vice Chancellor and then went on to comprehensive classroom teaching in London. Love of learning and teaching, illuminated Harry's life and inspired young and old around him. I don't know how this type of missionary teaching is generated – for example in Durkheim's Third Republic in France or in Newsom's Hertfordshire – but I see it as the spear-head of central and spiritual remoralisation. Of course, we shall need big salary increases for teachers, but the respect of the local community as against absurdly highly-paid managers, administrators and businessmen are no less essential. Of course, we shall need a General Teaching Council to raise morale as in Scotland. At all events we must have talent in front of the children if we want a civilised and prosperous tomorrow.

I could never quite make out where Tony Crosland stood on education. He was a large, formidable, aggressive, outspoken man: always like the biggest and rudest boy in the playground, so likely to be feared. In Birmingham he came to see me and Geoffrey Ostergaard about our study of democracy in co-operatives. Gaitskell had given him the job of healing an ailing arm of the working-class movement while he was temporarily dislodged from the House of Commons. He had won South Gloucestershire in 1950, lost it in 1955, worked for Gaitskell and re-entered parliament in 1964, as the member for Grimsby. He spent a short time in George Brown's Department for Economic Affairs and then became Secretary of State for Education in January 1965. It was obvious to me that he was not especially well informed, which is not in the least surprising since he had been reared in the private sector and at Trinity College, Oxford (which was much the same and much despised by Balliol next door). He wasn't at all fond of the universities for much the same reasons, though he was very definitely one of the left-wing intellectuals and indeed belonged with distinction to the last generation of highly educated PPE politicians. More recently this route has closed and the brains come from Scottish Law Schools. To outward appearances at least, immediately before the Second War, Crosland was a clever playboy, arguing with Dennis Healey and carefully nurtured by Philip Williams.

Yet no less certainly he was committed to educational expansion and reform – the one to generate an informed democracy, the other to release opportunity for children from the stranglehold of wealth. It was all in the context of revisionism (in which he was a latter-day Bernstein, tutored by Williams) whereas I held the same educational ideals out of direct experience of a working-class scholarship schooling and never thought it worthwhile to argue with communists. Education for Tony, as expounded in *The Future of Socialism* (1956) was the motor of revisionist modern socialism – the path to high productivity and to high participation. He was, unconsciously, a follower of the youthful Alfred Marshall who had expounded similar views in 1872 to Cambridge undergraduates though not calling it socialism, either revisionist or mainstream. In that theoretical sense I never doubted him though I respected his economics more than his sociology (which seemed to come mostly from liberal Americans like Bell and Lipset).

In any case I knew that his burning personal ambition was to make an impact on economic policy and he wanted to control a central economic ministry. Harold Wilson was, of course, punishing him for his loyalty to Gaitskell by sending him to what they both regarded as a rather secondary position. All rather confused, I thought. Nevertheless it did give him a seat in the Cabinet and theoretically, that is according to his own academic theory, it was a key ministry for socialist engineering.

Again such social engineering implied careful re-appraisal of the connection of schooling to work, and here Crosland was again handicapped by his background. Like most public or grammar school boys, he systematically

misunderstood the whole area of so-called further education, which, especially
in those days, constituted a vast apparatus of second, third and nth chances
for those, mostly working-class men, who had 'failed' the grammar school
11+. So once again the British, especially the English, failed to pursue the
essentially socialist target of a 'first-class world work force'. The technical
schools were allowed to decline: the vocational qualifications were allowed
to persist in the obscurity of City and Guilds and regional associations –
both somehow suggesting medieval or provincial irrelevance. The delayed
and debilitated drive towards university expansion was allowed to avoid
industrial cities altogether, and to appear, not as the Victorians insisted at
the centre of population growth, but instead at pre-industrial green field sites
named after places which could have been Oxford or Cambridge had it not
been for minor accidents in the history of the country.

True the Industrial Training Boards were encouraged to some extent.
Tony set Maurice Kogan, the energetic ex-secretary of Bridget Plowden's
committee, to foster them. But he also relied heavily on Toby Weaver to
advance the doctrine that something called the public sector (in fact local
non-university colleges) could be recognised by central government and
given a boost on the grounds that they would respond readily to expansion
plans while 'autonomous' universities would not. Some of us, including Fred
Dainton and Asa Briggs, pointed out that this was a calumny. The principle of
binary development was announced in a speech at Woolwich. Here is Susan
Crosland's (1982) account.

> Toby Weaver was now the senior official concerned with higher educa-
> tion. He proposed the binary policy to Tony. Tony seized it, amended
> it, made it his own. Near the end of April 1965 he made the famous
> Woolwich Speech – putting in some offensive remarks bound to upset
> people. 'Let us now move away from our snobbish caste-ridden hierar-
> chical obsession with university status,' was one. The next thing was
> to determine where to move from there. With the help of Weaver and
> others, he invented the polytechnics as a make-weight to the universities
> – 'which took courage, was revolutionary, and was right,' Weaver
> said. Tony had to struggle for the intellectual cohesion with which
> he defended the binary policy to democratise higher education; he
> succeeded in altering the terms of the debate: the Robbins attitudes lost
> their dominance. The polytechnics – related to the needs of technology
> and industry – were to stand alongside the universities, not inferior but
> different. In 1966 thirty polytechnics were created.

We modified the principle towards a more pluralistic reality the following
year, but the damage was already done. I never saw the Woolwich speech
until after it was delivered. Moreover, Tony stuck to his and Toby Weaver's
prejudice that the binary division was correct. He still believed in it when
I talked to him in Oxford in 1976, though he knew that I was a unitary
advocate. Neither of us knew at that point, though it was predictable, that
eventually a Tory government would abolish the binary system by the simple

device of allowing all institutions of higher education to call themselves universities while funding them as if they were polytechnics. In this way the established and internationally acknowledged excellence of the British traditional universities (Scottish Redbrick, New and Oxbridge) was publicly destroyed while international statistics recorded a huge leap in enrolments to 30 per cent of the relevant age group. In Tony's youth it had been 3 per cent. Quite apart from the Open University, which Harold Wilson installed Jennie Lee to cultivate, the truly radical possibility of 'another Robbins', advocated for example by Robin Marris, was ignored, and a debate about who should pay by what mechanism still goes on.

Still worse, the case against Crosland could be extended also to secondary schooling. Although she never intended it, Susan Crosland, in her much applauded biography (S. Crosland, 1982), gave every lazy or reactionary journalist or politician a devastatingly effective 'sound bite' by quoting a crude outburst from her tired husband to her at Landsdowne Road.

> He was driven mad by the obtuseness of those who claimed grammar schools did not affect comprehensives despite the undeniable fact that the former creamed off the more gifted children. Following a dinner with four of the teachers' associations – 'Joint 4' – his tread was ominous as he mounted the stairs. He stopped at our bedroom door. 'Good evening. You'd better come in the study.' I put my novel aside and got smartly out of our bed, wondering what had caused this latest vexation. 'If it's the last thing I do, I'm going to destroy every fucking grammar school in England,' he said. 'And Wales. And Northern Ireland.' 'Why not Scotland?' I asked out of pure curiosity. 'Because their schools come under the Secretary of State for Scotland.' He began to laugh at his inability to destroy their grammar schools.

His true opinions are more soberly stated later on the same page. But any serious students of Crosland's educational thought would be better advised to read his own *The Future of Socialism*, or *The Conservative Enemy*, or *Socialism Now*, where he makes it crystal clear that his anger was directed first and foremost against 'public' (i.e. commercial) not grammar schools. 'I have never been able to understand why socialists have been so obsessed with the question of grammar schools, and so indifferent to the much more glaring injustice of the independent schools' (Crosland *The Future of Socialism*, 1956, p.261). He really agreed with me that comprehensive schools are essentially the policy of taking grammar plus technical schooling to all our children. Moreover he had insisted in *The Conservative Enemy* that a Labour Government must give high priority to the reform of the public schools. The objective must be to assimilate them into the state system. The public schools should give most of their places to children who do not pay. A token number of free places was quite unacceptable. 'We must either have a radical reform or none at all.' A Labour Government should proceed if possible by agreement. To impose a scheme which wholly changed the character of the schools would cause all the teachers to leave. If the public schools refused to accept voluntary reform, then the Government must legislate. 'The object of legislation would be not to prohibit all private fee-paying, which would be an intolerable restriction of personal liberty, but, by regulating the conditions under which education is bought and sold, to secure a more equitable distribution of educational resources between different classes of the nation'.

It was, however, never completely clear where his prejudices ended and his calm political analysis began. One, perhaps too fanciful, way of putting it is to say that his politics were an extension of infantile struggle with his father – an exclusive Plymouth Brethren sectarian. Too crude no doubt, but I was once struck by his exaggerated respect for Eric Ashby's tall, unbending rectitude. Tony explicitly told me he was afraid of him. I also sometimes thought that Tony's educational politics were a complicated internal battle between his love/hate for Oxford and his wish to identify with his Grimsby constituents.

I might go further and declare the whole experience of Crosland politics applied to education as a disaster were it not for three things. First, although putting economic policy first, Tony was searingly honest once he attended to the problem before him – and that he did in Curzon Street where the civil servants loved him.

Second, when I became his adviser on the sociology side, having learned a lot about education in Britain, the OECD countries, and the USA, I was influenced by Philip Williams (by that time an established fellow of Nuffield College) who I guess, recommended me. Philip was a sobersides in ordinary matters though a passionate anti-Marxist Gaitskellite, labour supporter. These characteristics together with his extreme devotion to Tony from undergraduate days, enabled me to overcome distaste towards the politician as a person. For Crosland not only had the external stigmata of an exaggerated Oxford voice and flamboyant dress but was also a profligate drinker and philanderer. All this was doubtless understandable as a reaction to the Plymouth Brethren background. So Tony's love of freedom was fetishist, driven, immoderate. Alcohol, cigars, women, even opera, were avidly consumed, Life's candle was burned at both ends and in the middle, and so did not last long even with his tremendous physique. Because he was physically, a big man, others tended to fear him. He wanted to see himself as the proponent of libertarian socialism and me as a stern egalitarian. I didn't see it like that: I saw us both as both. But the English sin in education, I thought, was inequality while his great fear was that we might impose unfreedom on those who wanted to send their children to schools in the private sector.

I never wanted the Public Schools Commission and thought that Newsom and Donnison could more profitably employ their time. He thought a full enquiry was politically obligatory. I believed a bargain could be struck (he thought imposed) based on calculations of the cost of boarding (in state boarding schools) and otherwise insisting on equal expenditure per head, and involving the abolition of charitable status. This surely would have met his libertarian scruples. But underneath he was reluctant and convinced that nobody really cared about such things. All polls, he kept saying, show education to be low among popular political priorities. This may have been true then: it is certainly not so now.

Third, his successors were much worse. Patrick Gordon Walker apparently didn't know what to do with an inherited adviser. I felt like Charlie Chaplin in *City Lights* where a toff would get drunk and take Charlie home, swearing eternal comradeship, and then have him thrown out in the morning as a person unknown. Ted Short was not much better.

Shirley Williams took the job more seriously. I remember defending her stoutly against civil servants (in 1968 when she came as Minister of State) who claimed that she behaved more like an executive officer than a minister of the crown. When she eventually became Secretary of State in the 1970s I scarcely saw her. She never invited me to return to my previous advisory role. And then for me there was the fatal night at a hotel in Bath in 1982 when she and Peter Jenkins (Guardian) tried all evening to persuade me to join the Social Democratic Party. I don't think Crosland would ever have joined.

In any case today we have to remind ourselves that a socialist future is still possible in education, meaning priority for investment in children – in their families, their pre-schooling, their primary schools, their essentially grammar secondary education, and the open Californian opportunity on opportunity for tertiary college and life-long learning. A combination of progressive graduate taxation and also progressive general taxation would give us the necessary funding. The idea of learning banks has come in the 1990s. My fear is that economic liberal propaganda, the casino philosophy, and cheating the social services and the income tax collector, may have undermined popular willingness to pay the taxes needed to support the welfare state which we affirm, in principle, that we want for the country. There are even, I must sadly add, signs of lack of resolve among the Labour Party leaders, driven no doubt by the paramount importance of office. The Harman case in 1996 was a jolt. Blair's own choice, admittedly for a Catholic school where only interviews of prospective parents stand as a selective device, can be defended only by rather tortuous logic. Among the leaders resolute unification of family with party loyalty much surely be a necessary basis for long-run confidence from a democratic electorate.

Though I never worked directly with John Tomlinson, I was always aware of his support for my now unfashionable views. He was a sturdy Cleggite. We were both implausible members of what came in the eighties to be dismissed by the Right as the educational establishment. I hope and believe that our time will come again. If not I fear that Britain will descend to barbarism and that provincial children of the working class will never know that, once upon a time, enlightened school reformers were energetically building one nation of civilised and skilful citizens and workers.

REFERENCES

Crosland, C A R (1956) *The Future of Socialism*, London: Cape.
Crosland, S (1982) *Tony Crosland*, London: Cape.

Halsey, A H (1996) *No Discouragement: An autobiography*, Basingstoke: MacMillan.

Halsey, A H (1956) Genetics, Social Structure and Intelligence, *British Journal of Sociology*, 9, 15–28.

Kogan, M (1971) *The Politics of Education*, Harmondsworth: Penguin.

Thomas, H (ed) (1968) *Crisis in the Civil Service*, London: Blend.

15

EDUCATION MANAGEMENT IN HARD TIMES

Maurice Kogan

Professor Maurice Kogan is Professor of Government and
Joint Director of the Centre for the Evaluation of Public
Policy and Practice at Brunel University. He was Acting
Vice Chancellor of Brunel University from 1989 to 1990.

It is a good time for prophecy; prophets flourish at times of disorder and
break-up. It can be fairly said that the educational management scene is not
far from that state. Fifteen years ago none of us could predict that we would
experience not only Bosnia but also Kenneth Baker, Kenneth Clarke, John
Patten and a host of Savanorolas and Rasputins, all prepared to visit their
own version of good thinking on the schools. How interesting, too, that those
producing chaos are those who profess belief in order and control.

There are different ways in which education leaders and administrators
can seek to change the world. A long while ago Harry Rée celebrated one
version, the finely balanced humanism, creative constructivism and implicit
condescension of the founder of the Cambridgeshire Village Colleges, Henry
Morris (Rée, 1973). There were many others with green fingers – Alec Clegg
of the West Riding of Yorkshire, Stuart Mason of Leicestershire and John
Newsom of Hertfordshire, of whom it was said that he went about the
county with a trumpet in one hand and a trowel in another. I recall a
visit with Edward Boyle, then the Parliamentary Secretary, at the end of
the 1950s to a local authority where we attended the farewell ceremony
to a long standing Chief Education Officer. He recounted how, when he
had first come to the small, industrial and slum ridden county borough
some decades before, he had asked himself, 'What good can come from
Bootle?', but was now able to point to its new schools and how the service

was bringing the full educational experience to its people as provided for in the 1944 Act.

Others will give testimony to John Tomlinson's contribution to British education as an administrator, academic and as a leading figure in so many initiatives at the national level. He has been unfortunate in his time in that his particular brand of analytic power, empathy with good practice and practitioners and public action through consensus have not been compatible with the change models of the last two decades, but his influence has been pervasive and, if coined in a period of difficulty, will prove to be money in the bank for better times.

His value system and motivation are compatible with the position taken in this paper. He has described his reasons for becoming an educational administrator in the following terms:

> I have always been interested in the overall scheme of things and how that changes, develops and can be helped to improve . . . It . . . was clear to me . . . that the mission of the public education system is part of the mission of improving society and people's lives and I wanted to be in on that. I did not want to go into politics. I thought education was a much better way of trying to live that kind of good life.
> (Bush *et al.*, 1989, pp. 150–160)

He went on to describe how the life of the administrator changed as local politics became more polarised in the mid-1970s, although never perhaps in Cheshire to the point experienced in one county borough in 1980, where the Policy and Resources Committee felt it necessary to announce:

> It is incumbent on all local authority officers . . . to do all within their power to see that the policies of the council are acted upon with integrity and great haste . . . The Council will do all within its powers to make the local authorities (*sic*) officers reach a high level of job satisfaction coupled with proper remuneration for their work. It will, therefore, NOT tolerate ANY ACTION BY ANY OFFICER designed to hinder or frustrate any of its policy matters . . . We expect to be advised NOT LED, we expect to be supported, NOT HINDERED . . . WE CAN NOT AND WILL NOT tolerate less.

It goes on to say that:

> in principal (*sic*), the staff posts require formal qualifications, such qualifications should be kept to a minimum, thus allowing primary consideration to be given to the individual applicant's social awareness akin to our policy. 'Appointments and advertisements will be handled by a central committee' to ensure that potential applicants are aware of the philisophy (*sic*) of the council.   (Bush *et al.*, ibid. p. 53)

This debasement of the creed of public service was carried forward by others from other ideological stand-points in the 1980s. It will be recalled that a junior minister, one of the few conservatives to lose his seat at the 1992

General Election, thought that the reduction of the number of LEA staff would produce a 'suede dividend' because all education officers wore suede shoes. He made this remark before Kenneth Clarke became secretary of state. More serious than 'jokes' was to be the wholesale denigration of local education authorities as oppressively bureaucratic and wasteful. Some were; most were not.

The education service lost many able people throughout these changing times, but educational research and analysis gained from the acquisition of John Tomlinson who went on to serve with distinction in leading the Warwick University Institute of Education. He remains in my mind's eye as I sketch out some thoughts on the role and styles of local education authorities of the future, in much the way that he has done in his own books and those shared with Stewart Ranson.

CHANGING POLITICAL AND MORAL ASSUMPTIONS

We have already noted that educational management depends on what it is allowed to do by the political and legal context within which it works. To consider its future therefore entails looking at the changing political and moral assumptions within which it might work.

Many of us were brought up, no matter what our party allegiances, on variants of Welfare State beliefs. These beliefs persist virtually as a folk memory and part of our innate moral dispositions:

- The state should act to remedy the effects of the worst inequalities.
- The common good is best constructed and advanced by the exercise of a combination of political policy making and professional expertise.
- The specification of the common good requires rational construction and systematic negotiation and cannot rely on happenstantial political or market processes.

These assumptions differ from Thatcherist or Marxist notions which assume that conflict, and its softer version, competition, is the most effective engine of change. They derive from traditions incorporating elements of Christianity and secular moralities such as those advanced by Durkheim, the Fabians, T H Marshall and Titmuss which insist that people must live and work together and that social solidarity should carry them beyond the pursuit of their own interests. Reciprocity, altruism and community have been the moral premises which legitimised officials to plan, connect, lead and allocate.

It was from within the welfare state, however, in the 1960s onwards, that criticism arose that this model assumed too much power for expertise and too much unempowered dependency for clients. The ethical base and objectives remained the same whilst more care for the psychology of delivery was argued. That critique did not get very far. The groups in power – professionals, politicians, unions – remained confident of their mandate to prescribe. The present government have been destructive of good things, without giving sufficient thought to their replacement. But in causing a shift away from provider power, they have achieved what previous regimes found politically difficult to do.

Present arrangements for governing education start with objectives and specify mechanisms that radically change the mandate of educational management. They push the social and collective ethic into the background on the grounds that if the state enables individuals and self-motivating groups to maximise their own advantages, the whole society will be more productive and better off. The collectivity will be better if it does not act like one. The state, including LEAs and their managers, then takes second place. It performs those functions that cannot be performed through the market, and residual control functions.

The new frame allowed by the government is not consistently in line with either the Welfare State or with a market model. Ministers have not aimed to reform so much as to cripple LEAs, by the encouragement given to schools to opt out, and thus reduce their resource base, by the requirement to progressively yield ground to the Funding Agency and by the requirements to strip down their own capacity through the operation of local management of schools. In all of these matters they evinced an antipathy beyond that so far extended to other parts of local government or to the structures that run the NHS.

REBUILDING THE MANAGEMENT TASK

Those who believe in the importance of locally based elected government for education must try to go forward from both the critique made from within the Welfare State and the rational elements of the latest government proposals. A starting point for those committed to such an aim is to ask what are the 'irreducible' functions of LEAs, what can the schools not do without help from somebody intermediate between them and the centre. There are very few irreducibles, but as Philippa Cordingley and I (Cordingley and Kogan, 1993) noted in our study of local government functioning, there are several activities which are essential or highly desirable. Taking them all in all, they add up to a sufficient justification for retaining or reformulating an intermediate entity. Many public institutions are allowed to continue with far less justification. There are:

- those functions going beyond the range of one school. An obvious example is securing continuing educational advice of the kind provided by advisory services. The functions of expert career and psychological services are other examples.
- those functions not suitable for purchase in the open market. An example of this would be legal services. Very few lawyers in private practice will have the expertise to advise and provide services that need knowledge of the enormously complex law of school attendance, statementing, teacher employment and the like, although there are some small non-education

authorities that use private firms of solicitors. A further example does not easily fit any one category. If, for instance, a school were to burn down, the whole resource of a local authority could swing into action to make sure that education continued to be offered.

- those functions requiring connections with other sectors of public service – child abuse is an obvious example, but broader span public provisions of all kinds as well.
- appellate and advisory functions other than those likely to be provided by an individual and implicated school. It seems crystal clear that a legitimised public body beyond any of the interested parties must be available for adjudication and disinterested advice.

Our field work also revealed an expressed need for leadership, networking and convening among schools. It is unlikely that the multiple expertise and resources required to perform these essential and desirable functions are likely to be available to authorities which are both disempowered and under-resourced.

Public authorities are needed to go well beyond these somewhat minimalist functions. Thus in my recent acquaintance with one local authority, I have been impressed by its sense of the need to present a vision in which the local authority acts as an agent of school improvement. Here the schizoid attitude of government has helped not at all. Local authorities are held responsible for standards, but the change model is that of schools acting in an entrepreneurial mode, building up power through competition with other schools and driven on by demands of their own local customers. We thus have conflicting models, one of which would omit the local authority to the maximum possible extent.

Thus the Audit Commission's hope that in losing an empire the LEAs might find a role (Audit Commission, 1989) seems frustrated at every turn. Sharing with a quango a duty to provide schooling and progressively giving it territory so that the electively legitimised and professionally construed public interest will disappear altogether is creating a quagmire of confusion and uncertainty. And it is a device seemed designed to attenuate confidence and a sense of self-worth in those who have to live with it in the public service.

Need these functions, minimalist or beyond, be administered by an elected body? Leaving aside the moral and expressive case for democracy – not always well exemplified, as we have seen, by those elected – there is a functional case, namely, that without elective democracy hard choices between conflicting priorities are not legitimated. Elections legitimise all sorts of funny people as councillors but technocrats have no legitimacy at all to prioritise simply on the basis of their own expertise.

If this seems to lead me back to a fully empowered LEA, I want also to take seriously the changes, some destructive but others creative, promoted by the central government since the late 1980s. What shifts in values or assumptions do such changes imply? I should like more empirical evidence on this but, putting the best construction on them, the shifts could be:

- from client dependency on professional judgements to consumer power

- towards greater autonomy for schools and other services at the base of the system
- using mechanisms which make a selfless use of the market mechanism in place of, or alongside, prestructured planning.

If one attempts to combine those propositions with the Welfare State assumptions noted earlier, three possible modes of educational management become apparent. One is a reformed 'managerial and planning role'. The second is that of 'provider or a purchaser in a quasi-market'. The third are various forms of a 'normative mode' – working through analysis, information and advocacy. My ideal would be to use all three in a reinforcing and virtuous cycle.

Managerial and planning role

Under the present arrangements, many LEAs must share with the Funding Agency the duty to plan for sufficient places and schools. The LEA has the final responsibility to ensure that all children attend school or are otherwise suitably educated. It will retain responsibility for special education, and statementing and for certain other specific services.

Most of these functions are concerned with planning rather than provision and, in maximising what is left of planning and distributive powers, LEAs must take on board the lessons of the later days of the Welfare State. This would require negotiation and partnership with the newly empowered governing bodies and the building of connections between otherwise free entities: a combination of two modes – analysis and legitimation.

On both counts, 'needs analysis' scores high. It can give a secure empirical and operational base for planning. It also entails wide span consultation. Here we can surely note movement from traditional educational management. In times of relative plenty – they were never bountiful – it was easy to assume that professionals should set up benign provision for which the clients would then be recruited. Even if the professionals know best – and they often do – the very act of asking the clients what they want, before the system converts wants into authorised wants or needs – itself secures support and legitimacy for plans. Consultation gives voice to conflicting interests. But if expressed and brought into the analytic frame, the information about dissent, as well as positive information about needs, can be ultimately internalised. It then contributes to both analysis and legitimation.

How to assess needs? It requires patient work, movement back and forth from the misty areas of affect, feeling and values, all of which attach to beliefs in desired states of the human condition, and forward to feasibility. It will not produce an aggregate of similar units. Some statements will be numbers and time frames, and other will be words, although it is frequently possible to put rough and ready figures on words. One then finishes up with statements made in more than one mode. These cannot be tight synopses of all of the information that one has gathered, but reveal, in some kind of order, an eclectic range of knowledge that can be put to use.

As the needs analysis moves into the planning stage, political decisions, based on both values and defined needs, help form priorities. And then the rest of the cycle can be followed: planning of provision, ensuring or enforcing provision, securing its adequate support through training and the like and, ultimately, evaluation.

Evaluation, too, is best multimodal. In the past it often has not been well done. The connoisseurial forms – of professionals making impressionistic judgments based on their own experience – still remain essential, but must include much more. If testing is considered it is important that it should go into it. But it should also include careful assessments of impacts, would markedly increase both quantitative and qualitative. Then we could know whether needs are being met. Evaluation would help set up a reiterative test and change process for needs. It would enable us to see whether preferred value positions are being sustained in action.

These planning activities are possible within the present restricted mandate, even if the resource base is shrunken. Many are already part of thinking for the future in many LEAs.

Provider or purchaser in a quasi-market

There is also a great deal of confusion about markets. The purchaser-provider mode is simply a mechanism rather than an independent set of values. It can, but need not, embody a profit motive and the values associated with that. But, as we have it in the NHS and in some parts of local government, its essential core is a contract – to provide something in terms of its quality, quantity, timeliness and cost. Such a notion is not alien to the public service ethic. But it may lead to poor functioning where services must be continuous, and cannot be broken down into their components – how does one contract for spending time with parents or severely disturbed children? Over what period of time should a contract for creating, installing and evaluating a full curriculum extend?

In any event, LEAs were discouraged from replacing their management with those of purchaser functions as was allowed to the former district health authorities, health service trusts and social service departments, although, nevertheless, there has been some movement of this kind. If the contractual model is to gain force, there are lessons to be learned from experience elsewhere. There will be many immature providers and purchasers, for example, and broking between them will require expertise. In the health service, trusts and GP fund holders are still groping towards a needs assessment mechanism which will inform purchasers and help providers meet their contracts. All of this is different from classic public tasks of management.

Normative mode

There are also questions of style and ethos within a normative mode of management. Working with autonomous schools means drawing on the strengths of both sides, but the structures for it are weak. Head teachers learn to be many things, but adding so many managerial tasks at the same time as they are deprived of local authority support will deepen the loneliness at the top. The heads of other, perhaps competing, schools, are also involved with complex universes of their own. The non-authoritarian outsider, able to tap into the expertise of the whole authority, might well provide the moral leadership and networks they otherwise lack. Analysing the new needs of the institutions and providing the convening and facilitating roles must be a management priority. Advocacy, knowledge generation and dissemination functions are essential resources for schools which have so much to carry. But all of this would be on the basis of partnership rather than condescension.

THE NEW PROFESSIONALISM

These modes add up to a new professionalism which would recognise that old boundaries have crumbled and some funny new ones have been put in their place. The new management needs a sure grasp of the new political and institutional topology so that work can progress across boundaries. It needs to rest not only on professional and technical knowledge but also on the exploitation of 'Ordinary Knowledge' which is itself part of what has been termed Usable Knowledge (Lindblom and Cohen, 1979) – the knowledge which derives from the reading of clients' wants, the often tilted perceptions of journalists and the like. Its potency is akin to the power of the 'unreal' economy in economics. The unreal economy depends on sentience rather than analysis but ultimately can affect the real economy through causing changes in prices which are thus made less secure on objective facts of production and trade. Thus if politicians or the press or parents say that educational standards are low, even if unproved, that is part of the universe of knowledge that has to be faced.

New professionalism in educational administration needs new knowledge in the forms of needs assessment and multimodal evaluation. It needs a good dose of action based political science. Legitimation means making shrewd judgments of balance between the competing values and interests of the funding agency, local authority councillors, governors and heads, and the primary clients. It needs the acquisition of skills of advocacy, critique, consultation and consensus building.

We live in a difficult time, made virtually impossible in the recent past by some of the action of a biased central government. Local government managers if they want to survive will have to learn to make constructive use of ambiguities, and to not assume that any certainty will remain so for very long. Howard Davies has expressed the view that in five to ten years some of the uncertainties will give way to a reformulated local government. He said that about five years ago now. Components of that new settlement, both structural and behavioural, need to be formulated now. And if LEAs fail – or are not allowed to develop these approaches – the many and disconnected bodies put in their place will have to learn to do so.

REFERENCES

Audit Commission, (1989) *Losing an Empire and Finding a Role: The LEA of the Future*, HMSO.

Bush, T, Kogan, M & Lenny, T (1989) *Directors of Education: Facing Reform*, London: Jessica Kingsley Publishers

Cordingley, P & Kogan M (1993) *In Support of Education: The Functioning of Local Government*, London: Jessica Kingsley Publishers.

Lindblom, C E & Cohen, D K (1979) *Usable Knowledge*, Yale University Press.

Rée, H (1973) *Educator Extraordinary: The Life and Achievement of Henry Morris*, Harlow: Longman.

16

VALUES IN EDUCATION

Mary Warnock

Baroness Warnock DBE is a philosopher. She was an
Oxford University Teacher from 1949 and Headteacher
of Oxford High School from 1966–1972. She has been a
Member of the House of Lords since 1985.

The Jesuits probably had it about right: you need to catch children well
before they are seven if you are to get them indoctrinated. And the book of
Proverbs is equally optimistic: 'Train up a child in the way he should go, and
he will not depart from it.' But do we approve of training and indoctrination?
Certainly we used not to . . . (by 'we', I mean those interested in the theory of
education). Twenty years ago, many thousands of words were written about
the distinction between education and training, the desirability of neutrality
in teachers, and the difference between education and indoctrination. It is
striking, looking back on that time, how things have changed. Education is
no longer supposed to be somehow value-free and if I here take it for granted,
without argument, that education must necessarily concern itself with values,
and that school is the place where, more than any other, values should be
taught, I shall not be so much frowned upon as I would have been twenty
or thirty years ago.

However, though I take this for granted, I find a certain difficulty in this
way of expressing what it is that I assume. I find difficulty, that is, in managing
the noun 'value', as a matter of syntax. I shall try for the most part to use the
word in the sense in which, we are told, all animals, in learning their way
about the world, also learn certain values. In categorising our perceptions into
identifiable and re-identifiable things we all, flat-worms as well as humans,
incorporate values into our categorisation, in accordance both with the nature
of our species and with our individual experience. Thus, for example, being

members of the species *Rattus Rattus*, all rats like certain kinds of food; but individual rats can learn by experience how to pursue food in a particular maze, or how to avoid electric shocks to their feet in a particular cage. That is to say the species *Rattus Rattus* has some values inherited, and common to all rats; but each individual member of the species can identify, by experience, not only the general value but particular, and sometimes new and unforeseen manifestations of it. Values in this sense are kinds of things that are nice or nasty, to be pursued or avoided, by any animal that can move.

However, though this is the 'proper' or fundamental sense of 'value', values are often spoken of as good things, and so the word 'valuable' means 'such as to be valued highly', rather than to be valued either high or low. This need not constitute a real problem. For though you may be able to give someone the idea of what is good for them to eat without deliberately giving them the idea of what is poisonous or disgusting, yet in the case of more abstract concepts such as Homo Sapiens alone is capable of forming, you cannot teach someone what constitutes honesty, say, without an implicit contrast with dishonesty, both of which are values in the proper sense, one high the other low. I shall have more to say about this below.

To return, then, to school: it is the place, self-evidently, where children are most likely first to learn the intellectual values such as honesty, reliance on evidence, clarity in communication, impartiality. For many children it may also be the first, and indeed the only place where aesthetic values can be experienced and discussed; and because school is where most children first have to work and play with people who are not members of their family, under the eye of grown-up people other than their parents, it is also the place where social values can best be taught . . . such values as politeness, fairness, punctuality, obedience, tidiness, cleanliness and many others. Few would dispute this. But, I believe that, in addition, interlocked with all these values, and not truly separable from them, there are moral values; and no one who is not prepared to introduce children explicitly to moral values, proclaiming them, in so many words as moral should contemplate entering the teaching profession.

This sounds a formidable thing to take on. Yet we know that it must be taken on. There is no one who is not horrified by the crimes committed by young children, and the outrages of which they are capable. The law is not enough to prevent them. Indeed the law cannot be effective unless, behind it and propping it up, there exists a more or less consensus morality, the only truly civilising power in society.

I shall argue that, although consensus has a bad name, and sometimes suggests a weak compromise reached by a kind of global committee without anybody's true conviction, yet a consensus morality is essential to society and even to the law itself; and it is such a morality that teachers are obliged, by the nature of their profession to teach.

Why is it so difficult for teachers to face their obligation to teach moral values? Why is it that their first reaction is to deny that this is their business? Either they say that it is a matter for the family; or, more specifically, they ask who are they to dictate morality to their pupils, even if they are prepared to keep decent order in the classroom or playground? Moral values, they say, are a matter for the individual.

This kind of reaction, in my view, implies a false distinction. A code of rules, introduced into school to ensure that it runs smoothly, or that it presents a decent face to the outside world, is one thing, it suggests. Morality, on the other hand, is something personal, which each must choose for himself. For a teacher to enter this private territory would be intrusive or arrogant. Just as we should think it wrong for teachers to try to convert the Muslim children in their class to Christianity, so, vaguely, teachers feel morality is diverse, and must be left alone, whether or not it is derived from a religion (though it may be the lurking fear that morality cannot be separated from religion that makes teachers so uneasy). The very word 'morality' induces in many young teachers an acute embarrassment. Adopting what is called 'high moral tone', or 'moralising' is to be avoided at all costs, as is 'being judgmental'. Moral words are generally not much in use among the young. People who are caught in some delinquency incline to admit that they have done something foolish or silly, not something wrong. A sense of guilt is thought, on the whole, to be inhibiting and undesirable. The thought that one is a sinner is inimical to the improved 'self-image' which teachers believe to be essential if their pupils are to do better at school.

This reluctance to use the old vocabulary of morals, to talk about virtues and vices, good and evil, temptation and sin may, as I have suggested, be partly accounted for by the connexion between these words and Christian dogma. Their use may immediately seem to smack of piety, or sanctimoniousness. Moreover such concepts are probably unfamiliar to people who do not go to church and for whom the words of the liturgy are not anywhere even vaguely banging around in their heads. And even if they were, to use them, with their Christian associations, might seem to be irrelevant, or insulting to people of other faiths.

There are other, more philosophical influences at work. In higher education, and of course this includes the education of teachers, there exists a fairly widespread and radical relativism, an aspect of postmodernism, reinforced by some kinds of feminism, which derives from the belief that there is and can be no single 'privileged' point of view that will reveal a truth about the way things actually are. The world itself is a construct, and any construction of a world is possible. Nothing is certain save that things seem different according to how you wish to talk about them, what story you decide to tell. To pretend that there is the possibility of one truth is the result of a will to dominate; it is to impose a single interpretation of experience on everyone, and call it the truth. This relativism is associated, in philosophy, with the powerful influence of Nietzsche, and later with the fashionable Derrida, and his disciple, Richard Rorty; in theology with Don Cupitt; and in feminism by writers too numerous to cite. It is expressed sometimes in the form of hostility to a 'canon' of literature, to which all children ought to have access; sometimes in an objection to the teaching of 'standard English'; but most often in a refusal to accept any suggestion of absolute or universal moral standards. Of course moral relativism was familiar both to Plato and Aristotle. It is far from new. But it is an issue that teachers must be prepared to face.

We are constantly reminded, and with benign intent, of the multicultural nature of our society, and the urgent need, therefore, for toleration. We are told not to assume that the standards of the 'white middle class male' (as the feminists put it) are, or ought to be, the standards universally to be adopted. The emphasis on tolerance tends to make teachers believe that all moral views should be given equal weight. But to suggest this is to imply a more radical view still, namely, that morality itself is an out-of-date concept. For what was morality but an insistence on rules to be obeyed by everyone, always, and though the heavens fell? Take this away, it may be argued, and morality collapses. If we do not believe in 'absolute values' we cannot believe in morality at all. This view may seem to get some support from a kind of vaguely accepted determinism, thought, perhaps, to be 'what science tells us'. Many people are half-persuaded by a theory which rejects the idea of responsibility, bad behaviour being the result either of faulty genes, or of social deprivation, or both, but in any case not meriting blame (except insofar as blame itself may function as a tool in behaviour modification). There are those who believe that the more we know about the genetic map of the human race, the more human behaviour will seem inevitable, not susceptible to education to change or improve it in any individual case. Yet it is plain that morality has a function, a positive use, whatever else one may think of it. For the idea of morality essentially consists in that of a community of persons who want to be good, who want to behave well rather than badly, and to do so whatever inducements are offered them to do otherwise. And so the idea of morality must be rescued if civilised society is to continue. Laws themselves have no force, and will not be obeyed, if there is no moral sense that obedience to the law is demanded by something other than the law itself. After all, the criminal law is nothing but an external force, seeking to deter people from doing what most of us would be restrained by conscience from doing, even if we were tempted, such as stealing, or injuring other people or defrauding them. The criminal law is necessary where conscience fails. And the criminal law applies to everyone in society, whatever their colour or race, whatever their degree of social deprivation.

But equally conscience, the desire to behave well, and the shame at behaving badly, is held to be common to everyone, or at least capable of being developed. In subjection to the law and the obligation to keep within its bounds we are all in the same boat. We therefore should not be so much overawed by the differences between people and their points of view that we forget the common elements in humanity, what are the preferences, likes and dislikes, loves and hates which all humans share, and which form not only the basis of the criminal law, but of the moral sense which must lie behind it. These common loves and hates are, as I suggested at the beginning, what we may refer to as Values. We value being allowed to live without fear of violence; we value enjoying our own possessions without fear of theft. We value the affection, trust and security of our families, and we value a degree of civilisation in society such that we may pursue our own interests and our tastes; in peace.

What threatens these values are the passions of humans, their greed, their selfishness, their aggression, and their consequent indifference to others. It therefore seems to me perfectly possible that, right from the beginning in Nursery and Primary schools, children can be taught to restrain these passions, and to recognise that not to do so is wrong. Gradually they can be introduced to an ideal of behaviour, in which people are good to one another, and think of other people as having interests, likes and dislikes, wishes and plans as important as their own. And such thoughts need to be presented not as a set of rules but as a preference for good over evil, and a striving to attain it. Such teaching calls for a re-invention of the vocabulary of morals which teachers can use without feeling embarrassed, or ashamed of seeming old-fashioned, or too remote from their pupils.

For it is the very idea of morality that needs to be taught, the idea, as I have suggested, of wanting to be good rather than bad; and this is the idea central to all systems of morality, however they may differ from each other in the actual content they give to the ideas of 'good' and 'bad'. There are of course different views about such content; but not such radically different views as is sometimes supposed. The threat that we live under at the present time is not that there are many different moralities in society, but rather that there are many people in society who have no concept of morality at all. Their guiding principle is that they must have what they want, whether this is the satisfaction of beating up a person who annoys them, or making a dubious gain on the stock market. The notion of being tempted to do what one should not, and with an effort of restraint, will not do, is unfamiliar to them.

One difficulty that teachers very properly feel about the teaching of morality is that, especially with young children it has to be done partly by example. And yet, this is not really a difficulty: it is a part of professionalism. A professional teacher must be scrupulously fair; must be punctual, must be hopeful, must be clear-headed and courageous. All these, and other virtues are part of being a good teacher. But though the exercise of such virtues on the teacher's part may influence her pupils, example alone is not enough. There is a need to put moral values into words, if they are to be adopted and understood.

One centrally important way of teaching children to absorb moral values and adopt them as their own is through the telling of stories. It is plainly much easier to use a moral vocabulary about events that are seen as a whole, in a ready-made framework, as they are in a story, rather than in the messy and unfinished business of everyday life. A story is, as it were, an artificially intelligible slice of life; and the clarity of the values incorporated in the story, the conflict and the resolution of the conflict which make up the plot, the satisfaction in the triumph of good over evil, make stories crucial to the development of a moral sense in children, however young. I believe that we ought not to be afraid of Moral Tales, nor of using the names of the virtues and vices to describe the characters. People in stories should be truthful or liars, brave or cowardly, honest or dishonest, selfish or unselfish. Of course as children get older subtleties of plot and of character can be introduced; and children will soon seek them out for themselves. But at the beginning, and especially for children who have never heard such words before, it is through stories that moral words can be made familiar, without which it is impossible for any internalised morality to develop. For what is at issue here is the development of certain abstract concepts, and without words these cannot be developed. A story is absorbing and memorable because it relates a particular series of events happening to particular people; yet the general can be seen through the particular. *The Little old Woman who Lived in a Vinegar Bottle* had amazing things happen to her. Yet when in the end the Fairy took all her new possessions away, saying that she was impossible to please, 'the more you have, the more you want' a general and recognisable concept is finally articulated. This power to see the general in the particular is the power of imagination. And children need to have this developed, above all their faculties, by their teachers. Some psychologists hold that children are incapable of understanding abstract ideas until they are well on towards the end of their primary school life. This seems to me to be a misleading way of putting it. As they develop competence in the use of abstract words, or their related adjectives, such as 'greedy', 'ungrateful' and so on, so they gradually come to be able to think more in abstractions, but always (and I believe all through their lives, unless they are mathematicians) helped in such thinking by illustrations, exemplifications of the general in the particular. It is thus through stories that the child's imagination can be educated to envisage possibilities, and think about things other than those immediately in front of his eyes, and so come to have the power to envisage an ideal to which he can himself aspire. For out of a concept of something admired – courage, say, or truthfulness or loyalty – may develop a positive wish to exemplify such virtues. And this is to adopt an ideal which is the same as to want to be good rather than bad.

I have suggested that teachers find it easier to deploy moral concepts in the context of stories than directly, in classroom or playground. There is a danger in this. It is possible to distance moral issues so far from the real world that children may fail to feel that the distinction between good and evil has any application to themselves. Most primary school children, for example, are entirely familiar with the wrongness of cutting down rain forests, or slaughtering elephants for their tusks, of over-fishing, or emitting oil into the sea. Environmental issues are perfect for teachers: it is not embarrassing at all to castigate the baddies, and uphold a vision of nature unsullied and unpolluted. Again, it is easy to pick on villains from the past, Hitler, for example or Stalin, and use them as convenient targets, the embodiments of evil. The inadequacies of such images for the teaching or moral values is that a child is too far distanced from involvement. He has no choices himself of whether or not to cut down a rain forest or empty bilge into the stream nor of whether to become a dictator, or seek to take possession of Europe. Such activities are both too impersonal and too large-scale to be more than emblems of evil. What is lacking in such stories is any sense of personal temptation, and the power to resist it. And without this there can be no beginnings of morality.

The idea of temptation, as I have already suggested, seems to me to be central in the teaching of moral values at school. For whether we believe that morality grew up originally as a social device, or as a God-given law, the fact is that morality is essential as a way, the only way, that humans can countervail against the evil that would arise if everyone followed their own selfish passions. Not all the natural instincts of humans are destructive; they have natural sympathies with other animals, especially other humans. But their natural sympathies are limited. Morality enables them to enlarge their sympathies, and to envisage general goods, or create universal ideals.

In order to understand this, even children have to learn that they have such natural passions, that they may be led by them into doing what they immediately want, rather than what they ought to do: that is to say that they may be tempted. They also need to learn that they can, if they will, overcome temptation. I believe, incidentally, that learning this is far more conducive to a good self-image, or high self-esteem than the depressing belief that we cannot help being as we are, doing what we do. One way of increasing self-esteem, as we are all told, is to encourage children to discover what they can do, like climbing rocks, or playing musical instruments, and praising them for doing it. But another way, just as effective, is praising them for not doing what they might easily have done, and probably wanted to do, like snatching back a toy taken from them by another child, or losing their temper under provocation. Determinism is the most hopeless philosophy, if taken seriously. It removes all will to strive, whether for intellectual or moral improvement. It is demeaning to feel helpless to improve.

In order to get children to understand that there are temptations, and that these temptations may be overcome, I think that teachers should talk to them about themselves, not as individuals but as humans. I am not suggesting that the teacher should embark on a psychological disquisition, but rather that, from time to time, and as the opportunity arises, he should give his pupils some images of themselves. He might do worse than to start with the Pilgrim's Progress: or he might produce some modified version of Plato's tripartite soul, by means of which the central idea of a conflict between different parts could be introduced. Best of all perhaps he could give them an image of themselves like that which Bishop Butler argued for, in his sermons delivered to the Judges at the Roll Chapel in 1726. Human beings, he said, are composed of a mass of particular likes and dislikes, passions and aversions chaotic and potentially contradictory. But among these there are two steady principles, one benevolence and the other cool self-love. He was certain that humans do care for other people, it is part of their nature to do so, so long as this motive is not swamped by other immediate passions. Equally, humans do, and should, care for their own long-term interests. They care, for example, for what other people think of them, for their reputation; and when they sit down in a cool hour, they realise that it is contrary to these interests to behave badly, to let people down, to bully them, to prove themselves too greedy or ambitious. Even children can be moved by the thought 'do I really want to be looked on as a cheat, or a bully?' Reflecting on the kind of figure you cut is part of cool self-love. The two great principles are therefore not always, indeed not often in conflict with each other. Both are more important than the particular and immediate passions, but above both sits conscience which has the ultimate authority, and must in the end be consulted in case of conflict or uncertainty. And if the child asks 'what is conscience?', then the teacher must say it is the voice you would be ashamed to disobey; it is the feeling that you must do this or refrain from that. This is obviously not a profound or a philosophical answer; but, once again, it can be illustrated by means of stories. It can come to make sense through the intelligible, understandable actions of good humans, as stories portray them, and through the equally understandable but not admirable actions of bad or weak humans, who succumb to greed or other passions.

Of course there are many children who come to school already equipped with some such hazy ideas; but there are far more who come without them. Even if those psychologists to whom I have already referred are right, and such a concept as conscience or obedience to an inner command is unintelligible to a small child, nevertheless I believe that there are ways in which a teacher can prepare children for the formation of such an idea, and that unless they are so prepared, the idea may never take root; and if it does not they, and ultimately we all, are lost.

The point of these pictures of man, Plato's or Joseph Butler's is that they are supposed to be true of all humans: that is what they are for. They tell us about human nature in general, and this is a shared nature common to everyone. Of course I am not denying that there exist in the world profound moral disagreements, some of which are doubtless ineradicable. People will probably always think differently about abortion, about the proper role of women, about freedom of speech, about sexual freedom and about thousands of other issues; and they not only think differently, but they feel with overwhelming conviction that their opinions are right. Ideals do, and will, always conflict. My plea is simply that teachers take their eyes off these formidable problems, and start with children nearer home, with their own natures, their own probably quite trivial temptations and their ability to overcome them. It is on such topics as these that teachers must be brave enough to speak in moral terms.

Teachers who are themselves convinced and practising Christians may in some ways have an easier time, if they take up their duty to teach children moral values. For they will at any rate have the concepts ready to hand (and the vocabulary in which to articulate them). They will have some understanding of sin and temptation, mercy and forgiveness, faith, hope and charity. But in other, and I think more fundamental ways, their task is probably more difficult. For, except in very rare circumstances, they cannot explicitly derive the moral values that they try to teach from a Christian source. For if they did so, those who have a different religion, or those who cannot even begin to take religion seriously at all, might reject the moral teaching along with its supposed religious base. They must separate morality from religion (even if they personally hold them to be intimately, even necessarily linked). Yet they must not underestimate the differences between Muslims, Hindus, Jews and Christians; they must not appear to be saying that it does not matter in which of these faiths your roots are down, for this might be insulting and off-putting to everyone who was brought up in some religious tradition or other. What is demanded of them if they are to fulfil this part of their obligation to their pupils is that they should become moral philosophers, in order to justify the morality they must teach. What they have to do is seek out the human values that are common to everybody, simply in virtue of their humanity – the things that human animals pursue and the things that they avoid, given their powers – so much superior to those of other animals – for abstract thought, for imagination and for sympathy. The secularisation of society has not in fact destroyed such common values. But they need to be brought out into the open and articulated, if they are to be taught; and they need to be taught, if they are to be embraced. And to ensure that children are taught early to embrace them is not only what we demand from the teaching profession, but is also our only hope for the future.

ENDPIECE 4

Justice Shallow

Justice Shallow was a regular contributor to *Education*
until its demise in 1996.

My dear Silence

I fear I have been a poor correspondent of late, due mainly to that idleness which I wear constantly like a comfortable old jacket, but, in part, because, these last weeks, we were pre-occupied at County Hall with the appointment of a new chief education officer. I thought that the present incumbent had been with us for only eighteen months or so, whereas it turns out that he has given us seven good years, and feels that the time has come to exchange the meagre satisfactions of public life for the richer ones of leisurely breakfasts, extended holidays in term time, and reading for an Open University degree in some obscure and impenetrable subject such as the life and works of Dionysius the Areopagite.

The chief executive, a man whose crude ambitions would make Sejanus look like Mary Poppins, insisted that our search for a replacement should be in the hands of a headhunter. Where do these appalling people come from, and how can they justify the vast sums of money we are expected to heap on them for compiling lists of wholly unsuitable and inadequate candidates? This fellow produced a crop of possibilities reminding me of nothing so much as the pressed men whom Jack Falstaff found with us in Gloucestershire – Mouldy, Shadow, Wart, Feeble and Bullcalf – each about as fitted for the soldier's life as a grim Victorian matriarch would be for a sprightly bordello in a Wild West frontier town. We fought the suggestion that they should be subjected to psychological testing, which would have introduced yet another shaman into our selection process, and ended up, no doubt, with a tally of degenerates, psychotics and joggers. It continues to fascinate me that our chief executive, who so frequently lectures us on the merits of prudence and economy in our affairs, should be in thrall to these witchdoctors and rune-casters, and prepared to buy their flatulent advice at a budget level which, if applied elsewhere, could significantly enhance the pupil–teacher ratio throughout the county, or pay for the armed forces of a minor European principality.

The subsequent discussions ebbed and flowed like a tide over the Essex mudflats, and were just as murky, but we eventually short-listed four people – not many, I agree for so important a post, yet, as far as we could tell, they represented the cream from the watery, flavourless milk served up to us. On the assumption that the interviewing committee was made up of half-witted geriatrics who would lose their way driving down the M1, we were offered a page of questions we might like to ask. Now no sensible member would ever repine at the idea that officers should do all the hard, preparatory work in any situation, but when that work turns out to be as intellectually challenging as an airport novel, then members must assert their authority, and consign such documents to the nearest shredder. Happily, our chairman, fierce, bald and short of breath like one of Sassoon's scarlet majors, announced in clear Anglo-Saxon terms that we were quite capable of framing our own questions, that we would not award marks for answers as though we were examining spotty youths at Key Stage III, and that we would rely on our instincts and experiences which, on the whole, had served us quite well when making officer appointments on previous occasions. At the phrase 'on the whole', he shot a glance at the chief executive who noticed not at all, since he has a hide from which an exocet missile would bounce like a pingpong ball.

The evening before the interviews was given to dinner with the candidates, that ordeal by knife and fork to which, I understand, aspirants to All Souls fellowships are exposed. Ours was a strange affair, sometimes dismal, often hilarious, and decidedly unredeemed by the meal we were offered, and wines certain to dissolve the fillings in your teeth. The wretched visitors squirmed throughout as though their chairs were fashioned from barbed wire, and were reduced either to lugubrious silence, or to inane, endless chatter. I asked one chap what he did in his spare time, and, perhaps to impress, he replied that he had no spare time as the job took up his every waking moment. I urged him to read Roy Jenkins' life of Gladstone which tells the story that on the day he presented his 1859 budget, that stern, unbending man read a good deal of Tennyson in preparation for a long, critical article he was to write about the poet. It was evident from the glazed look in the eyes of my dinner companion that he knew nothing of Jenkins, little about the Grand Old Man, and less about the strange Poet Laureate from Lincolnshire. And, which is likely, he probably prized the more his detailed knowledge of Section 298 of the 1993 Education Act than his frail acquaintance with sundry poets lounging on Parnassus.

This is, old friend, as you might expect of me, an insufferably pompous and patronizing line to take, but, that evening, and from such fragmentary evidence, I began to feel dark and chill shadows lying across my hopes of a happy outcome. On the morning of the interviews, wearing such expressions of inquisitorial severity as would have stirred the envy of Torquemada, we arranged ourselves in the small committee room and began. I will not bore you with the details of a fairly humdrum day. All the candidates were expected to make a ten minute presentation on some anodyne topic, and then had fifty minutes of grilling – not quite the right word, however, since it carries with it a sense of harsh, relentless questioning of the 'we-have-ways-of-making-you-talk' variety. It was so hard to come to grips with what they were trying to tell us – somewhat like wrestling with a vast feather duvet – for every answer was couched in that coded language, management-speak, whose practitioners converse in cliché, jabber away in jargon, and argue in acronyms. I later asked the chief executive precisely what are the meanings of T.Q.M., culture change, out-sourcing, empowerment and core competencies, and he looked at me pitifully, as might a senior wrangler at an innumerate seven year old. I still await enlightenment.

My sadness was that we heard next to nothing about schools and children. That may be naive and sentimental on my part, and I do understand, in these rigorous times, that we all need to develop an understanding of the bottom line, and a proper regard for effective management – not, I suggest, that these concepts and practices, though then clothed in different words, have ever really been alien to our stewardship – but you and I know, and so in their hearts do they, what the purposes of all these frantic activities are. They should find a means of giving expression to that, and not appear as supine victims of techno-fads, without philosophies, and as brutal to the English language as Vlad the Impaler was to those who offered him mild advice on how to govern. They were all decent people in whom humane and intelligent administrators were struggling to get out, and their tragedy was to set before us what they thought we expected of a chief officer – which is as devastating a criticism of us as it is of them.

It is undoubtedly a sign of age that I began to compare our hopefuls with the CEO's you and I have met, heard and worked with over our years in local government. Some are now in Abraham's bosom, and I doubt that one in twenty of present assistant education officers would show a flicker of recognition were their names to be mentioned – Mason, Morris, Newsom, Broad, Longland, Barraclough, Lionel Russell, Lincoln Ralphs, Alec Clegg: or the somewhat later group of George Cooke, Bill Petty, Dudley Fiske and Barry Taylor. I have heard it argued that, because theirs were years of growth and a concomitant optimism, the officer life was as sunny and undemanding as that of an aristocrat during the ancien regime. Well, I cannot imagine that building schools, with considerable flair and on time, to meet the post-war boom: or moving from all-age schools to a primary–secondary modern–grammar system: or organizing a massive expansion of further education – for example – were all achieved without great effort and skill. What they did have, and rare indeed today, were education committees which gave them their head, and Ministers of Education who had the sense to work with and through local government. The result was an admirable individuality and idiosyncracy, and, after stagnant years, a tidal surge of progress instead of the melancholy, long, withdrawing roar now sounding along the desolate shore of education, littered as it is with the flotsam and jetsam of shipwrecked hopes, and clogged with the fetid oil of central bureaucracy. Or words to that effect.

Will this present cadre of officers generate anything like the epic tales of their predecessors, stories which, with the harp and the drinking horn pass round the moot halls of the High Kings – though, more likely, in the four-ale bar of the pub nearest to County Hall? I have long cherished the one of Alec Clegg, who took to committee a project of which his chairman disapproved. Such, of course, was the might of the political machine that the scheme was flatly rejected and when the chairman said, 'There, I told you that it wouldn't go through', Clegg replied, 'Ah, but you haven't seen the minutes yet.' To be fair, I daresay that there will still be anecdotes, something along the lines of how the Assistant Director (Business Units) outwitted the word-processor, but will those stories have lessons and nourishment in them?

I blame the government – to be blamed for everything is what governments are for. In its wooden-headed reformist zeal, it emasculated local authorities, putting their kings in chains and their nobles in links of iron, there to sing their impotence in shrill tones, and leaving chief officers to struggle manfully – this is fast becoming a tangled, politically incorrect sentence – against demotion to post-boys and biddable clerks. Secretaries of State, in these last dozen years or so, have had a poor opinion of CEO's whom they judged to be sly agents of the KGB, wearing lavender silk shirts, and reading Swinburne rather than the stock-market statistics. What a wonderfully comic gallery those ministers of the crown were! Keith Joseph seemed to be as surprised at finding himself in Elizabeth House as Marcel Proust would have been to wake up one morning in command of a crack infantry division in the Imperial German army. Yet he had the sense to think things through, and move cautiously, consolidating his position before the next advance. How unlike the approach of his successor, Kenneth 'Look on my works ye mighty and despair' Baker, whose reforms – not all of which were totally ludicrous – galloped through the House of Commons like the Mongol hordes of Genghis Khan, laying waste years of trust, cooperation and sensible progress at local level in favour of an unwieldy mix of crude dominance from the centre and hobbled delegation to institutions. It is hard to remember the order of succession thereafter. I am sure that a man called John MacGregor was in there somewhere, and that Kenneth Clarke gave us a laugh or two for a short while. I definitely recall John Patten who was, I believe, a well-meaning fellow, but utterly without discretion and common sense. A.J.P. Taylor, the historian, once said that he had extreme views weakly held. Patten had weak views extremely held. Dons, with few exceptions, make successful politicians, for they treat the nation as though it were a pack of badly dressed, idle undergraduates, best disciplined by fines, sarcasm and frequent examinations. Patten might have found greater fulfilment and usefulness as second master of a traditional grammar school in the corner of some county that time forgot. The present incumbent, Mrs Shepherd, seems slightly better than most, but has to give too much of her time to a campaign against the Bourbons of the Downing Street Policy Unit who think that education has gone to the dogs since Wackford Squeers hung up his cane and joined OFSTED.

I can understand ministers being inept performers as economists, diplomats, businessmen or educationalists. They are, after all and like us, feeble amateurs caught in the toils of some pretty complex problems. What I cannot forgive is their being such hopeless politicians. They have effectively destroyed local government, thus shattering their own local power bases, and alienating those foot-soldiers without whom electoral wars are not won – the envelope-lickers, subscription collectors and door-steppers. Just as surely, they have put CEO's into neutral shutting government off from sound, practical advice, and leaving to rust the skills of men and women who actually do know how to make things work, or, at least, in Robert Bolt's words, how to minimize the inconvenience of things.

In his play about Thomas More, Bolt has many shrewd things to say about the use and abuse of power, and how the children of this world are in their generation wiser than the children of light. I once heard him quoted to great effect by John Tomlinson, another of those CEO's who, by his speeches at conferences, caused elected members like us to remember, for that hour at least, that we were engaged on something of more consequence than dancing to the badly-composed gavottes of Secretaries of State. Tomlinson is a most interesting man. He was CEO in Cheshire, one of those distant counties which you and I see as a sort of Ultima Thule, peopled by anthropophagi and clog dancers. He then became a professor at Warwick, in its infancy a distressingly radical university, but now much sought after by the sober middle classes for their ewe-lambs. The road from CEO to professor has become a well-trodden one, but none the less surprising. My own image of professors was set by early reading of the Beano and Dandy in which such men – and always men – are drawn wearing hairy tweeds, smoking foul pipes, bald heads crashing up through untrimmed shrubberies of hair, and speaking in thick central European accents. How disillusioning to meet today's Jermyn Street-shirted, Saville Row-suited, cut-glass accented academics, at home as much in the salon as in a seminar. After years of circumspection, however, having to guard their tongues lest they give political or public offence, they now, like Gladstone after the death of Palmerston, can come amongst us unmuzzled. Unlike lesser mortals, though, who having left local government turn to excoriate it, Tomlinson has praised LEA's – feeding the hand that had occasionally bitten him, as it were – for he saw them as part of a Grand Alliance of children, parents, teachers and universities who would fight not against governments – transient and unworthy opponents at best – but against those older, more persistent and resourceful enemies: ignorance, bigotry and indifference. For the assault, he has marshalled his talents, as would any good general, to hammer away on the right and on the left, and then storm through the centre of the enemy's defensive positions.

On one wing stand his writings – books, pamphlets, lectures – on a wide range of issues, and full of ideas which hook in the memory. Like W.S. Gilbert's Private Willis, he is an intellectual chap and thinks of things that would astonish you. I have read a fair amount of his work, which you will find surprising, since you know of my view that much writing about education is as arid as the Kalahari. And I have heard him lecture on, I think, three occasions. He eschews rhetorical bombast, and sets out his propositions in terms that even I can understand. It is persuasion without pedantry, and, thank goodness, never too solemn. Cheerfulness is always breaking in.

On the other wing lies his chairmanship of innumerable committees. We two have been much exposed to committees during our life, and, on Judgement Day, St Peter will, I trust, count that for virtue, and usher us straight into paradise's hall. I would not willingly embrace the chairmanship of any committee – the phrase is redolent of airless rooms, pointless points of order, windbags, and curling sandwiches. Professor Tomlinson's hobby is growing dahlias, so he would understand my rather strained horticultural image when I say that committee work, in my experience, produces few blooms but many earwigs. Yet he, by contrast, thrives on it all, tackling difficult subjects and situations, leaving members feeling that they have added to the sum of human happiness, and producing reports which say something and lead somewhere.

In the centre we have his work in Cheshire and latterly at Warwick. CEO's are often clumsily pigeon-holed. Overlooking the categories clown and desperado, Harold Macmillan said that prime ministers were either scholars or swordsmen. Tomlinson's professional life shows him to be equally proficient in both these latter roles. He left Cheshire a much better place than he found it, in its system of administration as in its set of values. No doubt the same will be true of his years at Warwick. Few of us, and then only in moments of extreme lucidity, can understand where the frontiers lie between a university's Institute of Education and its Department of Education, but the common purpose is, at different stages of their careers, to produce good teachers, and it is not an ignoble purpose. Whatever else we may need in education, we first must have, working in it and for it, the best possible people, doing their utmost for their pupils, and supported in intelligent, civilized ways. An OFSTED report has told us that, in teaching, compassion is not enough. Perhaps; but, without it, you would have a very dehydrated person indeed, and when, as in John Tomlinson's case, you find compassion, passion and great technical competence, then you meet a formidable figure.

Old friend, I have maundered on for too long, so let me end with this. In a deep cave, in some remote mountain fastness, like Frederick Barbarossa and his knights, sleep those great CEO's of the past, their beards growing through the table, dreamlessly waiting for the call of the battle trumpets. We need their spirit to return to infuse our work, and enable us once more to grasp that education, whatever other admittedly useful aims may be set for it, is there to help the young to see visions, and the old to dream dreams.

Your optimistic friend.

LIVING EDUCATION: REFLECTIONS AND CONCLUSIONS

Peter Mortimore

Professor Peter Mortimore OBE is Director of the Institute
of Education, University of London. He was a Professor at
Lancaster University 1988–1990 and Director of Research
and Statistics for the ILEA 1979–1985.

THE PURPOSE OF THE BOOK

The tradition of giving a Festschrift to an academic who is retiring from
a university post stems – as the word indicates – from Germany. In our
British culture it is a fairly recent but growing trend. In some disciplines, such
volumes are written mainly for insiders – those who have worked with, or even
competed with, the person for whom the book is written. The language of the
book can be technical and its contents may be unintelligible to most general
readers. The book can signal an appreciation of many years of collaboration,
a respect for a worthy adversary or even a gracious reconciliation.

In the world of education which, in this context, means the world of
policies and organisation of schools and colleges, the curriculum, teaching
methods and the study of effectiveness, the Festschrift cannot be so exclusive.
These parts of the education system touch most of us – as pupils, parents,
governers and tax payers – and are widely discussed in the media. In this
field, the Festschrift has to make a contribution to the general understanding
of education, as well as seeking to honour its recipient.

The authors who have contributed to *Living Education* come from no single
school of thought. They have different political views and different attitudes
towards many social issues. They are united, however, by two things: an
intense interest in the education system and a respect for the contribution
made to it by John Tomlinson.

THE FOUR THEMES

It would be repetitive to summarise each of the issues that have been addressed so eloquently by the authors of these chapters. The following is intended simply to highlight a selection which is particularly pertinent to the concerns of John Tomlinson. As is fitting, in a volume dedicated to such a positive person, this selection has been made in order to promote a critical appraisal and to propose improvements rather than to gloat over past mistakes. Science progresses by the challenging of established facts by new investigators with fresh (or newly interpreted) evidence. Educational science should be no different. That it draws on a variety of parent disciplines (psychology, sociology, history, economics and philosophy) and mixed methodologies (quantitative and qualitative) – rather than being a weakness – is an illustration of its strength. As in the physical sciences, the need for integration, synthesis and a holistic view are increasingly being recognised.

1 Organisation of Education

The period of educational history covered by John Tomlinson's career – as so clearly illustrated by Viv Little's introduction and by John Mann's and Stuart Maclure's chapters – accommodates numerous changes. Naturally these changes have been explored, in this book, from an educational perspective but their source has also been traced by some contributors to more fundamental economic or political trends. Thus the acceptance of the limits of the growth in public services, caused by the oil crisis of the 1970s, and a growing disillusion with the process of planning, have led the government to create an education market.

In the establishment of this market, local education authorities have been compelled to privatise – or at least to demonstrate a willingness to embrace market forces through compulsory tendering and the institutionalisation of the 'client-contractor' relationship – and to delegate many of their powers downwards to governing bodies. Despite the enforced nature of the changes, a number of LEAs have adapted their roles successfully so that they have taken on the new roles expected of them by central government, whilst keeping faith with their local government mission. Ranson's chapter demonstrates not only that this is possible but that there are good theoretical reasons for it.

For individual schools, the change has been equally radical. The notion of the 'common school' as the basic unit of 'a national system locally administered' has been banished. Instead, diversity has been pursued. Survival in this newly created market has also meant, as Tony Edwards points out, the legitimation – for many schools – of an exclusive focus on the well-being of a single institution. There has been a corresponding abatement of concern for the good of the locality, or for the well-being of the community of schools that make up the local education authority. The search for consensus, which had been a guiding light since 1944, has been abandoned. It is true that the guiding light had not always lit a path to cohesion; Stuart Maclure has illustrated the contradictions as well as the insularity and complacency that were also characteristics of the pre-market period.

As Maclure and Mann argue in their chapters, the abolition of the Schools Council symbolised a change of political mood. The policy makers of government were no longer to be inhibited by what they saw as the counter-influence of the players in the system. Why should government provide a platform for its critics? Without one, it could be bolder and force radical changes through the new powers that have been conferred on successive secretaries of state since 1988.

For those who supported such change, the negative side of consensus politics – the delays and the sectional interests – provided ample justification for creating a new system more in tune with a modern, radical government which sees its principal duty as pleasing its supporters rather than representing the country as a whole. Yet, as Maclure suggests, perhaps the real reason for the demise of the Schools' Council was its existence, in a relatively small country, *outside* central government. If Maclure is correct, his argument does not augur well for the long-term future of the many quangos and agencies that have been created over the last eight or so years.

The paradoxical nature of these changes is well illustrated by the empowering of school governing bodies to change the character of their schools whilst, simultaneously and contradictorily, shackling of them to a statutory National Curriculum and a regular testing programme (with publication in league tables of school by school results). The head teacher of today is both freer than his or her predecessor and more constrained. The visits of inspectors from OFSTED (the Office for Standards in Education) tend to alarm them considerably more than did the earlier visits of either Her Majesty's Inspectors of Schools or LEA advisers. Whether or not this is a good thing will become clear as we gain a longer-term view of whether, after inspection, the quality of learning in the school improves so significantly as to justify the stress on the health of the staff – including the head.

Clearly it is right that our education system should be dynamic rather than static and those who hark back to the old ways tend to do so using rose-tinted glasses. There are, however, too many concerns about the negative impact of many of the changes for them to be lightly dismissed. If there was confidence that each reform had been introduced in good faith, it would still be hard to enlist the full support of practitioners; prejudice for the known and a natural conservatism are powerful forces against change. In cases where there is a suspicion that the real motivation was to settle scores – with the teachers' unions or the LEAs – then the chance of successful implementation diminishes sharply.

Barber, in his inaugural lecture at the Institute of Education, drew attention to the argument of Francis Fukuyama (1995) 'that a nation's well-being . . . is conditioned by a single, pervasive cultural characteristic: the level of trust inherent in the society'. It is this loss of trust, perhaps, that is the greatest problem faced by those who manage and who work in the education service in England today. The government does not trust its teachers and they do not trust their government. Lack of trust leads to a lack of faith between the parties and spreads to those outside. Thus the media has little faith in the education system. Parents – whilst frequently trusting the teachers of their children's schools – have little faith in teachers collectively.

An additional problem for everybody concerned with the education system, and with other public services, is the feeling that positive 'spins' have to be put on all government actions. Listening to a government spokes-person listing its achievements induces scepticism. If only mistakes and inadequate progress could be admitted, practitioners would be less likely to become cynical.

The messages of this first section of the book are that:

- while change is inevitable, its likelihood of success will be enhanced by trust in those most affected by the proposed changes
- piecemeal change and the creation of numerous agencies may well lead to a system lacking cohesion and a clear sense of direction
- the reduction of LEA powers are having serious repercussions on the quality of education in some schools
- it is never too late to save the day and those working in the education system – when motivated to do so by the opportunity for collaboration – are skilful in creating new models of provision.

2 Curriculum Development and Practice

The curriculum lies at the heart of the education system. Once perceived as a 'secret garden,' in which only teachers were permitted to wander, it has become a battlefield on which different forces skirmish. Reference has already been made to the demise of the Schools Council. In this section of the book two chapters focus directly on the curriculum as a whole whilst one deals with the Arts in education and another with provision for the under-fives.

Margaret Maden's chapter stems from her involvement with the OECD (Organisation for Economic Cooperation and Development) and its review of the lessons of curriculum change in twenty of the most developed countries in the world. She describes the themes that this work has identified: a new attitude towards intelligence; a greater emphasis on student outcomes; and an increasing concern for those with special needs or who are suffering from the impact of social or economic disadvantage.

The OECD work also highlights the steps that it considers need to be taken before wide-scale curriculum change: the development of clear objectives; specification of agreed values; and the engagement of the major stakeholders. These three steps most certainly did not occur before the implementation of the English National Curriculum. Perhaps it is as a consequence of this omission that Denis Lawton is able to argue that the resulting product is so deeply flawed reflecting, as he shows, a confusion of approaches, a lack of coherence and a failure to move us towards a national (or an international) consensus.

Lawton describes the attempts that have been made to patch up the worst problems of the National Curriculum – including the valiant efforts of Sir Ron Dearing – but few would consider that the vast amounts of the education budget that have been devoted to its development represent good value for money. In many ways, the curricular choices currently offered to young people are similar to those which were condemned so vociferously in 1987! The need for a greater component of moral and of civic education – also highlighted by Maden – remains, as does the unhelpful divide between academic and vocational education and the absence of any real commitment to life-long education. It is significant that there should be so much common ground between criticisms made on the basis of a national analysis and the comparative work of an international agency.

The English curriculum movements of the 1970s were inspired by the work of the Schools Council, much influenced by the work of John Tomlinson. They had moved a long way towards the creation of a coherent, forward-looking model which would have fitted well with the OECD principles. It is ironic that this model was so completely rejected by a government itself in search for a coherent approach. With a more discerning strategy, much of it could have been saved. The HMI Curriculum Matters documents could have provided some of the solutions to today's problems of an overcrowded and fragmented curriculum.

Notwithstanding these serious criticisms, the National Curriculum still represents an opportunity to offer our young people an entitlement to the best practice. It holds out a hope that we can harness expert knowledge to create a tapestry of appropriate knowledge, skills and experience – parts of which can be woven by the young learners themselves. The active involvement of the learner, not in a foolish 'free-for-all' but through carefully planned and monitored routes, fits well with the latest theory of seven relatively independent intelligences proposed by Howard Gardner (1983; 1993) and with David Perkins' (1995) suggestion of the existence of 'reflective' and 'experimental' as well as of 'neural' intelligence.

Eric Bolton's chapter on the Arts draws attention to the precarious and peripheral role that they hold within our education system. He argues passionately for their inclusion on a more whole-hearted basis. Representing, as they do, some of the highest and the most spiritual accomplishments of mankind, the Arts have a full part to play in education. They can provide valuable teaching aids to other parts of the curriculum and to the acquisition of complex skills but they also deserve space in their own right. As Bolton suggests so persuasively, some of the latest developments in science are pointing towards a more holistic view of the world's phenomena – a view which can be complemented by insights provided by the Arts. Again, this resonates with the new views of intelligence. Paradoxically, much of the support for the Arts in schools has come from local education authorities. Many of the great youth orchestras and bands, opera and dance programmes and the vitally important instrumental lessons only exist because of the commitment of education committees to this aspect of education. John Tomlinson's Local Authority of Cheshire was no exception and his influence extended the role of the Arts. He also played an important role in the work of the Gulbenkian Foundation and its 'Arts in School Project.' Some LEA support still exists (Nottinghamshire's support for the youth programme of the Nottingham Playhouse and the funding of numerous projects by the Council for Local Education Authorities are good examples) but much has been lost through the abolition of the Inner London Education Authority, the local government reorganisations that have separated cities from county councils and increasingly strict funding delegation formulae for all LEAs.

Provision for the under-fives is also a contentious area, as the chapter by Tricia David illustrates. Lack of serious investment, fragmentation of services between education and health departments, a limited view of the way intelligence develops, and political interference have all hampered the creation of a coherent and integrated system such as exists in other countries. David also highlights the false dichotomy between learning and play that has been promoted by some critics of so called 'progressive methods'. In her view, the overlap between learning and play is desirable and leads to the 'joy' of learning so evident in observations of well structured nursery provision.

David draws to our attention some of the difficulties of the voucher system. Despite assurances to the contrary, the early experience of the pilot scheme has not been reassuring. Practitioners are concerned that much educational time will be wasted chasing the necessary bits of paper. It also appears inevitable that some sections of society will be better able to use the new system than others. As a result, it is feared that the capacity of nursery provision to offer a good start to young children from disadvantaged families will be reduced. Time will tell if these predictions are over-gloomy, but it does look as if the lessons of the implementation of the National Curriculum have not yet been fully learned.

The messages of this second section of the book are that:

- a command and control attitude still prevails within the education system and practitioners' experience is not yet sufficiently valued
- a number of present policies are contradictory and prevent the establishment of a coherent system akin to those in other developed countries
- the Arts are still viewed with suspicion by government despite their educational potential
- the needs of the under-fives – for so long ignored – are being addressed though the adoption of market principles but these threaten to reduce the inclusiveness of the initiative.

3 Education and Industry Links

Traditionally, the worlds of school and of work have lived apart. Charles Handy has captured exquisitely the shock of the seemingly well educated young person starting his or her first job, only to discover to their horror that learning (or at least, learning which is of relevance), rather than finishing, is just about to start. The predominant pattern of the nineteenth and early twentieth century was of factory owners sending their sons to Oxbridge, whilst recruiting as workers those with the minimum of schooling. It was not until the 1970s, when much of our industrial heritage was in trouble, that the anti-industrial culture of our nation was seriously addressed by educationalists, as the chapter by Kenneth Adams and Eric Bates demonstrates. Our nation was underachieving at school and, at the same time, was failing to prepare our young people for a more sophisticated workplace. The rest of the world had moved on and had resolved many of the differences between school and work. In the case of some Asian countries, moving on meant leap-frogging over industrialisation and beginning to pose the threat that, in its latest form, Geoffrey Holland describes so vividly.

The efforts to bring together the two worlds of business and education have not been easy, as Adams and Bates and the chapter by John Eggleston illustrate. There have been some successes, but there have also been a number of failures. Later initiatives have vitiated the success of earlier efforts. Young people have shown preliminary interest before rejecting relevance for the established status of ordinary school subjects. Nevertheless, as Eggleston argues, a number of interesting developments have taken place: work experience, link courses, work simulation and (probably the best known) the ambitious Technical and Vocational Education Initiative.

The chapter by Geoffrey Holland illustrates with great clarity the nature of the challenge facing our education system. It also points to the penalties being inflicted on our manufacturing industry by an amateur approach to training. If the wastage described by Holland could be reduced or even abolished, there would not only be a better educated workforce but a less frustrated population. But, as is made plain, more of the old is unlikely to bring about change; new methods of learning – drawing on the motivational power of new technology – are needed.

Whether more vocational education is 'the answer' to disengaged and demotivated young people is unclear. Indeed, there is a trend for some young people to use vocational qualifications as an alternative gateway to the academic system, as the evidence of an increasing proportion of university applicants with new vocational qualifications demonstrates. Perhaps we should be paying closer attention to the Handy message (and that proposed in the earlier section by Lawton) and changing the education we offer to *all* young people. Rather than offering academic to some and vocational to others it might be more sensible to focus on a new approach to learning which covers both and which gives more power to the learner.

The messages of this third section of the book are that:

- traditional attitudes towards vocational education have changed little and it is still seen as irrelevant for pupils who are good at academic learning
- average standards of English school leavers still lag behind those of other nations
- teachers should draw on new theories of intelligence to lift the expectations they hold about their pupils
- new approaches to learning – including a greater use of new technology – are needed.

4 Professional Concerns

This section of the book includes a fascinating historical account of an attempt to change the system by someone who was there; Chelly Halsey's chapter should be required reading for all special advisers to government. The section also encompasses a forward-looking piece by Michael Barber which reinforces the twin themes, first introduced by Holland, of increasing international competition and the need for better learning and higher standards within our own system.

Echoing the theme of an earlier section of the book, Maurice Kogan analyses the consequences for local democracy of the recent changes in the governance of education. The critique of quango rule and its lack of accountability reinforces the earlier cry of Justice Shallow that there are simply too many people trying to run the show. Kogan's plea is for the sheer practicality of some form of local government involvement in education. This plea is eloquently taken up once more by Justice Shallow whose images of the great chief education officers of the past, awaiting their call whilst their spirit inspires both young and old, conjure up pre-Raphaelite paintings and remind us of the cyclical nature of art forms and of public attitudes.

An additional theme of this section is that education has to deal with both academic and moral concerns. The academic message has been a constant theme throughout the book, but the moral concern (introduced by Lawton) has been less obvious, although John Tomlinson has always argued that schools can and should provide children with experience of living in an ethical society. Resisting the temptation to cry moral panic, Mary Warnock argues that teachers need to pay adequate attention to the teaching of values. She recognises that this can be difficult and that promoting a particular set of values does not sit easily with some aspects of modern life. Nevertheless, she argues that it is essential and that the means to undertake this task, incorporating the separation of religion and moral teaching, must be found by today's teachers. This point harks back to an interest of Tomlinson's in the elucidation of the values which underpin the practice of teaching itself.

The messages of this final section of the book are that:

- the education system must be forward looking but lessons from the past about the difficulties of change must not be forgotten

- ideology should not be permitted to inhibit practical democratic solutions
- education has a moral purpose and schools have a vital contribution to make to the development of pupils' values
- education must serve the needs of all young people rather than just those of a privileged few.

ARE THE NATIONAL ISSUES RAISED IN THIS BOOK SIMILAR TO, OR DIFFERENT FROM, THOSE FACED BY OTHER COUNTRIES?

The earlier discussions on the OECD curriculum work have partly answered this question and have demonstrated a commonality of concerns. Consideration of a recently published Report (*Learning: the Treasure Within*) prepared by an international commission on behalf of UNESCO (the United Nations Educational, Scientific and Cultural Organisation), provides additional evidence that many of the issues raised here are not particular to this country.

The UNESCO Commission – led by the former French Minister for Economy and Finance and ex President of the European Commission, Jacques Delors – spent two years collecting information about the aims and standing of education and focusing on its outcomes. It identified seven powerful tensions in the work of education systems. The tensions are between:

- the global and the local
- the universal and the individual
- tradition and modernity
- long-term and short-term considerations
- the need for competition and the need for concern for equality of opportunity
- the extraordinary expansion of knowledge and human beings' capacity to assimilate it
- the spiritual and the material.

Tension between the global and the local

This tension has been reflected in several of the comments made by contributors about the English system and its relationship to the rest of the world. How those responsible for, or involved in, education should relate their particular situation to that of others in similar institutions in their LEA, other parts of the country, or even in relation to schools or colleges in other parts of the world is not easy to resolve. Should the head or governors of a school that, because of its particular funding arrangements, has a healthy surplus of income over expenditure worry if a neighbouring institution – or a similar one in another LEA – faces financial difficulties? Is it altruism beyond the call of duty or a last vestige of idealism for people to be concerned at the inequity of the situation? If a school, in addition to its privileged funding basis, is also able to choose a majority of its pupils, unlike the other institution which has an intake of young people solely from disadvantaged backgrounds, should the head and governors care about this double discrepancy?

Such moral dilemmas are currently being experienced by people working in and for our schools. Of course, this situation is part of the dilemma faced by everyone living in a society where the distribution of wealth is increasingly skewed, as John Tomlinson's early work for the Court Report (discussed in Mann's chapter), demonstrated so clearly. But today the situation is more serious. According to the 1995 Rowntree Inquiry, 'Between 1979 and 1992, the poorest 20 to 30 per cent of the population failed to benefit from economic growth – a reversal of the trend from 1945 onwards.' This fact has implications for all aspects of life but, perhaps, particularly for education and health. According to Wilkinson (Observer, 8.9.96) 'In Britain, people in the poorest areas have death rates that are – age for age – four times as high as people in the richest areas.'

This disparity in income and its relationship to education and health is an even greater international problem: the gap between the richest 20 per cent of the world and the poorest 20 per cent grew between 1960 and 1994 from a ratio of 30:1 to over 60:1.

Tension between the universal and the individual

This tension has surfaced less obviously than others in this book although it can be inferred from some of the arguments of Edwards, Mann, David, Halsey and Warnock. Schools are made up of collections of pupils and staff. The staff have always to balance the needs of an individual pupil with those of his or her classmates. This applies to academic work, as well as to the acceptability of pupil behaviour. Many heads and governing bodies are facing just such dilemmas as they review their policies and their actions on both whom they accept into schools and whom they exclude. The UNESCO Commission stresses the need for education to be 'inclusive' of all people; a sentiment that would be warmly welcomed by John Tomlinson.

Tension between tradition and modernity

As we move towards the new millennium it is particularly appropriate to consider whether this tension can be found in our own system. A number of the contributions address the matter. Some do it directly (notably Barber, Holland and Lawton); others indirectly (Edwards, Maden, David and Kogan). The critical question seems to be whether the policy makers responsible for our system are facing in the right direction – and whether this should be forwards or backwards? The writings of John Tomlinson reveal the problem: on some issues we need to preserve the glories of the past whilst on others we need to change and adopt new attitudes. The problem, as always, is choosing which course to take.

Our aspirations for high academic standards (for as many as possible); our British tradition of pastoral care and the focus on the development of the whole child (including an awareness of values) an increasing concern about the need for equal opportunities; the delegation of financial management to the school level; the rapidly developing sets of partnerships (between teachers, parents, governors and schools and universities and the business and industrial communities); the growth of school improvement led by practitioners; the intake into the profession of energetic and talented teachers; and the continued upgrading of initial and continuing teacher education, are surely worth fighting for.

The residual problem of low expectations and a fixed view of intelligence; the idea that learning stops at the end of formal education; a backward looking curriculum which divides people into sheep and goats and older students into vocational and academic; poor environmental conditions and a lack of up-to-date books and learning resources; the low social status of teachers; the excessive rigidity of the organisation of learning; a dependence on established orthodoxies in teaching styles (from whatever source); inadequate resources; an inspection process which is purely top down and which seemingly prefers failure to success; and the establishment of a selfish single-institution culture for heads and governors, are less desirable.

Having chosen which traditional features of our system are worth fighting for and which should be abandoned, is it possible to design a way forward which takes account of trends in economic, social and political developments?

Tension between long-term and short-term considerations

Modern politics in democracies is bedevilled by this tension. The transience of politicians' terms of office forces them to focus on the short-term. In contrast, nations such as Singapore have demonstrated the value of long-term educational planning. Such situations are easier to create and sustain where one party is likely to be re-elected regularly. Paradoxically, this country has been governed by the same party for seventeen years (over half the time of the independent existence of Singapore) but, even so, successive Secretaries of State have seldom had the confidence to take a long-term view with regard to financial commitments, even though they have done so in legislating their favourite policy objectives.

The main problem is a lack of continuity and this – to a large extent – is due to the lack of a national consensus or even the will to move towards one, as a number of the contributors to this book have argued. As long as political parties favour adversarial postures and consciously strive to find 'clear water' between their policies and those of their rivals, a consensus cannot be created and short-termism will continue.

Tension between the need for competition and the need for concern for equality of opportunity

This tension was addressed directly in Barber's chapter. It has also surfaced in earlier discussions in this chapter. It is fundamental to the debate about the future direction of publicly-funded schooling.

Competition undoubtedly influences the behaviour of both teachers and pupils, just as it does in the world of commerce. It leads to increased motivation and inspires creative thinking. But what if the competition is unfair? What if those who, favoured through some historical factor or geographical accident, are then further rewarded? What if those who are already coping with a heavy burden find that it has been increased? How, in such cases, can the concern for equity be upheld?

A market forces argument built on competition works well with inanimate objects. It has been adopted by government through the publication of league tables and their influence on parental choice of applications. But can its principles be applied so surely to individual pupils if it is schools which are doing the choosing? Who but the most noble head teacher will choose a 'hard to teach' pupil? Who will welcome a pupil with known behaviour difficulties? Who will retain a young person who has already demonstrated their emotional instability? The UNESCO Report accepts the notion of diversity of provision but sees it as a means rather than an end. It warns against the use of systems based on the diversity of pupils.

Research on effective secondary schools has stressed the value of a 'balanced' intake of pupils, on the grounds that institutions with such a balance are in a position to promote the achievement of all. The alternative, in which some schools become academic and commercial winners and others become losers, has already led to the establishment of 'pecking orders', with those at the bottom gaining reputations as sink schools. This situation is not rectified easily, as the reputation of a school tends to outlast the reality.

Having created such a problem, it is difficult to see a ready solution. The LEA, as it was in John Tomlinson's day as a Chief Education Officer, would have had powers to intervene by restricting growth in some schools and fostering it in others but, today, this is seen as interfering in the market and such powers have been removed. The problem will not disappear: choice, once given, can seldom be removed. A future government (of whatever political party) – hopefully working with the education community – will have to find a solution to how the universal requirements of an educational system and the particular needs of an individual can best be balanced. It may well be that the only way forward is by schools, rather than becoming more and more diverse, striving to become more and more like each other. In which case it will be essential that they do so by copying good practice in order to improve rather than through any 'levelling down' process.

Tension between the extraordinary expansion of knowledge and human beings' capacity to assimilate it

Of the seven tensions identified by UNESCO, this is the one that has had the least detailed discussion (although it has been implied a number of times) in this book. This omission is understandable since the authors have tended to focus on events that have taken place during the career of one person. It is a tension, however, to which John Tomlinson frequently alluded in his speeches and writing and one which cannot be avoided. Knowledge is increasing at an extraordinary rate and developments in computing, and its various applications, mean that both the volume and the speed of knowledge creation will increase still further. Will humans be able to assimilate much of this new knowledge?

Fortunately, part of the new knowledge concerns the functioning of the human brain. Work in the United States, for instance, by Caine and Caine (1991) or by Coveney and Highfield (1995) has demonstrated that scientists have previously underestimated the capability of the human brain. The brain is a complex mixture of electrical and chemical connections. The latest research shows that these are far more extensive than was thought and that the brain extends to literally hundreds of thousands of millions of synaptic connections. Close collaboration between neurologists, psychologists and educationalists under *The 21st Century Learning Initiative Programme* (in which a key role is being played by John Abbott, an English ex-head teacher and the founder of 'Education 2000') is leading to a better understanding of the brain and of how learning takes place (Abbott, forthcoming). It is sincerely hoped that such work will lead to the discovery of ways to make people better learners.

Even with significant progress in learning how to learn, no human will be able to keep up with the flow of new information in any specialist area. Skills in knowledge identification and management will increase in importance. What are now seen as librarian or data search skills will be needed by ordinary learners. Of course, basic knowledge and skills will still be essential. But, in addition, schools will also need to provide courses in skills such as knowledge management.

Tension between the spiritual and the material

The final tension identified by UNESCO has been well aired in this book – directly in the chapter by Mary Warnock – and indirectly in a number of other contributions. For nations which are largely secular but which have cultures deeply infused with religious ideas the tension is clear; for those nations where there are competing and irreconcilable religions which possess opposing value systems, the problem can be more severe. Science has often been seen as opposing the spiritual, but modern thinking appears to be less dogmatic and it is recognised that the question of values –

whose values and *which* values – lies at the heart of much modern scientific work.

Schools cannot and should not avoid the teaching of values. Yet, as the SCAA (School Curriculum and Assessment Authority) initiative in this field has shown, a complete consensus is unlikely. Individual head teachers and governing bodies may have to wait a while for clear guidance. Yet, in practice, the outlook is not so gloomy. Most schools are run according to rules which are based on clear values: respect for others and the condemnation of bullying, cheating, abusing others because of their differences, vandalism, drug abuse and many other unacceptable behaviours. Teachers – more than many other groups – also know the power of modelling good behaviour. They understand that there is no such thing as a neutral model – one is either good or bad; teaching groups reflect the best and worst characteristics of their teachers. Hence much of the effective transmission of positive values is done through the setting of good examples, rather than through direct teaching in assemblies or religious lessons.

Teachers also have to cope with questions of public morality. How can they help their pupils to make sense of newspapers which pontificate about morality in schools whilst publishing so much unsavoury material for the vicarious pleasure of the readers? How can teachers deal with the hypocrisy of so many in public life? How can they explain the selfishness and greed of modern societies without being accused of being *political*? As Warnock argues, they can use stories to help transmit values and, if there has been a tendency for teachers to focus more on discrimination and environmental neglect than on other areas of morality, this balance needs to be adjusted.

Edwards quotes John Tomlinson's 1993 statement that the kind of schooling we decide to offer our young is the clearest public statement we can make about the kind of society we want them to build. If that is true, our policy makers need to take note – urgently – before they inflict further long-term changes on our system. The lesson of the last ten years is that change must be thoroughly thought through and its planned (and even its unplanned) consequences must be evaluated.

HAS THE BOOK GENERATED NEW KNOWLEDGE AND CLARIFIED OUR THINKING ABOUT EDUCATION?

The various chapters of this book have created new knowledge about the education system and about how it has worked in the past, is working today and – most importantly – how it might work in the future. Our society faces many dilemmas. There are no magic potions, blueprints or panaceas. The authors of the chapters in this book, as has been noted, represent no one school of thought. Each has drawn on his or her own knowledge and experience to make their own arguments. The modern world is too complicated for any simple or simplistic solution to work. Nevertheless, the common themes that have run through these chapters provide both a critique and ideas for progress. The authors have also conveyed the flavour of much of the work and the achievements of John Tomlinson whose dedication to different roles within the education system has inspired them to write their chapters. As Justice Shallow has so skilfully noted, compassion, passion for education and great technical competence are not always found in the same person; where they are, it is a cause for celebration.

REFERENCES

Abbott, J (forthcoming) *The 21st Century Learning Initiative Programme.*
Barber, M (1996) *How to do the Impossible*, Inaugural Professorial Lecture, London: Institute of Education.
Caine, G & Caine R (1991) *Making Connections: Teaching and the Human Brain*, Addison Wesley, Washington.
Coveney, P & Highfield, R (1995) *Frontiers of Complexity*, London: Faber & Faber.
Fukuyama, F (1996) *Trust: the Social Virtues and the Creation of Prosperity*, London: Penguin.
Gardner, H (1983) *Frames of mind: the Theory of Multiple Intelligences*, New York: Basic Books.
Gardner, H (1993) *The Unschooled Mind: how children think and how schools should teach*, London: Harper Collins.
Perkins, D (1995) *Outsmarting IQ; Emerging Science of Learnable Intelligence*, Boston: Collier MacMillan.
Timmins, N (1996) A Powerful Indictment of the Eighties, The Rowntree Inquiry, *Independent*, 10 February.
UNESCO (1996) *Learning: the Treasure Within*, International Commission on Education for the Twenty-First Century, Paris: UNESCO.
Wilkinson K (1996) Inequality Kills, *The Observer*, 8 September.

REFERENCES

Abbott, J (forthcoming) *The 21st Century Learning Initiative Programme.*

Ackroyd, P (1995) *The Poems of William Blake,* London: Sinclair-Stevenson.

Adey, P S (1988) Cognitive Acceleration – Review and Prospects, *International Journal of Science Education,* 10, 2, 121–134.

Adey, P S & Shayer, M (1990) Accelerating the Development of Formal Thinking in Middle and High School Students, *J. RES. Science Teaching,* 27, 3, 267–285.

Adey, P S & Shayer, M (1993) An Exploration of Long-Term Far-Transfer Effects Following an Extended Intervention Programme in the High School Science Curriculum, *Cognition and Instruction,* 11.

Anning, A (1995) *The Key Stage Zero Curriculum: a response to the SCAA draft proposals on pre-school education,* London: ATL.

Ashton, D (1993) Understanding Change in Youth Labour Markets – A Conceptual Framework *British Journal of Education and Work,* 6, 3, 5–24.

Audit Commission (1989) *Losing an Empire, Finding a Role: the LEA of the Future.* Occasional Paper No. 10. London: HMSO.

Ball, C (1994) *Start Right: the importance of early learning,* London: RSA.

Barber, M (1994) *The Making of the 1944 Education Act,* London: Cassell.

Barber, M (1996) *The Learning Game: Arguments for an Education Revolution,* London: Gollancz.

Barber, M (1996) *How to do the Impossible,* Inaugural Professorial Lecture, London: Institute of Education, December.

Barth, R (1990) *Improving Schools from Within,* San Francisco: Jossey Bass.

Baynes, C F (1968) *The I Ching or Book of Changes – the Richard Wilhelm Translation.* Third edition. London: RKP.

Baxter, A (1987) Job Designs, progressive education and the correspondence between work and schooling, *British Journal of Education and Work,* 1, 1, 33–44.

Beckett, F (1996) Going back to Dotheboys Hall, *The Guardian,* Education Supplement, 27.8.96.

Bennett, N (1987) Changing Perspectives on Teaching Learning Processes, *Oxford Review of Education,* 13, 1.

Blair, A. (1994) Speech to conference in Manchester (unpublished).

Bolton, E (1993) Imaginary gardens with real toads. In C. Chitty & B. Simon (eds) *Education Answers Back: critical responses to government policy,* London: Lawrence and Wishart.

Bowlby, J (1953) *Childcare and the Growth of Love,* Harmondsworth: Penguin.

Bowles, S & Gintis, H (1976) *Schooling in Capitalist America,* London: Routledge & Kegan Paul.

Bredekamp, S (ed) (1986) *Developmentally Appropriate Practice in Early Childhood Programs Serving Children from Birth through Age 8,* Washington DC: NAEYC.

Bredekamp, S (1993) Developmentally appropriate practice. Position statement presented at NAEYC Conference, Anaheim, November.

Brighouse, T (1996) *The Need to Go Beyond the National Curriculum, RSA Journal,* CXLIV, 5470, June.

Bruner, J (1960) *The Process of Education,* Boston: Harvard.

Bruner, J (1977) *The Process of Instruction,* Cambridge, Massachusetts: Harvard University Press.

Bruner, J & Haste, H (eds) (1987) *Making Sense,* London: Methuen.

Bruner, J (1990) *Acts of Meaning,* Cambridge, Massachusetts: Harvard University Press.

Bull, C & Gardner, H (1984) *Frames of Mind: The Theory of Multiple Intelligences,* London: Heinemann.

Bush, T, Kogan, M & Lenney, T (1989) *Directors of Education – Facing Reform,* London: Jessica Kingsley Publishers.

Caine, G & Caine, R (1991) *Making Connections: Teaching and the Human Brain,* Addison Wesley, U.S.A.

Caldwell, B & Spinks, J (1988) *Leading the Self-Managing School,* Lewes: Falmer.

Caldwell, B J & Spinks, J M (1992) *Leading the Self-Managing School,* Falmer Press: Lewes.

Careers Research and Advisory Centre (1979) *Schools and Industry.*

Carnie, F, Large, M & Tasker, M (1995) *Freeing Education: Steps towards real choice and diversity in schools,* Bath: Hawthorn Press.

Coleman, J (1990) Choice, community and future schools. In W. Clune & J. Witte (eds) *Choice and Control in American Education,1,* Bristol, Pennsylvania and Basingstoke UK: Falmer Press.

Cooke, G & Gosden, P (1986) *Education Committees* AEC Trust, 75.

Cordingley, P & Kogan, M (1993) *In Support of Education: The Functioning of Local Government,* London: Jessica Kingsley Publishers.

Coveney, P & Highfield, R (1995) *Frontiers of Complexity,* London: Faber & Faber.

Clyde, M (1995) Concluding the debate. In M. Fleer (ed) *DAP centrism: challenging Developmentally Appropriate Practice,* Watson: Australia, Australian Early Childhood Association.

Crosland, C A R (1956) *The Future of Socialism,* London: Cape.

Crosland, S (1982) *Tony Crosland,* London: Cape.

Dahlberg, G & Asen, G (1994) Evaluation and regulation: a question of empowerment. In P. Moss, A. Pence (eds) *Valuing Quality in the Early Years,* London: Paul Chapman.

David, T (1990) *Under Five – Under-educated?* Milton Keynes: Open University Press.

David, T (1992) What do parents want their children to learn in pre-school in Belgium and the UK? Paper presented at the XXth World Congress of OMEP, Arizona 1992.

David, T (ed) (1993) *Educating our Youngest Children: European Perspectives,* London: Paul Chapman.

David, T (in press) Nursery education and the National Curriculum. In T.Cox (ed) *The National Curriculum and the Early Years,* London: Falmer.

David, T, Curtis, A & Siraj-Blatchford, I (1992) *Effective Teaching in the Early Years,* Stoke-on-Trent: Trentham Books.

Deloache, J S & Brown, A L (1987) The early emergence of planning skills in children. In J. Bruner & H. Haste (eds) *Making Sense,* London: Methuen.

Denning, T (1995) *Information Technology and Pupil Motivation,* Keele: Keele University.

Department for Education (1995) *Improving Schools Initiative,* London: HMSO.

Department of Industry (1977) Industry, education and management. A Discussion Paper. London: DoI.

Department of Industry (1980) *Industry/Education Liaison,* Industry/Education Unit: Department of Industry.

Department of National Heritage (1996) *Setting the Scene, The Arts and Young People.*

Dept. of Trade & Industry (1994) *Competitiveness: Helping Business to Win,* Government White Paper, London: HMSO.

DES (1978) *Report of the Committee of Enquiry into the education of handicapped children and young people* (Warnock Report), London: HMSO.

DES (1989) *Aspects of Primary Education: The Education of Children Under Five,* London: HMSO.

DES (1990) *Starting with Quality* (Rumbold Report), London: HMSO.

DfEE (1996) *Work and family: ideas and options for childcare,* London: DfEE.

DfEE (1996a) *Nursery Education Scheme: The Next Steps,* London: DfEE.

Donaldson, M (1978) *Children's Minds,* Glasgow: Fontana.

Douglas, M H (1975) Industrial Design and Production Projects in Secondary Schools, *Studies in Design Education and Craft,* 8.1.

Edwards, D & Mercer, N (1987) *Common Knowledge,* London: Methuen.

Edwards, T (1988) Schooling, liberation and repression. In P. Gordon (ed) *The Study of Education: 3, The Changing Scene,* London: Woburn Press.

Edwards, T (1989) Benefits, costs and risks: some expectations of the National Curriculum, *Curriculum* 10, 2, 65–70.

Eliot, T S (1958) The Lovesong of J.Alfred Prufrock in *Collected Poems 1909 – 1935,* London: Faber & Faber.

ESRC Sponsored Research (Grant RWO 231879) – Report (1994) *The New System of Government for Education,* Swindon: ESRC.

FEFC (1996) *Inclusive Learning.* Report of the Learning Difficulties and/or Disabilities Committee. London: HMSO.

Fitz, J, Edwards, T & Whitty, G (1986) Beneficiaries, benefits and costs: an investigation of the Assisted Places Scheme, *Research Papers in Education* 1, 3, 169–193.

Flew, A (1991) Educational services: independent competition or maintained monopoly? In D. Green (ed) *Empowering Parents: how to break the schools monopoly,* London: Institute of Economic Affairs Health and Welfare Unit.

Forrest, G (ed) (1996) *Experiences of Work: Current Issues and Developments,* Warwick: SCIP.

Fukuyama, F (1996) *Trust: the Social Virtues and the Creation of Prosperity,* London: Penguin.

Fullan, M (1991) *The New Meaning of Educational Change,* London: Cassell.

Galton, M (1989) *Teaching in the Primary School,* London: Fulton.

Galton, M (1995) *Crisis in the Primary Classroom,* London: Fulton.

Gardner, H (1983) *Frames of Mind: the Theory of Multiple Intelligences,* New York: Basic Books.

Gardner, H (1993) *The Unschooled Mind: how children think and how schools should teach,* London: Harper Collins.

Gewirtz, S, Ball, S & Bowe, R (1995) *Markets, Choice and Equity in Education,* Buckingham: Open University Press.

Gibran, K (1926) *The Prophet,* London: William Heinemann.

Gleeson, D (1993) Legislation for Change: Missed Opportunities in the Further and Higher Education Act, *British Journal of Education and Work,* 6, 2, 29–41.

Goleman, D (1996) *Emotional Intelligence, Why it can matter more than IQ,* London: Bloomsbury.

Green, A & Steedman, H (1993) *Educational Provision, Educational Attainment and the Needs of Industry, A review of Research for Germany, France, Japan, the USA and Britain.* NIESR

Griffiths, T (1995) *European Partnerships: European Work Experience,* Warwick: SCIP.

Grubb, W and Lazerson, M (1981) Vocational Solutions to Youth Problems: the

Persistent Frustrations of the American Experience, Educational Analysis, Vol. 3, no. 2, pp. 91–104.

Halsey, A H (1958) Genetics, Social Structure and Intelligence, *British Journal of Sociology*, 9, 15–28.

Halsey, A H (1993) Changes in the Family, *Children and Society* Vol. 7, no. 2, p. 125.

Halsey, A H (1996) *No Discouragement: An autobiography*, Basingstoke: MacMillan.

Hamner, T & Furlong, A (1996) Staying on: the effects of recent changes in educational participation for 17–19 year olds in Norway and Scotland, *Sociological Review*, 44, 4, 675–691.

Handy, C (1994) *The Empty Raincoat*, London: Hutchinson.

Hargreaves, D (1994) *The Mosaic of Learning: Schools and Teachers for the Next Century*, London: DEMOS.

Hargreaves, D (1996) Diversity and choice in school education: a modified libertarian approach, *Oxford Review of Education* 22, 2, 131–141 and 155–156.

Haviland, J (ed) (1988) *Take Care, Mr Baker*: a selection from the advice on the Government's Education Reform Bill which the Secretary of State for Education invited but decided not to publish, London: Fourth Estate.

Heaney, S (1995) *The Redress of Poetry*, London: Faber & Faber.

Hillgate Group (1987) *The Reform of British Education*, London: Claridge Press.

Hirst, P (1993) *Associative Democracy*, Oxford: Polity.

Huff, P, Snider, R & Stephenson, S (1986) *Teaching and Learning Styles*, Ontario Secondary Teachers' Federation (OSSTF).

Hughes, M (1993) *Flexible Learning Evidence Examined*, Network Ed Press.

Hunt, D (1982) The Practical Value of Learning Styles Ideas. In J. W. Keefe (ed) *Student Learning Styles and Brain Behavior*, Vancouver: Reston.

Hutt, S J, Tyler, S, Hutt, C & Christopherson, H (1989) *Play, exploration and learning*, London: Routledge.

Institute for Public Policy Research (1993) *Education: A Different Vision*, Institute for Public Policy Research and Rivers, London: Oram Press.

Jamieson, I & Lightfoot, M (1981) Learning about Work, *Educational Analysis*, 3, 2.

Katz, L (1987) Quoted in 'Burnout by five' *Times Educational Supplement*, 18 September.

Katz, L (1995) *A global view: an agenda for tomorrow and the future*. Paper presented at the RSA Start Right Conference, London: September.

Kavanagh, D (1987) *Thatcherism and British Politics: the end of consensus*, London: Oxford University Press.

King, R (1978) *All things bright and beautiful?* Chichester: Wiley.

Kogan, M (1971) *The Politics of Education*, Harmondsworth: Penguin.

Labour Party (1995) *Diversity and Excellence*, Labour Party: London.

Lally, M (1991) *The Nursery Teacher in Action*, London: Paul Chapman.

Lawlor, S & McKay, F (1993) *English and Work Experience: An active learning resource for schools*, Warwick: SCIP.

Lazerson, M (1971) *Origins of the Urban School*, Cambridge, Massachusetts: Harvard University Press.

Levacic, R (1993) Local Management of Schools as an organisational form: Theory and Application, *Journal of Education Policy*, 8, 2, 123–141.

Levacic, R (1995) *Local Management of School: Analysis & Practice*, Milton Keynes: Open University.

Levin, H (1989) Education as a public and private good. In N. Devins (ed) *Public Values, Private Schools*, Lewes & Philadelphia: Falmer Press.

238   *References*

Lindblom, C E & Cohen, D K (1979) *Usable Knowledge*, Yale University Press.

Linton, M (1996) Minister rue 'gaps' in child care, *The Guardian*, 29 August, p.10.

Little, V & Tomlinson, J (1993) Education: Thirty years of Change – for Better or Worse? In *Children and Society*, 7, 2.

McLean, V S (1991) *The Human Encounter*, London: Falmer.

Maclure, S (1984) *Educational Development and School Building 79–80*, London: Longmans.

Maden, M & Hillman, J (1995) Lessons in Success in National Commission on Education *Success Against the Odds*, London: Routledge.

Madood, T (1992) On not being white in Britain: discrimination, diversity and commonality. In M. Leicester & M. Taylor (eds) *Ethics, Ethnicity and Education*, London: Kogan Page.

Manpower Services Commission (1981) *A New Training Initiative*, London: Manpower Services Commission.

Miller, S (1973) Ends, means and galumphing: some leitmotifs of play, *American Anthropologist*, 75, 87–98.

Moss, P (1996) Perspectives from Europe. In G.Pugh (ed) *Contemporary Issues in the Early Years*, London: Paul Chapman.

Moss, P & Pence, A (eds) (1994) *Valuing Quality in the Early Years*, London: Paul Chapman.

Moyles, J (1989) *Just Playing?* Buckingham: Open University Press.

Naisbitt, J (1994) *The Global Paradox*, London: Nicholas Brealey Publishing.

Narayan, N (1996) Muslims set schools a spiritual test, *Observer*, 25 February.

National Commission on Education (1993) *Learning to Succeed*, London: Routledge.

Nunes, T (1994) The relationship between childhood and society, *Van Leer Foundation Newsletter*, Spring 1994, 16–17.

OECD/CERI (1994) *The Curriculum Redefined: Schooling for the 21st Century*, Paris: OECD.

OECD/CERI (1995) *Teachers and Curriculum Reform in Basic Schooling*, Paris: OECD.

Perkins, D (1995) *Outsmarting IQ; Emerging Science of Learnable Intelligence*, Boston: Collier MacMillan.

Plant, R (1990) *Citizenship and Rights: Two Views*, London: Institute of Economic Affairs.

Plaskow, M (1985) (ed) *Life and Death of the Schools Council*, passim, London: Falmer.

Prais, S & Wagner, K (1986) *Schooling Standards in Britain and Germany*, NIESR.

Pugh, G (1988) *Services for Under Fives: Developing a Coordinated Approach*, London: NCB.

Pugh, G (ed) (1992) *Contemporary Issues in the Early Years*, London: NCB/Paul Chapman.

Putnam, R (1993) *Making Democracy Work*, Princeton University Press.

Pyke, N (1996) Vocational Training Rejected, *Times Educational Supplement*, 18, 10, 9.

Ranson, S (1992) *The Role of Local Government in Education*, Harlow: Longman.

Ranson, S (1995) From Reform to Restructuring of Education. In J. Stewart & G. Stoker (eds) *Local Government in the 1990s*, London: Macmillan.

Ranson, S & Tomlinson, J (eds) (1994) *School Co-operation: new forms of local governance*, Harlow: Longman.

Rée, H (1973) *Educator Extraordinary: The Life and Achievement of Henry Morris*, Harlow: Longman.

Rees, T L & Gregory, D (1981) Youth Employment and Unemployment: A Decade of Decline, *Educational Analysis*, 3, 2.

Reich, R (1993) *The Work of Nations*, New York: Simon & Schuster.

Robinson, P (1996) *Rhetoric and Reality, Britain's New Vocational Qualifications*, London: Routledge.

SCAA(1995) *Draft proposals for desirable outcomes of preschool learning*, London: SCAA.

SCAA (1996) *Nursery Education Desirable Outcomes for Children's Learning on entering compulsory schooling*, London: SCAA.

Schweinhart, L J & Weikart, D P (1993) *A Summary of Significant Benefits: the High/Scope Perry Preschool Study through Age 27*, Ypsilanti MI: High/Scope Foundation.

Seldon, A (1995) The economic fundamentals. In R. Murley (ed) *Patients or Customers?* London: Institute of Economic Affairs Health and Welfare Unit.

Sexton, S (1988) *A Guide to the Education Reform Bill*, Warlingham: Institute of Economic Affairs Education Unit.

Sexton, S (1992) *Our Schools – Future Policy*, Warlingham: Independent Primary and Secondary Education Trust.

Shorrocks, D (1992) Evaluating Key Stage 1 Assessments: the testing time of May 1991, *Early Years* 13, 1, 16–20.

Simon, B (1965) *Education and the Labour Movement*, London: Lawrence Wishart.

Simon, B (1981) Why No Pedagogy in England? In B. Simon & W. Taylor (eds) *Education in the Eighties: the central issue*, London: Batsford.

Singer, E (1992) *Child development and daycare*, London: Routledge.

Skinner, W G (1970) Link Courses in Colleges of Further Education, Part 1, *Survey 4*, Staffordshire, Keele University (for Schools Council) April.

Sutton-Smith, B (ed) (1979) *Playing and Learning*, New York: Gardner Press.

Sylva, K, Siraj-Blatchford, I & Johnson, S (1992) The impact of the UK National Curriculum on pre-school practice: some top-down processes at work, *International Journal of Early Childhood*, 24, 1, 41–51.

Tate, N (1994) Off the fence on common culture, *Times Educational Supplement*, 29 July.

The Times (1995) Three kind mice. (Editorial) *The Times*, 12 September.

Thody, A (1995) The governor citizen; agent of the state, the community or the school? In A. Macbeth, D. McCreath & J. Aitcheson (eds) *Collaborate or Compete? Educational partnerships in a market economy*, London: Falmer Press.

Thomas, H (ed) (1968) *Crisis in the Civil Service*, London: Blend.

Thring, E (1883) *The Theory and Practice of Teaching*, Cambridge University Press.

Timmins, N (1996) A Powerful Indictment of the Eighties, The Rowntree Inquiry, *Independent*, 10 February.

Timmins, N (1996) *The Five Giants: a biography of the welfare state*, London: Fontana.

Tizard, B & Hughes, M (1984) *Young Children Learning*, London: Fontana.

Tobin, D, Wu, D & Davidson, D (1989) *Preschool in three Cultures: Japan, China and the United States*, Yale University Press.

Tomlinson, J R G (1962) *Additional Grenville Papers 1765–1765* (ed), Manchester: Manchester University Press.

Tomlinson, J R G (1979) Address to Convocation on 14 November 1978 as Director of Education, Cheshire. Cheshire Education Committee.

Tomlinson, J R G (1979) An educationalist looks at health education, *International*

Journal of Health Education, 22, 3.

Tomlinson, J R G (1980) Reflections on Curriculum Development (The Charles Gittens Memorial Lecture), 19 February.

Tomlinson, J R G (1980) The Schools Council: address to the Professional Association of Teachers, 29 July.

Tomlinson, J R G (1980) Charter Fellows' Presentation Ceremony (College of Preceptors), 15 October.

Tomlinson, J R G (1980) Reflections on Education and Medicine (The Lockyer Lecture to the Royal College of Physicians), 16 October.

Tomlinson, J R G (1980) The Director's Bin (Article from *Education in Cheshire*).

Tomlinson, J R G (1981) Present State of the Curriculum Debate in England (Address to American Association of School Administrators), 16 December.

Tomlinson, J R G (1981) Ideas into Action, or The Empire Strikes Back (Address to Secondary Heads Association), 31 March.

Tomlinson, J R G (1981) Education in the 80s (Address to Royal Society of Arts), 3 June.

Tomlinson, J R G (1981) The Schools Council: A Chairman's Salute and Envoi (Schools Council Lecture to British Association), 1 September.

Tomlinson, J R G (1982) The Profession of Education Officer: Past Pluperfect, Present Tense, Future Conditional, *Sheffield Papers in Educational Management 25*.

Tomlinson, J R G (1986) Public education, public good. Inaugural Lecture, University of Warwick, 2 June.

Tomlinson, J R G (1991) Comprehensive Education in England and Wales, 1944–1991, *European Journal of Education*, 26,2,103–117.

Tomlinson, J (1993) *The Control of Education*, London: Cassell.

Tomlinson, J R G (1994) Professional Development and control: a General Teaching Council. In H. Bines & M. Welton (eds) *Managing Partnership in Teacher Training and Development*, London: Routledge.

Tomlinson, J R G (1995) Teachers and Values in *British Journal of Education Studies*, 23, 3, 315–318.

Tomlinson, J R G (1996) A statement of Ethical Principles for the Teaching Profession, unpublished draft GTC (England and Wales).

Tomlinson, J R G & Little, V M (1996) A Code of Ethical Principles for the Teaching Profession, unpublished paper, UCET Ethics Working Party.

Trevarthen, C (1992) An infant's motives for speaking and thinking in the culture. In A. H. Wold (ed) *The Dialogical Alternative*, Oxford University Press.

UNESCO International Commission on Education for the Twenty-First Century (1996) *Learning: the Treasure Within*, Paris: UNESCO.

Vygotsky, I. (1978) *Mind in Society*, Cambridge, Massachusetts: Harvard University Press.

Walford, G (1995) The Christian schools campaign – a successful educational pressure group? *British Educational Research Journal*, 21, 4, 451–464.

Walford, G (1996) Diversity and choice in school education: an alternative view, *Oxford Review of Education*, 22, 2, 143–154 and 159–160.

Walker, G (1995) To Educate the Nations, Harry Rée Lecture, Settle, UK (unpublished).

Watts, A G (1981) Schools Work and Youth: An Introduction, *Educational Analysis*, 3, 2.

Weiss, M (1993) New guiding principles in educational policy: the case of Germany, *Journal of Education Policy*, 8, 4, 307–320.

Whitty, G (1989) The New Right and the National Curriculum; state control or market forces? *Journal of Education Policy*, 4, 4, 329–341.

Whitty, G, Edwards, T & Gewirtz, S (1993) *Specialisation and Choice in Urban Education*, London: Routledge.

Wilkinson, K (1996) Inequality Kills, *The Observer*, 8 September.

Williams, S (1996) *Snakes and Ladders – A Political Diary*, Tape: BBC Worldwide Ltd.

Willis, P (1978) *Learning to Labour*, London: Saxon House.

Yates, A & Pidgeon, D (1957) *Admission to Grammar Schools*, London: NFER.

Yates, C (1987) Teaching Correlational Reasoning to 11–13 Year-Olds, *Journal of Biological Education*, 21, 3, 197–202.

Zigler, E (1987) Formal schooling for four-year-olds? No. *American Psychologist*, 42, 3, 254–260.

INDEX

nurseries, 99, 107
nursery education, xx, 98, 99, 100,
    101, 107, 131, 136
nursery schools, nursery classes,
    99
Nursery Voucher Scheme, 100
National Union of Teachers,
    (NUT), 58
National Vocational Qualifications,
    (NVQ), 134

objectives, 35, 60, 61, 76, 82,
    83, 84, 135, 136, 137, 138,
    145, 150, 158, 162, 195, 196,
    222, 229
Open University, 25, 47, 109, 110,
    177, 183, 189, 211
opting out, 28, 32, 33, 34
Organisation for Economic
    Co-operation and Development
    (OECD), 71, 72, 73, 74, 75, 76,
    77, 78, 79, 80, 182, 190, 222,
    223, 227

Parliamentary Scientific
    Committee, 148
Patten, John 193, 214, 215
patterns of management, 37
pedagogies, 80
pedagogy, 21, 52, 84, 86
performance indicators, 32
playgroups, 99
Plowden Report, 13
pluralism, 59, 60
pluralist, xx
pluralistic society, 22
politics of education, 182, 185
polytechnics, 167, 188, 189
postmodernism, 204
preschool, 102, 108, 110
primary schools, 54, 121, 146,
    149, 191, 206
privatisation, 36, 37, 39, 40,
    46, 220
producer monopolies, 16
producer self-interest, 17

profession, xviii, 29, 53, 56, 59,
    60, 61, 77, 132, 151, 203,
    210, 229
professional expertise, 29, 195
professionalism, xviii, xx, 49, 59,
    60, 113, 134, 144, 200, 206
progressive general taxation, 191
progressive graduate taxation,
    191
public expenditure, 40, 60,
    131, 137
public interest, 17, 18, 19, 20,
    22, 197
public schools, 189
public servants, 16
public services, 16, 17, 185,
    220, 222
purchaser-provider, 35, 199

qualifications, 12, 64, 88, 100,
    129, 130, 136, 151, 156, 163,
    188, 194, 225
quality assurance, 32, 38

Rée, Harry, 181, 186, 193
Reform Bill, 18, 25
Registered Nursery Education
    Inspector, 100
relativism, 204, 205
Robbins Report, 188, 189
Rowntree Inquiry 1995, 228
Royal College of Arts, 147
Royal Society, xvii, 9, 48, 62,
    143, 147
Royal Society of Arts (RSA), xvii,
    9, 48, 62, 109, 127, 143, 144
Ruskin speech, 12, 48

School Curriculum and Assessment
    Authority, 19, 81, 106, 232
school governors, 20
school improvement, 175, 197, 229
Schools Council, xiv, 10, 11, 12,
    15, 17, 48, 55, 57, 58, 59, 62,
    81, 141, 143, 152, 153, 158,
    164, 165, 221, 222, 223

value rationality, 41, 46
value-added analyses, 32
values, xix, xx, 15, 21, 22, 24, 27,
    29, 31, 41, 44, 51, 53, 76, 85,
    92, 106, 107, 108, 118, 125,
    141, 153, 154, 162, 180, 184,
    197, 198, 199, 200, 202, 203,
    204, 205, 206, 207, 208, 209,
    210, 216, 222, 226, 227, 229,
    231, 232
vocational education, 5, 75, 135,
    151, 223, 225, 226
vocational identity, 153, 155,
    156, 163
vocational qualifications, 129, 130,
    188, 225
vocationalism, 74
vouchers, 224

Warnock Report, 105
welfare state, 195, 196, 198
White Paper of 1987 (Better
    Schools), 96

White Paper 1992, 18, 20
White Paper 1996, 20
whole class teaching, 86, 88
Wilson, Sir Harold 183, 187, 189
Women into Science and
    Engineering, 147
work experience, 143, 150,
    153, 154, 156, 157, 158, 159,
    160, 225
work simulation, 157, 161, 225
workplace, 14, 99, 125, 174,
    176, 225
world citizenship, 180
World Competitiveness Report,
    128
World Economic Forum, 128
world of work, 150, 156, 157, 158

Young Engineer for Britain, 146
Young Enterprise, 146
Youth Training Schemes, 121